AFTER FREEDOM

AFTER FREEDOM

The Rise of the Post-Apartheid
Generation in Democratic South Africa

Katherine S. Newman
Ariane De Lannoy

BEACON PRESS ■ BOSTON

Beacon Press
Boston, Massachusetts
www.beacon.org

Beacon Press books
are published under the auspices of
the Unitarian Universalist Association of Congregations.

17 16 15 14   8 7 6 5 4 3 2 1

Many names and identifying characteristics of people mentioned
in this work have been changed to protect their identities.

This book is printed on acid-free paper that meets the uncoated paper
ANSI/NISO specifications for permanence as revised in 1992.

Text design and composition by Kim Arney

Interior photos © Jillian Edelstein

Library of Congress Cataloging-in-Publication Data
Newman, Katherine S.
    After freedom : the rise of the post-apartheid generation in democratic South Africa /
Katherine S. Newman, Ariane De Lannoy.
        pages   cm
    Includes bibliographical references and index.
    ISBN 978-0-8070-0746-4 (hardcover : alk. paper)
    ISBN 978-0-8070-0747-1 (ebook)
1. Post-apartheid era—South Africa. 2. Democracy—South Africa. 3. South Africa—
Social conditions—1994– 4. South Africa—Economic conditions—1991– 5. South
Africa—Race relations. I. De Lannoy, Ariane, author. II. Title.
    DT1971.N49 2014
    968.065—dc23

                                                        201304193

❖ ❖ ❖

For Siya and Mpendulo

SIXTY-SEVEN YEARS AFTER THE END of the Civil War, Hortense Powdermaker, an adventurous young Yale University anthropologist set out for the small town of Indianola, Mississippi. Located in the heart of the Delta region, the home of King Cotton, a territory largely unfamiliar to Americans, Indianola was a county seat at the center of the Jim Crow South. Officially and openly segregated, the town was in the grips of a social system that bore a strong resemblance to what would become the apartheid regime of South Africa, already well under construction beginning with the passage of the Colour Bar Act in 1911.

A former labor organizer for the Amalgamated Clothing Workers, Powdermaker was interested in learning about the long aftermath of the Civil War in the South, and about how black and white people had adjusted—or not—to the stresses of living in close proximity but in a separate, rigidly hierarchical social world.[1] Indianola at the time was blanketed by "Whites only" signs: on buses, benches, and store entrances. The local movie theater restricted black people to the balcony. White hospitals refused black patients, who had to seek medical care in their own community. Powdermaker herself had to find a way to move back and forth between two worlds that seemed to use every conceivable mechanism to avoid dealing with each other, outside of strictly instrumental relations of the work world or the commercial sphere. Black women cleaned the houses belonging to white families. Black men, women, and children picked cotton in the fields of white landowners. White sheriffs with loaded shotguns loomed over the black world, and the Ku Klux Klan and its "midnight riders" in white sheets struck terror into the hearts of African American families. Social relations were deliberately minimized and carefully managed according to strict and legally enforceable codes that Powdermaker had to abide by if she was to understand these parallel worlds.

Her book *After Freedom: A Cultural Study of the Deep South,* whose title inspired our own, was published to acclaim in 1939. It was among the first to reach a broad audience interested in what had changed—and what had not—in the land of Jim Crow since the end of a bloody civil war fought in part to end slavery. Powdermaker's monograph became something of a landmark in anthropology because it was a trenchant analysis of what seemed a foreign country to many American readers. The Deep South had changed relatively little since the mid-nineteenth century. Entrenched racial animus persisted and so too did the police state that enforced the harshest aspects of what came to be known as "American apartheid."

Powdermaker's observations were poignant, disturbing, and not limited to race. Rigid segregation meant that on either side of the tracks in Indianola, class differences structured both the black and the white communities. African American doctors and preachers served the needs of their people but were elevated above them by their educational and occupational advantages. Their counterparts on the white side of Indianola saw themselves in the same stratified light. Hence, if race was the bold dividing line, class was its subtext. In fact, the stronger the separation of people by race, the more pronounced the internal differences by class. People who were thrown together on account of one characteristic, skin color, found ways to differentiate themselves from those whose neighborhoods, schools, and churches they were forced to share.

Racial division and the ugly consequences that follow remain alive in many parts of the United States today. Setbacks—from the gutting of the Voting Rights Act to the pernicious consequences of mass incarceration—are reminders of how far we have to go in our own long walk to freedom. Yet no one would argue that nothing has changed for the better. Fifty years after Martin Luther King Jr.'s historic march on Washington, there are black mayors, Ivy League university presidents, justices of the Supreme Court, and captains of industry in addition to the first black president of the country. Many of these leaders have seemingly sprung up from nowhere, but many too are the sons and daughters of elites who spend summers on Martha's Vineyard. Class matters in America's black community just as it does in its white world.

Is the country becoming more polarized and politically divided? Or are racial, gender-based, and other prejudices that seemed enduring in Powdermaker's day fading away? Younger, more tolerant generations have embraced forms of diversity that their elders could not abide. Gay marriage is the law in many states; it was unthinkable in Powdermaker's time. Is the glass half full or half empty? Where have we come from and where are we going?

Hortense Powdermaker gave us an enduring portrait of the United States in the early days of a long and tortuous transformation of the racial order. We hope to do the same for South Africa, in part by posing and answering similar questions. Twenty years ago, in 1994, South Africa celebrated its first free election. New voters, members of the majority population, which had been denied the franchise for generations, stood in line for as long as nine hours to reach polling booths. It was a democratic frenzy, appropriate to the end of a monumental struggle. Four years before, the proud figure of Nelson Mandela had emerged from Victor Verster Prison after twenty-seven years behind bars. Millions around the globe witnessed his walk to freedom as international media descended on South Africa to announce that apartheid was finished. A clenched fist held high and eyes beaming, Mandela strode along with his then-wife, Winnie, by his side while thousands of people in tears sang the anthem of the African National Congress, "Nkosi Sikelel' iAfrika" ("Lord Bless Afrika"), in Xhosa, one of South Africa's eleven official languages. Mandela's refusal to agree to deals offered him by anxious apartheid leaders, who had said they would cut his sentence in exchange for calling off strikes and protests, had increased admiration for him among his people and in the broader world.

On the day of the first democratic elections, international observers marveled that a country deeply torn by racial division and bathed in brutality was free from the violent explosions that many had expected would follow when apartheid collapsed. The street battles, torture chambers, water cannons, police murders of children marching in the streets of Soweto, economic sanctions, and years of exile had ended.

Since the 1994 elections, many books have been written about the human rights catastrophe that was apartheid, about the leaders who brought the system to its knees, and about the political concessions of F. W. De Klerk, Mandela's negotiating partner, who had represented the all-White National Party. A few books have covered the prospects of leaders of this new democracy, people who—like Mandela and his successors Thabo Mbeki and Jacob Zuma—have written its constitution and rebuilt its courts. More than one book has detailed the first use of a Truth and Reconciliation Commission (TRC) that exposed crimes against activists like Steven Biko without exacting any penalty besides public condemnation. Together these works detail parts of an extraordinary history. What they do not provide is an account of how ordinary people, particularly the South Africans who came of age during the post-apartheid transition, see the country that is their birthright: the "born-free generation."[2] Now in their late twenties and early thirties, these people were children during the old regime but by the time they came of age, apartheid was far enough in the past to have receded into the background. This generation has witnessed the birth of a new democracy, and it struggles with the meaning of the past but is no longer a prisoner of it. Their parents were on the front lines of that dramatic history, and their children have learned a great deal about their experience through private conversation. When tales of the struggle are told on television or among political leaders who seek public legitimacy by leaning on their sacrifices, many South Africans in their early thirties resonate to those stories. But these accounts do not belong to them. It is not their experience; it is their legacy.

It is to members of this new generation that the richest and most unequal country in Africa will belong.[3] In due course, some of them will be in charge of the nation's businesses, courts, universities, and newspapers. The less fortunate, those who were born in impoverished townships and have been unemployed and poor for years, will still need to raise a new generation of children who will look to them for guidance. Do South Africans who have watched the emergence of their new democracy feel optimistic about the future? Or are they disappointed by the enormous—some would say monumental—problems of inequality, poor housing, escalating crime, and schools that continue to deliver a brilliant education to a few and a substandard one to many? Do they have faith in the revolutionary party—the African National Congress, the party of Mandela—that brought South Africa to this democratic moment but "after freedom" confronts problems of corruption and capability? Is there really a movement toward a "rainbow" nation or is the specter of racial division ever present and intractable? Can people who were suppressed under apartheid for so long ever learn to trust the descendants of those who lorded it over their parents? For the minority White population, the questions of political representation and economic security remain just that: questions.

These are the very issues Hortense Powdermaker set out to explore in the US South eighty years ago. They are the issues that were on our mind as we embarked on research for this book, which took us from the center of Cape Town in the South Africa's Western Cape Province to desolate outposts of the Eastern Cape Province. Cape Town is a distinctive place from which to examine changes in the texture of life in South Africa after twenty years of democratic rule. The second largest city in the country, it is wealthier overall than much of the rest of South Africa, with a high proportion of its most successful manufacturing, high-technology, tourism, and finance companies.[4]

The region around Cape Town is now tightly integrated with the world economy, and trends that affect the country through trade and global competition are pronounced here. For the same reason, the city has long been a powerful magnet for migrants, both internal and international. Cape Town has more to offer economically than rural areas to the east and north where extreme poverty is widespread. People continue to migrate back and forward between these rural areas and Cape Town or the capital city, Pretoria, seeking more opportunities for work and education. Many end up in the burgeoning informal settlements outside the city centers.[5]

Despite its economic advantages, or perhaps because of them, Cape Town is a poster child for problems deriving from income inequality. UN-Habitat classifies the city as one of the most unequal in the world: approximately 40 percent of households are poor, with insufficient income to access basic necessities such as food and shelter.[6] The enormous gulf that separates the haves and have-nots is starkly visible in its patterns of racial segregation and the poverty of its Black population. At the same time, the Western Cape Province is the only province where the Coloured community, created by apartheid laws that deemed "mixed race" people a cut above their Black counterparts, is numerically dominant.[7] There is no other region of the country where one can appreciate the dynamic between the Coloured population and the new Black middle class or elites, the old White elites, and the massive Black population composed of the desperately poor.[8]

Cape Town looks in places like the colonial capital it was in the nineteenth century, with stately buildings fronted by pillars and the glorious Company Gardens stretching out before the Parliament. Partly surrounded by ocean at the southern tip of the Cape of Good Hope, blessed with a climate that rivals that of coastal California, dominated by majestic mountains, it is a stunning part of the continent. Yet a mere fifteen miles from this paradise are townships where more than half the residents live in shacks. Many survive without electricity or running water and endure horrific crime and endemic disease. It is emblematic of South Africa's rampant inequality that people could live so close to one another and yet be so far apart.

Seven individuals—the people of this book—provide a window on the meaning of multiracial democracy, its possibilities, and pitfalls ahead. Those looking out from Parliament's stately buildings and those who gaze warily from behind the makeshift door of a shack have different views of the years of political yearning and institution building. The views are also dramatically different depending on generation. People who lived through the struggle against apartheid can see progress, but younger people, the people of the book, wonder whether they can rely on the social changes that have transpired or whether they need to focus on what remains to be accomplished.

After Freedom is dedicated to Siyamthanda and Mpendulo Kweyama, the children of Ariane and her husband, Mdu Kweyama, who at four and seventeen represent the future of South Africa. Along with the rest of the world, they owe a debt (too large to be described) to the father of South African democracy, the late President Nelson Mandela.

CHAPTER ONE

The People of the Book

THANDISWA

The remote mountain pasture of the Kat River Valley in the eastern Cape Province is a stunning vista of dark green trees shading ravines where water flows to valleys covered in yellow mustard flowers. An unbroken carpet of grass cascades down the hills below the mountain, waving as the wind passes through the valley. Cattle graze on the mountain from early morning until dusk. Shepherds let them roam but call them in when the sun sets, coaxing the cows back down the mountainside to the "kraals," pens where they will spend the night. Thieves may be on the lookout for opportunities to abscond with these valuable animals, which are among the most important possessions of any rural family.

Round huts—"rondavels"—are posted around the kraals so that the cattle minders can keep a close watch on the herds. Some of these traditional dwellings are only six feet in diameter, just large enough to hold a bed and small fire. Although the climate is mild, the temperature in the high pastureland can dip well below freezing in the winter. Living in a rondavel can be a lonely affair. The romantic image of the pastoral community, where neighbors help one another and band together against the elements, doesn't always apply here. What some neighbors do to one another, or fear they are going to do, sets a tone of caution and distance that can erupt into damaging gossip and ostracism.

Thandiswa Boya lived in her family's rondavel on this mountainside for seven years, in the former Ciskei homeland created by the apartheid government. Arriving from Khayelitsha, a Black African township five hundred miles away, she was responsible for the care of her family's cows from the age of seventeen until she turned twenty-four.[1] She was three hours by foot from the nearest hamlet, Seymour, where she could—on occasion—visit people or a local shop. But her main responsibility was to look after the family savings account, eight cows. Worth several thousand rands each, cattle were the only property Africans were allowed to own in the apartheid years.

While the region once boasted large commercial citrus farms, mostly in hands of White South Africans, its demarcation as Ciskei in the 1970s led to

The rondavel in the Kat River Valley where Thandiswa spent seven years caring for eight cows, her family's "savings account."

the exodus of those farmers. With them went the jobs that sustained the workers of Seymour. All that is left now are miles of dead trees. A tobacco factory that once operated in the center of Seymour is now a moldering shell with broken windows. The local hotel now serves as a *shebeen* (an informal bar), and the only place in a dying town that shows any sign of life is the government office that dispenses monthly pensions and child allowances.

It is in this economically desolate region that Thandiswa led the herd out to pasture and brought them in at night, day in and day out. Left alone, surrounded by neighbors who were hostile or indifferent, with little food and nothing to do, she was imprisoned in open space. Years later, her bitterness over this abandonment is deep and abiding. Her life has been indelibly marked by the interruption she was forced to endure in her education. She returned to Khayelitsha from her seven-year exile a damaged soul, her sacrifice unrecognized by her father, who had been the one who had insisted she waste those precious years up on the mountainside.

When we met, Thandiswa was twenty-eight and the mother of two sons born to her from fathers who had not been part of her life since her children arrived. She was living near—yet a world away from— Cape Town's city center. With approximately 400,000 residents, Khayelitsha is a mixture of brick and plaster houses with modern conveniences—plumbing, heating, electricity—and informal houses, wooden shacks thrown together from scrap lumber, with roofs made of corrugated-iron sheets or plastic tarpaulins pinned down by the weight of old tires.[2] It is hard to believe that whole families live in these dwellings, typically only about eight feet square. As many as six people could be stuck in a shack without a toilet, bath, electricity, or heat. The structures spring up along rutted pathways, a rabbits' warren of lanes that muddy in winter, when rainwater floods into the shacks, leaving everything inside too moldy to salvage. All is lost every winter.

Thousands of Khayelitsha's shack dwellers are migrants from the Eastern Cape Province, where Thandiswa spent seven years cattle-minding. They have come in search of work, better education, or better health care services, all of which are in greater supply in the Western Cape.[3] Ramshackle dwellings stretch as far as the eye can see in many places; the makeshift houses cluster around the edges of formal settlements with durable buildings. The city works to provide basic services to many of these areas, but in the most informal ones people pay their neighbors in houses across the road for a little electricity, illegally diverted from the main wires to their shack.[4] This will provide enough energy to power a TV set or a toaster, though not at the same time and not the whole day.

In the years since apartheid ended and the "pass laws" that controlled the movement of Black and Coloured people were abandoned, a flood gate has opened, depositing in Cape Town thousands of newcomers desperate to escape the more punishing form of rural poverty they know. The lucky ones have steady jobs in the city of Cape Town as domestic workers, car guards (watching over parked cars), kitchen workers in restaurants, and even occasionally administrative staff. For these citizens of Khayelitsha, home may be a well-appointed zinc shack with curtains, a refrigerator, a functional television, and a real bed. The walls of these more comfortable dwellings are often covered in colorful wallpaper: newspaper sheets covered with ads for shampoo and motorcycles. The poorest residents have none of these creature comforts, only a bare wooden structure with a leaky plastic roof.

Thandiswa's house is in one of the older, formal neighborhoods of the township. Pale plaster, the color of milk, the house is bleached by the southern sun. There is no shade in the yard, nothing green anywhere near. The house is surrounded by sand. On one side there is a rusted gate, standing open. The windows are covered with "burglar bars"—wrought-iron barriers that keep the "smash and run" intruder at bay—and there is a security gate at the door. A forecourt in the front stretches to the next-door house, where two young men are hanging around, leaning against the door of an old car parked in the yard, watching the comings and goings at Thandiswa's house. She is not happy about their attention and waves them away when they make obscene remarks in a street dialect of Xhosa we do not understand (although she does). There is very little privacy to be had and White visitors are bound to provoke a stir. She beckons us inside, closing the iron gate across the front door.

The seven adults and three toddlers who live in Thandiswa's home share four beds. By local standards they are a large family, but they remain middle-income and their home reflects it.[5] It is a house, not a shack: it has multiple rooms, running cold water, electricity, and an indoor toilet. For thousands of Khayelitsha residents who must make do with far less, Thandiswa's home would be a dream come true.

When we first met, Thandiswa was mired in what seemed to be a para-lyzing depression and without a job or any means of supporting her family. Despite many efforts to find paid work, she is now largely dependent on the earnings of her father and government support for parents with children. Her days are endlessly monotonous, and the future will be—she is sure—just like the present: terminally boring. She is surrounded by kids all day, her own and her sisters', but she seems uninterested in them, listless in their presence. They try to catch her attention and get her to play, but she ignores them. Her two-year-old, Akhona, in turn often seems glazed.

In the years we have known her, Thandiswa has taken significant steps to change her trajectory on a number of occasions. Yet these moments of activity punctuate long months of stasis. She is desperate to take control of her life, but does not really know how, and her diary takes a turn toward the self-critical when nothing works out:

> Life is hard if you complain and do not make effort to improve yourself. I think I am very lazy; I become angry at myself sometimes. Sometimes I do go out there to look for a job, e.g., I once photocopied my CVs (about 6 times), and I visited different shops and places. Some promised to call me and they never did so, some simply said they are not employing people anymore. This whole process is exhausting, sometimes I just give up, and simpl[y] get into a taxi and I go home.[6]

When we got to know her better, we realized that Thandiswa was often fearful when it came to looking for job information, let alone actually apply-ing for employment. Too many times she had tried to find ways to better her education or land a job only to be disappointed. Periodically she spent entire days searching for work, walking from one store to another, her purse full of résumés. When rumors wafted past her that a firm might be hiring, she pushed past her self-doubt and made sure she was in line to drop off her résumé, buttonholed the hiring managers, and asked employees what else she could do to ensure she would be considered. Hundreds of jobless people from her township did the same; hence silence was the typical response.

Thandiswa's desperation to find work led her to become the victim of scams. Once she paid R550 for a two-week course that was supposed to train her to be a cashier, but she found out from a newspaper report that it was a fraud: other people had also been swindled. It could have been worse. She knew women who had paid thousands for a three-month course to become flight attendants, only to be left high and dry.

Her diary testifies to how frustrating the experience of looking for a job can be in a country where official unemployment has now crested over 25 percent but whose townships suffer far more.[7] In most, 60 percent are without work.

> What does hurt and has in the past, is when a job did not [require] any educational background, yet I still did not get it. I wonder, "Is my face smeared with shit? Why is it that when it's my turn to be interviewed I'm turned down and told that the job is only for men yet there are some women [with whom I was] waiting who got the job?"

These are jobs she could have done, she noted. All that was required was the desire to work. Leaving these interviews, tears would slowly well in her eyes and start to fall. As soon as she was outside, Thandiswa would quickly find a hidden spot where she could break down and sob.

AMANDA

Amanda says,

> I live a modern life. I go to clubs. I dress modern. I live in town. I eat out. I sit with you, a White woman, and we talk openly. There are no barriers. I don't feel I have to hold back. That was not possible in the olden days. This is modernity. I do not wear traditional dresses. I don't go to the office wearing nothing but beads to cover my breasts. I fit in.

Amanda is dressed for success. Her light-blue satin blouse matches her knee-length tight skirt. Color-coordinated shoes and a matching handbag complete the ensemble. Amanda's hair is platted into a thousand fine braids that hang down over her shoulders. Her wide-set, dark-brown eyes are framed with sparkling makeup. The effect is electric. She is every inch the contemporary, upscale Black girl, who could have walked off the pages of a glamour magazine, ready for an eligible young bachelor to buy her a drink in a trendy downtown bar. Gone are all traces of the poverty-stricken, segregated oppression of the township world. In their place: the future.

Amanda works for a major NGO headquartered in Cape Town that does advocacy work and educational outreach in public health. Her job brings her into close contact with the reality of poverty in places like Khayelitsha, where Thandiswa lives, but her personal life is insulated from these conditions. She is at the other end of the social universe.

A recent documentary produced by her NGO highlights the disastrous conditions in some of the worst informal areas of Nyanga, a Black township in Cape Town not far from where Amanda's half-sister lives. It features Amanda as the narrator, walking along garbage-clogged streams, looking in on people suffering from the end stages of AIDS or tuberculosis, urging viewers to get involved and contribute to charities that attend to the sick. Here she is a modern professional: engaged in serious work, albeit with a show business flare for the dramatic. Her ideal career is as a TV newscaster or actress.

Amanda's personal life is stranded between the poles of her material ambitions—expressed through her high heels and trendy life—and the vulnerability of her insecure station in the new Black middle class.[8] Amanda is not rich. When we first met, she was sharing an apartment in Sea Point, once a "Whites only" neighborhood of Cape Town that fronts the coast. The end of apartheid saw an influx of Black and Coloured South Africans, along with African nationals from other countries, into this previously forbidden area. Many of the original owners of these seaside flats fled the neighborhood in the late 1990s, when they realized it was no longer in a "Whites only" zone, and they became absentee landlords. Shops and restaurants with sidewalk terraces down by the waterfront closed down out of fear of the "crime and grime" their owners anticipated. Up on the hillsides, where mansions overlook the coast, White South Africans remained. But the main road, closer to the water, became a busy, noisy, street buzzing with cars, taxis, and buses. It is tree-lined for shade, and schoolchildren of all colors occupy the sidewalks—but so do prostitutes. Fancy clubs and good restaurants are nestled into streets not far from gambling houses and drug trafficking spots.

Around the corner from Amanda's apartment building, a revival of sorts is underway, spurred by investments that accompanied the 2010 World Cup competition, its first stop on the African continent. The Sea Point promenade, a green belt along the oceanfront, is one of the few places in town where skin color, culture, and class seem to fade away. White, Coloured and Black African families picnic in the grass and watch the big container ships that round the Horn of Africa on their way to the Arabian Peninsula. The deep blue sea crashes on the rock barriers that protect the land from the pounding, and a lovely breeze keeps the promenade cool, even on the hottest days in Cape Town. Children of all colors play together on the slides and roundabouts in the playgrounds or kick soccer balls. Well-heeled professionals jog past the homeless splayed on benches that line the promenade. Sea Point is a mélange that represents what the country was supposed to become: a spectrum of citizens safe in one another's company. In this particular neighborhood, that is exactly what has emerged.

It is one of the reasons Amanda fell in love with Sea Point. She reveled in the luxury of living near the water, and being close to the Victoria and Albert (V&A) mega-shopping complex and upscale double movie theater near the harbor, with its picturesque views of the water and Table Mountain. But living in such a trendy zone has cost her dearly. At first she had one room to herself in a three-bedroom apartment. Her room was tidy and stylishly decorated with colorful pillows, but at twenty-five, an age when many young professionals have whole apartments to themselves, one room was Amanda's entire private universe. And even this did not last long. Amanda and her roommates were illegal subletters, paying money to a man who claimed to hold the legal lease. He didn't bother to turn over their rent payments to the real landlord. Within six months, the whole arrangement came crashing down and Amanda was evicted.

She has bounced around ever since, moving for a time to a close-in suburban neighborhood, Rondebosch, near the University of Cape Town, and most recently far outside the city orbit to a new development about a forty-five-minute drive from the city. Amanda's fifth-hand car broke down more often than it was on the road, but when it was running she relied on it to take her to work in the city. When it wasn't, she leaned on a friend or joined her neighbors in the overcrowded taxi vans that routinely convey ex-urban dwellers back to the City Bowl where most jobs are to be found. Her new flat is a two-bedroom place in a modern, three-story block of apartments. The walls and floors are white, the latter made of stone. She has a flat-screen TV on the wall, a black faux-leather couch, and a gray shag rug on the floor. It is rather spartan but screams a kind of modernism with which Amanda wants to be identified.

Her new home is conveniently located near a new indoor shopping mall, with big-box stores and down-market clothing shops. It is not as luxurious as the V&A shopping mall in the city, but it would have been unthinkable as recently as twenty years ago for a Black woman in South Africa to live in an enclave like this. There were no such places. It took the growth of a Black and Coloured middle class in South Africa to create the demand for new gated communities.

Of course, for Amanda, mobility of this kind introduces complexities that are not always to her liking. "People think I'm a coconut," she complains. "You know, Black on the outside and White on the inside. . . . But I know my culture. I am a proud Black woman." It is not clear whether anyone actually accuses Amanda of deserting her roots or whether this is simply a critique that she perceives. Either way, it stings. Amanda and thousands of other fortunate Black people have enjoyed a degree of prosperity post-apartheid that has enabled them to streak past their poorer counterparts into occupations, housing, lifestyles, and forms of social interchange with other races that were largely impossible under the old regime.

AMBROSE

The community garden in Manenberg was supposed to be a little oasis of greenery in a dusty, forbidding corner of greater Cape Town. Volunteers turned the soil in long furrows and planted seeds for vegetables, fruit, and flowers. They strung a hand-painted sign above the entrance and carefully locked its gate to protect the garden. When plants started to sprout in the spring, the volunteers decided a pond was needed so that children could play in the water while their mothers sat nearby. Young men dug a hole, filled it with water, and circled the new pond with white stones. Someone located an old bench and placed it nearby. This was the closest thing this part of Manenberg had to a park other than the school playground, which was then, as now, on a more desolate stretch of sandy, barren land.

Little is left of the community garden today. A blasted, empty expanse, it is covered with broken beer bottles, empty soda cans, and plastic trash bags that blow up against the rickety fence. Garbage floats in the pond, filled now with stagnant water. Little kids still play here, dropping stones into the water, looking for fish, but they thread through scum. Tools that were kept in a shed near the garden have long since been stolen, and the shed itself is falling apart, its roof caved in and its walls leaning at odd angles, the paint on the boards weathered and peeling. Everything has gone brown. Not the dark brown of tilled earth, but the dry, cracked beige that alternates with the dirty gray of old cement, the color of Manenberg's apartment "flats."

These flats, which were built by the apartheid government for the Coloured population exiled from Cape Town's city center, rise up from the Cape Flats. The dusty plain is bisected by freeways, where cars and trucks belch out exhaust and shack fires caused by a careless match and spread by high winds can displace hundreds of families in the space of an hour. There are few properly paved streets in this part of Manenberg. Cars bounce on their shocks as they navigate through ruts and litter—old shoes, plastic containers, and crumpled paper.

Recessed from the street are blocks of apartment buildings, each three stories high. They form partial squares, open at one end, surrounding hard, black tarmac courtyards. The inner face of each flat looks down into the courtyards in a style reminiscent of a prison block. Apartment windows are covered with iron burglar bars and have long since gone translucent. Here and there, a broken window has been patched with newspaper or cardboard to keep the wind and dust from blowing through.

Residents have strung wire lines from one side of their courtyard to another so that they can dry their laundry in the wind that blows through the townships. From a distance, the clothes flapping in the breeze look festive, brightly colored cloth waving in the wind. Up close, though, the gaiety dissolves into disorder. The walls of the apartment blocks are covered with menacing graffiti announcing gang boundaries or asserting political slogans. Anything made of metal—gates, stop signs, cars—is rusted through. And there is a lot of metal in Manenberg because everything is gated. Anything that is not behind a security fence will not be left standing for long. Even the local library, a haven for the children of Manenberg, is surrounded by bars. Visitors must be buzzed in.

It is a work day in Cape Town, and those who have jobs have long since left Manenberg for the city in minivans that pack in fifteen people, carrying them from the Coloured township to the city's commercial districts and tourist zones, about twenty minutes away. In this part of Manenberg, the part that twenty-seven-year-old Ambrose calls home, few adults are employed. Instead they perch on top of overturned buckets that double as stools, clustered in knots outdoors along the rubble that passes for sidewalks. Children tear around the streets, chasing a worn ball or trying to open a hydrant to splash in. Every so often, they rush to their mother's side but are generally ignored. Manenberg's children are often expected to take care of themselves.

Born in Manenberg in the early 1980s, Ambrose is a tall, dark-skinned young man with a toothless grin. Some years ago, he decided to mimic a gruesome prison ritual practiced by gangs that rule the country's penitentiaries: initiates extract their front teeth—all of them—to mark themselves permanently as loyal soldiers. When Ambrose smiles, that yawning gap signals to potential employers and street toughs alike that he is part of a prison culture "on the outside." Actually Ambrose has spent no more than a year behind bars for five or six petty offenses, mainly assault and robbery. His record pales by comparison to the other men in his family tree. Ten of them—brothers, uncles—have either died behind bars or in violent attacks in the townships.

His mother tongue is Afrikaans, the language of the Boer population that battled the British for control of South Africa in the early twentieth century. It is the first language of South Africa's Coloured community, the largest ethnic group in the Western Cape. Defined by the architects of apartheid as the "mixed race community," Coloured people were favored relative to Black people but remained second-class citizens in almost all respects. It has left them in a politically ambiguous role in the years since apartheid fell.

Ambrose hangs out along the alleyways of the township and in the vicinity of a local nonprofit organization, which provides community support and functions as home away from home for him. Without a high school degree or a job, Ambrose has no other place to spend his time. He has occasionally found temporary jobs as a manual laborer, but they never lasted more than three months and paid poorly. Ambrose's mother, Felicity, thinks he could have done better. She was exasperated by her son, but at least for a few years she was loyal to him and made serious efforts to help him find a pathway to work. Three years after he was kicked out of high school, Felicity sent him to Cape Town College in the nearby, more middle-class Coloured township of Athlone for a degree in civil engineering. In the beginning, Ambrose thought this was his ticket out of Manenberg, but it wasn't long before the defects in his educational background began to show. He lost interest in his studies and failed. He tried again, this time seeking a painting and plumbing diploma at the same college, but didn't finish the required courses. School is simply not for Ambrose.

This is not to say that he is unwilling to work. He has painted buildings, worked at a bread company cleaning floors, and found his way to the Stellenbosch wine country, where he packed wine bottles into crates. Local community organizations have given him the occasional odd job sweeping the streets, but these jobs bring in little money, certainly not enough to pay rent. The cost of transport for these jobs can take up half his pay.

Ambrose rarely ventures beyond the limits of the township and knows nothing of Cape Town, despite its proximity. On very rare occasions he gets to go to one of the beautiful beaches along the seacoast. His face lights up at the thought of a day in the water. But for the most part, Ambrose is stranded in a place that doesn't want him. And the feeling is mutual.

DANIEL

Mandela Rhodes Place on a scorching hot January day. The rooftop deck by the pool is coming to life with oiled bodies and drinks with little parasols. One of Daniel Frederick's favorite hangout spots, this corner of town used to be rather grim, offering little else but daytime office blocks that turned deserted, gloomy, and downright dangerous at night. Today the neighborhood boasts several multibillion-rand developments erected as part of a planned revival of the city center. Cranes and building sites stand alongside shiny new apartment blocks and hotels, yet-to-be-revived Victorian houses, and scruffy inner-city areas that have not been incorporated into the gentrification plan. Real estate developers target foreign investors, business entrepreneurs, and tourists, but many of the new housing developments also manage to attract Capetonians who appreciate the prospect of walking to work, an easy "lock-up-and-go" lifestyle, safety, and proximity to cafes, restaurants, nightclubs, gyms, and open-air swimming pools on their rooftop decks.

Mandela Rhodes is a destination for yuppies who want to stroll along the pedestrian mall filled with little cafes and tourist stalls opposite the stately and venerable St. George's Cathedral. From the rooftop deck of his apartment building, Daniel watches the bustling on the street below. This is the Cape Town that Daniel and his wife call home. Like Ambrose, he is a Coloured man, but that is where the resemblance ends. We are a long way from Manenberg.

With his light-brown complexion and slightly Asian features, Daniel is still an anomaly in Mandela Rhodes Place. Black and Coloured people make up the majority of Cape Town's population, but there are no people of color on the roof deck except the occasional waiter or maintenance person. Unlike Johannesburg, where young Black professionals are an ever-growing part of the population, Cape Town does not have a sizeable middle or upper class of color. The chasm that separates Daniel from Ambrose testifies to the ways in which class has become an ever more powerful determinant of one's fate in South Africa. Race plays its part, but the accidents of family income and education increasingly determine where people within racial groups end up. Daniel often hangs out with a racially mixed crowd, but one made up of well-heeled young professionals. He visits all the trendy cafes, enjoying what he calls "a good life." He loves taking his wife out to a nice dinner in an upscale restaurant, where he fits right in, dressed sharply in name-brand clothes, shiny sunglasses, and an expensive watch.

Every day, Daniel strolls through the Company Gardens to his office, enjoying the manicured lawns, flowering trees, and the cool shade. It is a bucolic setting but it is also a public space that cannot be walled off from the "other," the street dweller that doesn't fit into this gentrified scene. The Gardens contain Tuynhuys, the South African president's official Cape Town residence, which is surrounded by a formidable security infrastructure. Dozens of cameras survey the lush, tree-lined lanes and green lawns. These same Company Gardens are home to dozens of vagrants, who use the lawns and benches as an overnight rest spot and public washing or eating place.

Daniel is aware of the inequalities that define Cape Town—and South African—life. After we gave him a camera to record for us his perspective of the world he inhabits, Daniel chose to take photos of the Parliament, referring to how things have changed for the better for people of color in the country, now having a vote and a voice and the ability to work their way up the socio-economic ladder. But his pictures also show homeless and poor people, whose lives are very different from his own. Apart from daily encounters with them on walks to and from work, he has very little contact with this part of South African society. Yet he knows it is there.

There are people in his own extended family who have not had his good fortune, but he rarely sees them. These relatives live in Coloured townships like Manenberg and do not visit Daniel or his family, who are now quite comfortably off. Daniel explains that he does not really know what to talk about with them about on the odd occasion that he does see them. He has no friends who still live in townships.

He lives the life that Ambrose would dream about if only he knew it existed.

BRANDON

Far removed from the city's hustle and bustle, all is quiet in the wide lanes of the northern suburbs. Many houses in the "Northerns" are large, some brick-faced, some plastered and painted nondescript beige. Some are smaller, single-story bungalows of simple design, but all are neat and proper, well kept. Manicured gardens, replete with kitschy statues and garden gnomes, dot the landscape. Some of the cul-de-sac streets have small parks. Everything here is easily accessible: large shopping malls, gas stations, restaurants, schools, and hospitals, all well maintained and impeccably middle class.

This is Brandon's home, the place where many members of his extended family still live. It is also the epicenter of what locals refer to as the community "beyond the Boerewors Curtain," literally the "Boer Sausage" Curtain. Brandon's culture celebrates the outdoor barbeque (or *braai*), not only for the taste of roasted meat but also for the conviviality of neighborhood and family gatherings where the cooking takes place over an open fire.

The northern suburbs are almost exclusively populated by White people, who form the backbone of the stalwart conservative ranks of Cape Town's political landscape. The dominant language in this area is Afrikaans, and many residents still support the politics of the old apartheid regime, though they would hesitate now to say so publically in the presence of outsiders.

This is no "rainbow nation." Most of the older residents want little to do with "the new South Africa." Many of them lost jobs when the post-apartheid government, looking to overturn decades of racial discrimination, imposed quotas designed to make way for the majority in the labor market. The resentment is high, laced with charges of hypocrisy that the African National Congress, which campaigned for colorblind policies, has now instituted forms of affirmative action that pivot on race. The Black Economic Empowerment legislation sets standards for multiracial business ownership. The Employment Equity Act requires companies to have plans to transform their employment profiles. Affirmative action measures in higher education have led to race-based admissions quotas at schools such as the University of Cape Town. Where is the fairness in this? many members of Brandon's community want to know.

Brandon is a beefy blonde man with a big smile, always nonchalant, with a pack of cigarettes close at hand, cracking jokes at every turn. He resembles Marlon Brando in *On the Waterfront*, with rough edges born of a working-class culture. His exterior is somewhat ironic, though, as his family is not actually blue collar in origin. Until he lost his job, Brandon's father, Ian, worked as a manager in the corporate world. Today he runs a pool service company, and Brandon has his own small home security systems enterprise, although he often struggles to make ends meet. Brandon speaks English with an accent that is hard to place, inherited from his Irish father and Dutch mother. Straddling the English- and Afrikaans-speaking White social circles in Cape Town, Brandon nonetheless thinks of himself as Afrikaans: he attended Afrikaans schools and grew up in this predominantly Afrikaans suburb, where he feels people are "more down to earth and honest," strict and conservative but also caring.

That caring rarely extends to non-White South Africans. With embarrassment, Brandon would recall the degrading, racist language he encounters every day in his own community. He took it upon himself to translate for us websites in Afrikaans that appeal to people who detest what has become of their country and who do not hesitate to speak of armed conflict needed to "take it back." Brandon spent many hours explaining "those ideas" to us—and perhaps to himself too.

There has been little movement in a more liberal direction in the community that Brandon thinks of as his own. Although skin color is no longer supposed to matter, residents of the Northerns tend to lose themselves in a discourse that places "them," non-Whites, in opposition to "us," White people. In focus groups and casual conversation, the older generation explain that "they" are "just too different." Accordingly, it just would not make sense to make friends across those dividing lines.

The increase in crime in the White areas since the end of apartheid has led many in the Northerns to build high walls around their houses. Iron barriers designed to repel intruders are everywhere. Some burglar bars are decorative or artistic, but others resemble bars on a prison cell. Either way, one cannot look outside of the windows to the landscape beyond without being reminded of the security state. Iron bars have become a ubiquitous feature of urban life for people of all colors.

The reality of high crime levels and reports on the increased number of murders of White South Africans—especially White farmers—made Brandon's Afrikaner community wonder whether "they really all hate us." Worldwide condemnation of apartheid left Afrikaners on the defensive, and while no one save the most extreme elements of the African National Congress were arguing for violent retaliation in the wake of the democratic transition, more than a few Whites understood why the logic of retribution might not be unthinkable.

One day, Brandon and his brother, Mark, were sitting around the *braai* and we asked Mark about his views of Black people. "One on one, I love Black people," he said.

> But as a race I kind of hate them . . . because they're always cocking up everything, in my opinion. That's the way I perceive it. . . . Like, before they were allowed to walk around everywhere, we didn't have crime. Now they're always just robbing people. . . . And I work with people, you give them a job, and they're nice . . . It's not all of them, but especially if we talk to builders and people . . . if you treat them too nice, they start taking advantage. . . . I'm also struggling with how I feel about . . . the natives.

Brandon joked, but in so many words agreed with his brother's stand. It would be wrong, though, to conclude that the brothers are no different from the Afrikaner generation that preceded them. Indeed, they themselves would draw a sharp contrast, describing their view as "liberal," rejecting the racist ideas of their elders. Yet, as one young White man told us, "Sometimes I struggle to really be as liberal and as nonracial as I want to be."

ANNA

Anna's bubbly personality is contagious and suits the artsy, trendy community where she works as a budding architect. In 2000, she moved from the national capital of Pretoria with her mother and sisters into Cape Town's leafy green suburb of Newlands. A quiet, upscale neighborhood fairly close to the city, Newlands looks like Greenwich, Connecticut, or Scarsdale, New York: big houses, lovely gardens, tall old trees that line clean and orderly streets. White, English-speaking residents jog along the paths of Newlands, walk their dogs, and stop for a quick chat with the doctors and lawyers who are their neighbors. Some of the best elementary and secondary schools in the country are within walking distance of Anna's house, which is one of the reasons why her mother, Karen, decided to move there after she divorced Anna's father.

Karen sent Anna and her two sisters to Westerford High School, a school known throughout the country for its high academic standards. Although they are fifth-generation German immigrants, Anna and her sisters all speak fluent German, English, and Afrikaans, an unusual expression of ethnic pride, as immigrants commonly lose their mother tongue within two or three generations. In Anna's case, it is perhaps even more surprising because the family didn't migrate to South Africa directly but instead (four generations back) were among the large population of German colonists who settled on large farms in Namibia, where Anna's grandfather still lives.

Anna enjoyed her protected life in the suburbs for a while, but eventually needed to "get out" and meet other people. She moved to Kalk Bay, a picturesque little town right on the False Bay Coast, a good forty-five-minute drive from Cape Town. Once a whaling station and marine research center, Kalk Bay is one of the most beautiful seaside towns of the Western Cape. It was for a time a fishing village with a community consisting of Khoisan people, Filipino crews who abandoned ship while passing through the Cape Point, and descendants of emancipated slaves who originated from Java, Malaysia, and Batavia (as Jakarta was known under the Dutch). The village was proclaimed a "White group area" in 1967, and thereafter Kalk Bay became much more spatially segregated, with an area designated for the "Coloured" fishermen and a White area for the English and the Afrikaners. The fishing families were either moved out entirely or at least away from the main road, slightly higher up the mountain, in court-like apartment blocks or "flats" not dissimilar to the Manenberg ones yet on a much smaller scale.

Unlike the townships on the outskirts of Cape Town, situated a distance from the center of the city, one need only cross a single road to get from the Coloured enclave to the "other" part of Kalk Bay, with its cobbled streets, art galleries, boutiques, and coffee shops. The harbor, which looks out on the sea and waves pounding on rocks, is decorated with fancy seafood restaurants that buy the catch of the day at the fish market on the dock. The pretty side of Kalk Bay is Anna's part of town, where she shares a flat with a roommate on the second floor of a picture-perfect whitewashed building. Neither high walls nor ugly electric barbed wire surround this complex, and there are no burglar bars on the windows. Anna despises those security measures and was attracted to her flat precisely because it doesn't have any of them. The apartment is simple, with a small kitchen, living room, and outside bathroom accessible via the balcony. She commutes from this haven to a small architectural firm in town where she has secured her first professional position.

Anna pursued architectural studies at the University of Cape Town after the racial quota system that determines university admissions refused her a place in the medical school. Opting for her second choice, she had long doubted whether architecture was really "her thing," and when we first met her she had decided to take a gap year and find an internship to figure out if this was the right profession for her. That she would attend university had always been a given in her family. Unlike Brandon and his siblings, Anna and her sisters were all pursuing higher education.

Anna's educational credentials, German passport, and strong work ethic constitute a potential pathway to outmigration. Though she loves South Africa, she is always eager to travel and once spent a year in Barcelona as an exchange student in architecture. After she graduated, Anna moved to Switzerland, eager to make a little money in a "first world environment." When she thinks about coming home to South Africa, she hopes that by then the lingering, troubling questions of racial inequality will somehow have been resolved.

SUZANNE

Greenmarket Square, a huge market in the middle of Cape Town catering to tourists, is crowded with shoppers on a sunny January Saturday. It is the height of the southern hemisphere summer, with a bright blue sky overhead and relentless heat shimmering off the cobblestones in the middle of the City

Bowl. Bounded by the streets of the commercial district, the square is jammed with stalls of artisans and traders selling goods from South Africa and beyond.

In the center of the square, we find one woman who is busy talking tourists out of their cash. Round faced, obviously pregnant, her head wrapped in a colorful scarf, Suzanne and her assistants actively entice shoppers who might otherwise pass them by. "Would you like to look at this bracelet?" an assistant inquires. "I can give you a good price." "How about this bowl, made by hand in KwaZulu Natal?" Suzanne urges. To foreign shoppers, Suzanne is but one of many selling similar wares. To those in the know, however, the lilt of her accent gives her away. She is not from this part of the world. Suzanne is Congolese, a refugee from civil wars, which have consumed much of central Africa. By the time we met, she had been in South Africa for eight years, the survivor of an epic journey of over 1,500 miles. Millions of migrants have come to South Africa in the decades since the end of apartheid, from countries as far away as Somalia and Rwanda and from as close as neighboring Zimbabwe. They have arrived in this prosperous, relatively peaceful country just in time to see the consequences of a worldwide recession slam into the economy, sending unemployment into the stratosphere. These are especially hard times for refugees and immigrants. The native-born, long since tired of waiting for the benefits of post-apartheid self-government, the houses and jobs they have been promised, are in no mood to tolerate the intrusion of foreign labor. Ambitious foreign Africans like Suzanne are looked upon as interlopers who have come to rob the rightful recipients of whatever the country's economy has to offer.

The subtext is familiar to Americans who hear right-wing complaints about Mexican workers who come across the southern border looking for jobs, medical care, and the spoils of a rich country, or to the French who hear from their politicians—from Nicholas Sarkozy, courting votes in a tough race, to Marine Le Pen, exploiting the brutal side of xenophobia—the refrain that there are too many foreigners. In periods of economic expansion, these voices are muted. Recessions bring them out in full force and the result is ugly.

Suzanne has grown to fear this atmosphere and so have her five children. Just before the World Cup in 2010, hosted by South Africa, a spate of horrific murders of immigrants consumed the attention of the country. Native-on-refugee brutality spread through the townships. Somali shopkeepers, who often run the "*spaza* shops" that feed the poorest neighborhoods, lost everything to arson fires. Young immigrant men were found with their throats slit. No one was talking, but everyone knew. The signs were everywhere: foreigners from other African countries were not welcome in South Africa.

The World Cup placed the country under an international spotlight. Fear of crime, an enduring problem in a vastly unequal country, grew even more intense as concern mounted over South Africa's ability to host a huge influx of soccer fans from all over the world. Police were put on the alert, and areas regarded as dubious were cleared—out of sight, out of mind—much to the dismay of thousands of shack dwellers who were turned out of their homes. Ironically, the attention riveted on the crime problem gave Suzanne peace of mind during the World Cup mania. But what would happen after that, when the event was just a memory? She did not want to think about it.

Like millions of refugees from war-torn regions, members of her family had to reinvent themselves, setting aside their old identities. Eduard, Suzanne's husband, a businessman in his native country, found work as a car guard in Camps Bay, keeping an eye on parked cars for tips. Suzanne took English lessons and with the help of a refugee organization formulated a plan to sell craft goods to tourists. Eight years later, with two more children in tow, the family lives in a comfortable flat in a mixed-race neighborhood. The children are thriving in school.

The drive and courage Suzanne needed to get through her refugee experience has fueled her ambition and success as a trader. Today women in Kwa-Zulu Natal work for her on contract, producing beaded bowls for Suzanne to sell in Cape Town. Once a year, she visits cloth markets in India where she buys sari fabric and ready-made clothing to sell at a marked-up price back in Cape Town. She has branched out, setting up multiple stalls in different markets, provisioning all of them herself and managing her growing workforce. Suzanne does not expect to work as a nurse again, the profession for which she was trained in the Democratic Republic of Congo, but she is proud of what she has accomplished, coming from nowhere with nothing.

At the same time, she laments that she has only two friends in South Africa. She misses her homeland but knows she will never be able to return. As she watches her children assimilate, she feels them becoming part of a society that has only uneasily accommodated to the presence of foreigners. She is a permanent refugee in a land that is ambivalent about her and periodically bursts into waves of xenophobic violence to underscore the point. She will never feel completely at home here.

THROUGH THE LIVES of Thandiswa, Amanda, Ambrose, David, Brandon, Anna, and Suzanne we explore how far South Africa has come in its quest to build a nonracial democracy and how far it has yet to travel. These seven South Africans are not members of the generation that fought against apartheid, they are its beneficiaries. For the Black and Coloured people among them, the opportunities available now were completely out of bounds for their parents and for the many generations that preceded them in the days when race sharply defined their fate. For the White South Africans, it is also a new day, one filled with greater constraints than were in place under the old regime. Where once white skin would almost certainly have been enough to guarantee the good life, education now matters more than ever. And while the lion's share of the country's wealth remains in white hands, it is quite possible for a man like Brandon to pass a lifetime in dead-end jobs.

The people of this book are poised to inherit a prosperous country that is nonetheless deeply troubled. Whether they find the inspiration to see its possibilities or lose faith in the future, they represent the generation that is about to seize the day, as the old leadership—especially Nelson Mandela—passes from the scene. Though each of them has a unique perspective and cannot in a strict statistical sense be considered representative of a nation as complex and regionally variegated as this one, they stand at distinctive points along the spectrum of race and class in Cape Town. It is through their generational experiences and ambitions that we will come to know South Africa on the twentieth anniversary of its first free election.

CHAPTER TWO

Apartheid Legacies

ALTHOUGH THE APARTHEID STATE OFFICIALLY began in 1948, segregation and racial discrimination began earlier in South Africa.[1] As far back as the nineteenth century, the descendants of the Dutch colonial settlers, the Boers, had already incorporated the idea of Black-White inequality into the Afrikaner Republic Constitution.

The first codification of that ideology was the Natives Land Act of 1913, defining 8.9 million hectares of the country as "Native Reserves." Unlike the Native American reservations in the United States, the South African reserves were explicitly intended to set aside a labor pool that would provide low-paid workers when needed and otherwise contain "excess Africans." That 1913 act made it illegal for African people to purchase land outside of these reserves.[2]

Urban racial segregation was also in place well before the apartheid government came into being. As far back as 1923, the Natives Urban Areas Act required local authorities to design separate neighborhoods for African people, "and to exercise a measure of control over the migration of the African population to towns." It was followed closely by the Slums Act of 1934, which insured that inner-city neighborhoods and dilapidated suburbs would be demolished and that the displaced African communities, deported to areas on the periphery of the city, would be grouped separately by race.

From 1948 onward, however, the official apartheid state would take segregation to even higher levels. The state's main objective was to support the superior position of the White minority in the country, in all spheres of life. Unskilled Afrikaners were to be protected from labor market competition.[3] Barriers were erected against any attempt to gain a political voice for the country's Black majority.

Under the rule of the White National Party, South Africa turned toward "total apartheid" through a set of race laws that would officially separate population groups and treat them differently before the law. The state would determine where people were allowed to live, what work they could look for, what schools they could go to, which beaches they could visit, what friends they could play with, and even which people they were allowed to fall in love with and marry.

The 1950 Population Registration Act required every person to be classified by race, based on lineage and on "physical appearance and social acceptability." From then on, people were to be labeled "White," "Indian," "Coloured," or "Black":

> "White person" means a person who in appearance obviously is, or who is generally accepted as a white person, but does not include a person, who, although in appearance obviously a white person, is generally accepted as a Coloured person.[4]

How curly is a person's hair? How dark is her skin? What language does she speak? The answers to these questions defined the legal rights of South Africans, and they divided families: sometimes siblings were classed differently from one another and children were classified differently from their aunts and uncles and even their parents.

The National Party went on to determine patterns of urban land use by race, creating the most thorough map of segregation anywhere in the world. The rigorous implementation of the Group Areas Act of 1950 mercilessly divided South African cities into separate White, Coloured, Indian, and African areas. The act required redesigning cities to hinder all but the most instrumental forms of contact between the various population groups. The races had to be separated by at least thirty meters of land, with no roads linking them.[5]

With the implementation of this legislation, prime real estate in the center of cities was proclaimed "Whites only"—Indian, Coloured, and Black people were uprooted and deported to the peripheries. Well-established, often racially integrated communities that had developed long before were dismantled, with neighbors and families torn apart and then resettled along racial lines in township blocks far from jobs, shops, and schools. While redrawing the country's cities, the Group Areas Board attempted to keep the impact on White people as modest as possible, while entire Indian, Coloured, and Black populations were forcibly removed and their land and property essentially stolen, never to be returned to the vast majority of them.

Far from the cities, influx controls were instituted to prevent rural Africans from coming anywhere near the urban areas unless they were needed for mining or agricultural labor. Following the Natives Resettlement Act of

1954, millions of Black people were moved to "independent homelands" (or "bantustans") such as the Ciskei and the Transkei, areas that were often poor, barren regions where it was impossible to grow enough food. "Pass laws" were introduced that required identity documents used to track the movements of rural Black people to prevent them from crossing into South Africa, which was now defined as another country. Anyone caught without a pass was subject to arrest.

To add force to the pass laws, housing for Black people in urban areas was severely limited. Men were forced into overcrowded, single-sex hostels. They were given bunk beds, seven or eight to a tiny room, if not left to sleep on the tops of tables used for communal eating. Workers were forbidden to bring their wives and children into the migrant zones. White families were not entirely thrilled with these controls because they found themselves unable to recruit servants as freely as many would have liked.[6]

What did this mean for the lives of the people of this book? How were they classified, and in which part of the country or the city did they live? The Fredericks were a case of a "split family." The descendants of Daniel's English grandfather and "Coloured" grandmother would all have to be classified as "Coloured."[7] This category referred to the direct descendants of the indigenous Khoi and San peoples, those brought to the country as slaves, and children born of relationships between members of these groups and Bantu-speaking people, or with European settlers.[8] That the Coloured group became an amalgam of so many different cultures and backgrounds, artificially placed together in a new census category, would lead to many debates over exactly what "Colouredness" represented, a problem that consumed attention for decades.

Because these were far from neutral classifications, there was tremendous tension and shame inside families like Daniel's as the privileges associated with one racial classification advantaged some and damned others. Daniel's aunt Bridgette was classified "White," while everyone else, including Daniel's father, who is also fairly light skinned, was deemed "Coloured." The statistics on individual requests for official racial reclassification as late as the 1980s show the desire of many to become "Coloured instead of African, or White instead of Coloured."[9] Because family lineage could thwart the attempts of light-skinned Coloured individuals to transform themselves into Whites, Bridgette cut all ties with her family after she was classified. No one in her new circle of White friends, not even her White husband, would ever find out her true mixed-race background. Daniel suspects that "she wanted to lose contact with the family so that people would not dig up her past and realize she was not White."

> We would hear through the grapevine that she was here, and then there. The family would hear that she was living with a White ID and was in Johannesburg. She would only call her mother every now and then, to stay in touch. She became the black sheep of the family, even though she was White now.

Bridgette stayed in touch secretly with her sister Jane, who of all the siblings was the closest to appearing white. "Aunt Bridgette's life was basically completely different from that of her siblings," Daniel noted. Because of her racial classification, Bridgette could buy land, shop in the best stores, sit on the best seats on the bus, and visit the best beaches and fanciest restaurants. If she wanted, she could get a better job than her family members could attain.

Ironically, the privileges of being White led Bridgette to relax too much in a family that prides itself on hard work and self-discipline. Unlike the siblings who devoted themselves to upward mobility in a racially restrictive environment, Bridgette failed to complete her matric (final) year of high school. Today she lives back in Cape Town but in a neighborhood that is much poorer than the Paarl community, where Daniel's parents live.

Ambrose's family is Coloured and to his knowledge has always been. Yet when he describes his heritage, the tortuous nature of apartheid social categories seeps into every comment. He is dark-skinned, with dark-brown eyes. To us, Ambrose cannot be distinguished from his African neighbors in the Black townships behind Nyanga Station in Gugulethu and Khayelitsha. Even so, he rejects out of hand the notion that he is of African blood. He refers to the San and Khoi—the original inhabitants of the Cape Province—as his ancestors and would be insulted if anyone were to think that he was Black. His native tongue is Afrikaans and he knows nothing of the languages of the Xhosa or Zulu peoples.

Apartheid "racial science" has left deep tracks in the psyche of South Africans. Ambrose is certain that Black people are less intelligent than "Brown people," his shorthand reference to Coloureds. It is not credible in his mind that Black Africans could run a country, and he points to the failures of the Zuma administration as proof.

Thandiswa's and Amanda's families would have stood no chance with a request for racial reclassification. Both women are originally from the Eastern

Cape, their mother tongue is Xhosa, one of the languages considered "Bantu" (African), and with their warm ebony skin colors and curly black hair, their appearance could only mark them as Black.

Anna and Brandon clearly fit the old requirements for the White designation. Anna's German family settled on Namibian farmland before moving into South Africa. Brandon's father is Irish, his mother Dutch, and the family considers itself Afrikaner. There are pronounced cultural and class differences between them, nonetheless. German immigrants were wealthier and more skilled, often land owners for whom the colonial experience was almost uniformly one of upward mobility. The Afrikaners were often lower-skilled laborers and less affluent. While Brandon's family was economically secure during the apartheid years, it was not as educated as Anna's. When apartheid ended and the barriers removed that had insulated White workers from competition from millions of Blacks, Brandon's family found itself sliding.

Subtle differences between ethnic groups within the White population hardly mattered under the old regime. Today they do matter, not only in terms of class position, but politically as well. There were, and still are, Afrikaner liberals who were staunchly opposed to the racial hierarchy that was apartheid, but most of the support for the National Party came from the Afrikaans community. English-speaking Whites descended from the British settler population were typically more middle class, and they often populated the ranks of White liberals, though they too could be found among defenders of apartheid.

Having developed as a fairly integrated city before apartheid, Cape Town would eventually exemplify the harshest consequences of forced removal. One particularly notorious example was the District Six community, described by its inhabitants in the 1960s as a vibrant, multiracial and multicultural inner-city area. Immigrant Whites, Muslim Malay Coloureds, Xhosa-speaking Blacks, and European Jews mixed easily in District Six. Many of Ambrose's neighbors lived there before they were summarily deported to the desolate flats of Manenberg on the outskirts of Cape Town. Life in District Six is remembered now in a museum that stands at the heart of the old neighborhood, filled with photos and memorabilia, adding a bittersweet tone to the indictment of the regime that tore this community from its moorings.

After removals and demolitions, District Six was abandoned and left derelict, as no one in power dared to decide its future. The expulsion had caused such controversy that any new residential development plan was almost automatically considered inappropriate.[10] Even today, District Six remains largely vacant, the church, mosque, and synagogue at the heart of the neighborhood are still silent, testimony to what was once there.

Protests against forced removals and bulldozing of Modderdam squatter settlements near Cape Town in August 1977.

It was in this segregated city that Brandon and Ambrose were born. Brandon's family settled in the Afrikaner-dominated northern suburbs, where life was free and easy, with shops, schools, and work opportunities close by. There was lots of space for children to roam on their own, build camps, and ride their bikes. Ambrose's family moved from an overcrowded house in the suburb of Kensington to Manenberg, where there were no shops, no proper infrastructure, no gardens or greenery. Even buying food required taking the train or bus.

Thandiswa's family moved from the rural Ciskei homeland in the 1970s or early 1980s, and Amanda moved into Cape Town in her late teenage years, in search of work, when the bans of the old apartheid system had already been removed. Amanda was born and spent her childhood in a township on the outskirts of Port Elizabeth, an equally segregated city.

The seven people of this book were children in apartheid South Africa. Now in their thirties, they remember *living* the segregation, not always understanding why they could not play with children of a different skin color or why they were served at a different counter in a shop in town. Those who lived in the townships recall the deprivation and hardship. Yet their past does not include forced removals and the abrupt end to a life that felt normal before and totally distorted afterward. Those kinds of memories live on among their older family and community members, for whom the removals were an extraordinarily painful upheaval. The elders speak of the sense of shock when arriving in townships with hardly any provisions, abandoned in the forgotten outskirts of the city.

Ironically, perhaps cynically, townships like Manenberg were developed around the concept of a "Garden City." Johnny Steinberg, a well-known South African journalist, captures the motivations of the original architects of apartheid:

> Flying over the Flats on the descent into Cape Town, you can see the clusters in all their glory: concentric layers of streets, turned in upon themselves, forming tight, hermetic circles, each surrounded by a barren wilderness of no-man's land. . . . With some imagination, you can just make out some of the benign intentions behind the original Garden City idea. The notion of inward looking clusters was meant to foster a village-like sense of community. Yet driving through Manenberg . . . one feels as if one has been locked into a maze, as if the ghetto is a dense universe. The idea of buttressing the clusters with greenbelts was intended to create open spaces in which the cluster-children would spend their afternoons. But the "greenbelts" of the Cape Flats are intraversable scrublands; the kids are locked inside the labyrinth.[11]

Coloured families like Ambrose's split up, the wealthier ones moving to areas with freestanding houses, and the poorer ones moving into flats. The disruption destabilized community life in a way that worsened with time. Children were left to fend for themselves while their parents became commuters between the outskirts of town and the city or one of the industrial areas. Without any stable authority structure, crime and violence crept into places like Manenberg and twisted the pathways of succeeding generations.

Daniel was born in the wine country, in its oldest city, Paarl, and lived his childhood in several areas of the town. He remembers living in lower-income areas but not in the kind of apartment blocks that dominate townships like Manenberg. Daniel's grandfather was originally from nearby Grabouw and did not live in what Daniel called a "township-like setup." The grandfather's family moved to Paarl when Daniel's father decided to attend school in the town. The men of the family—starting with Daniel's grandfather—managed to find work in Paarl and as a result were able to avoid the township experience. Even so, Daniel's mother, Christine, remembers how her family was forcibly removed from the center of town, which, she says, "then became a Whites-only residential and farming area." She was fourteen years old and had until then lived in the multicultural center of Paarl, where she recalls having had White, Coloured, and Black neighbors. The family, Daniel explained, was "shoved into the township" east of the Berg River, while White neighbors remained in the neighborhoods west of the river.

Daniel's father managed to build up his own business and wealth within the confines of the system and thus could keep the family out of the poorest areas of Paarl. Today, however, he laments the fact that he was only allowed to buy land in one specific area and not in the more up-market neighborhoods reserved for Whites, where real estate prices have now skyrocketed.

As in Manenberg, this newly created enclave consisted of neighbors who did not know one another. But the situation was not as dire as it was in "the Flats," and it seems that a sense of community grew rather fast. There were shops, for example, although the ones in this part of town were owned by Indian people. Soon Daniel's mother managed to find herself a job in a factory, and later she worked as a sales assistant. With the money she earned, she managed to move out of the township. Once married to Samuel, Daniel's father, a man with skills and a strong ambition to move up the socioeconomic ladder, she would look after their children. Although Daniel's early years were spent in poorer, segregated areas of Paarl, he recalls a far more middle-class life than Ambrose's. They are both Coloured, but Daniel was never lost in desolate blocks of flats, did not suffer the wages of gang battles, and instead had all the advantages of a caring family home and a stable neighborhood that was just a stone's throw from the center of Paarl.

As mentioned, neither Amanda nor Thandiswa are from Cape Town. Amanda moved to the city as a young adult, after the end of apartheid, but the story of the move to Cape Town by Thandiswa's family in the 1970s testifies to the restrictions on Black people who relocated from rural areas to the city during the heyday of apartheid.[12]

Thandiswa's father and mother lived in the Ciskei homeland in the early years of their family life. Black people were to have political rights only within separate nation-states such as the Ciskei and the Transkei, and they were to be treated as foreign workers if they lived and worked in "mainland South Africa." The goal was to reduce the presence of Blacks in areas that were to be under control of Whites. The resulting checkerboard federation was supposed to become something like a commonwealth of independent countries rotating around a motherland.

The homeland system faced several challenges, however. First, the reserves were scattered throughout the country and hence could not serve as the basis for separate states with any territorial integrity. Secondly, only 13 percent of all South African land was involved, a proportion too small to house the entire African population, particularly since the homelands were situated in economically unproductive regions that could not come close to feeding their people. As far back as 1954, the Tomlinson Commission suggested that additional land be sought if these nation-states were ever to be viable, but the National Party rejected the idea, and the government continued expropriating farms, transferring land from private owners to local government (but never to the "native" communities) or selling desirable land to White farmers. Africans outside of the homelands, who were considered "surplus to the needs of the White farming community," were forcibly removed and placed in the homelands. The aim of the entire operation was to keep White rural South Africa White. These policies led directly to the shredding of family ties, as an estimated 1.7 million people were displaced between 1960 and 1983. What those return migrants found upon arrival in the homelands was nothing short of appalling: hastily erected refugee camps, without sanitation and with little protection against the elements.

While the homeland policy was largely a move to prevent the millions of rural poor people from flooding into South Africa proper, it was also a politically motivated effort integral to the separation of the races, a "divide and conquer" plan to balkanize the African population by ethnic origin. Africans were broken up into linguistically diverse groups and then allocated to various homelands. The Xhosa people, to whom both Thandiswa's and Amanda's families belong, were divided into two groups, each provided with its own administration, one for the Ciskei area and one for the Transkei.

The Ciskei—an area that has "absolutely no basis in any ethnic, cultural, or linguistic fact whatsoever"—nestles between the Fish and Kei Rivers and contains only a small section of the eastern coast of South Africa.[13] It became a separate administrative region in the early 1970s and was declared independent by the South African government in 1981—independence never recognized by the United Nations or other members of the international community. As a consequence, however, Ciskei residents lost their South African citizenship.

Once a flourishing, fertile valley where White and Coloured farmers ran large-scale, irrigated farms, known as "one of the primary tobacco and citrus producing regions in the country," the Katberg region turned into a "dead valley" as White farmers left and Coloured ones were forcibly removed.[14]

Black and Coloured farm workers lost the jobs they had had on the commercial farms, but under apartheid law they were not allowed to use the land for farming.

The Ciskei consists of approximately 8,000 square kilometers, and in 1980 it had a population of about 650,000. Forced removals of "surplus people" into the Ciskei led to an influx of about 16,000 a year. Unemployment, poverty, and hunger rates were high. As far back as the 1950s, the population was already dependent upon imports for all its manufactured items, including clothing, and most of its food.

Thandiswa's family lived in the Kat River region in the Ciskei, where they owned a house and kept cattle. They left around the time when the land was expropriated to make way for the Black influx.

When we visited the area in 2009, most of the land lay uncultivated, the citrus trees gnarled by the sun and the absence of irrigation. We found a big

Elderly couple living on an abandoned citrus farm in Eastern Cape Province, an hour's walk from Seymour, where Thandiswa's sister lives.

farmhouse that was boarded up, its windows empty of glass, and grape vines in front of the house were withered. An old man and his wife came out of the front door in tattered clothes and explained that the farm had been deserted years ago. He had been a laborer on the farm and had decided to stay behind when the White farmer left. The tobacco factory in the heart of Seymour was in ruins—there had not been a crop for decades—and the entire region appeared abandoned.

Before Thandiswa's family left the region, they had kept a small vegetable garden and some healthy cows, but there was no work, neighbors had become jealous of their possessions, and allegations of witchcraft were on the rise. It was time to get out before someone got hurt. Yet leaving for Cape Town was a risky move. Although men were allowed to work as temporary migrant laborers, spouses and children were supposed to stay in the homelands. In 1955, the Western Cape Province was declared a "Coloured Labor Preference Area," and as a consequence, the city of Cape Town stopped building houses for Black people in the mid-1960s. Indeed, African people were moving in the opposite direction: thousands were forcibly removed from the Western Cape to the homelands. Overall, the policy failed dismally and Black migrants who

Students from the Seymour grade school showing off in front of the shuttered tobacco factory that used to employ residents of the town.

made their way back to the Western Cape ended up squatting illegally in increasingly violent settlements.[15]

Nevertheless, Thandiswa's family moved to the Western Cape, to Kuils River, where her father managed to find work on a farm. Her mother, Mam'Cethe, recalls the pass laws and the fear of being found in a settlement where she was not supposed to be. In 1952, the government stipulated that all Blacks over the age of sixteen had to carry a "reference book" that showed whether the person was legally allowed in an area. As an African woman under apartheid, Mam'Cethe had few rights; certainly she had no right to education and no right to own property. African women were not supposed to be in urban South Africa—unless they were domestic workers—and the fear and humiliation of arrest and deportation was constant and unnerving.

IN THE FIRST HALF OF THE 1980s, Thandiswa's family moved to a shack in Crossroads, an African township situated on the outskirts of Cape Town. Crossroads started out as a shantytown, erected by former farmworkers who, when ordered to leave, decided to build shacks on vacant land "by the crossroads." In the 1980s, this township gained a reputation for violence, mainly because different groups had been arbitrarily thrown together. Assaults were common, shacks made of wood scraps were set on fire, and hundreds were left homeless as the fires spread.

This was also the time (the end of the 1970s and beginning of the 1980s) that the Black population in all of South Africa's cities began to grow rapidly. Influx controls proved useless to stem the tide. Of the nearly two million people living in Cape Town, only 500,000 were White. Nearly a million were mixed-race Coloureds. More than 300,000 were African.

The influx control regulations were lifted in the late 1980s and only then was more land sought for Black Development Areas. These areas, however, were twice as densely populated as the Coloured or Asian Group Areas, and eight times that of the White Group Areas.[16]

Like Thandiswa, Amanda's family also has a migratory history that reflects the experience of Black South Africans. Amanda is originally from Port Elizabeth, an industrial town in the Eastern Cape. Today auto firms, clothing manufacturers, and textile and pharmaceutical industries are the main employers in the vicinity of Port Elizabeth. Amanda's grandmother was originally from Kimberley in the Northern Cape but had moved to Port Elizabeth in the 1950s to try to finish her high school education. After that, she married and settled into a house not far from where she lives now. She remembers all too well that the pass laws made the search for opportunities elsewhere almost impossible. Zondwa, Amanda's mother, recalls the hardships of living in shacks or small houses built by the government for Black people in East London, a township satellite of Port Elizabeth. People were crammed into spaces too small to hold them. There was never enough space and always the danger of fire.

On the other side of the racial divide, the majority of urban Whites were ensconced in wealthy neighborhoods of the central cities and the surrounding communities, like the northern suburbs of Cape Town where Brandon and his family lived. They had access to large plots of lands or nice, new, spacious apartments in the City Bowl.[17] Anna's mother and Brandon's family still reside in the suburbs today, albeit on different sides of the city. Anna's mother lives in Newlands, one of the most elegant and prestigious communities in the region, famous for cricket and rugby stadiums nearby. The Cape Town suburbs boast wide roads and large shopping malls, spacious houses with well-attended gardens, and good schools. Surrounded by walls and electric fences and attended by guard dogs, Newlands homes are elegant and expensive, but it is hard to overlook the fortress-like feeling of the neighborhood.

PERSONAL APARTHEID

By the 1980s, the geographically segregated apartheid city had become a fact on the ground. But segregation had been deemed necessary in all spheres of life if Whites were to survive in South Africa. Starting in the 1950s, regulations were introduced to isolate them from the rest of the country's social groups. For example, in 1953, the Reservation of Separate Amenities Act dictated:

> If a European has to sit next to a non-European at school, if on a railway station they are to use the same waiting rooms, if they are continually to travel together on the trains and sleep in the same hotels, it is evident that eventually we would have racial admixture, with the result that on the one hand one would no longer find a purely European population, and on the other hand a non-European population.[18]

This is the side of apartheid that people Thandiswa or Ambrose's age experienced. Daniel recalls that his family was not allowed on the same beaches as Whites, how theirs were "the dirty beaches" and how the "Coloured campsites" were different from those of Whites. Their neighborhood lacked swimming pools, while White areas always had them. Amanda thinks back on how she went to school and saw White children playing but was not allowed to join them.

Brandon and Anna felt awkward around the children of the domestic workers in their homes, children who were their own age but were treated so differently. Brandon recalls playing with them as if there was no such thing as segregation, only to discover that there were strict limits circumscribing those friendships.

For the older generation, "personal apartheid" is a vivid memory. African grandmothers who live near Thandiswa in Khayelitsha described the humiliation that was part of their daily diet. One elderly woman recalled how she could occasionally splurge on a first-class train ticket, but even that would not protect her from possible arrest should she get onto the train on the wrong side:

> If you had a first-class ticket . . . there was a "non-Whites" first class and a first class for Whites only. Even if you had a first-class ticket you would not come out of the same doors; you would have to turn back and use the doors of the third-class carriage yet you had a first-class ticket in hand. . . . And if the train was late and you quickly got in the first-class side of the Whites you would have to stand and you would be arrested because you are not allowed to stand there. You needed to stand by the door so that at the next station you could quickly go to the non-White first class.

The people of this book were children during this period, but even they had to figure out how to behave and what to think in the presence of those they were taught were irrevocably different. The climate of those times has left its traces that many battle with today, twenty years past the end of apartheid. In her book *Whiteness Just Isn't What It Used to Be*, Melissa Steyn describes her difficulties trying to understand—first as a child, later as a budding adolescent, and today as an adult in "the new South Africa"—the obsessive attention to the details of social segregation with which she was raised:

> The first time I ventured into our maid's room one afternoon as a little girl. . . . A white child just knew that one was not supposed to go into "their" places. . . . She sat holding her daughter's hand while we chatted. . . . "She's a real mother," [I realized]. Intimations of depths of her personhood, of a life quite separate from our home that I had unquestioningly assumed to be all that defined her, broke into my consciousness.

Another such moment was when I was older, in my early adolescence. We were moving, and I arrived home from school before my mother. I was to supervise the movers. A young "Coloured" man and I struck up a conversation. "Will I be raped?" The messages about the dangers of dark men, ingrained by socialization, tugged against my awkward impulse to reach out. He was doing his Junior Certificate, as I was, but by correspondence course, while working to support his studies. It was a shock to realize that this stranger and I shared interests as equals.[19]

The Group Areas Act had aimed primarily at enforcing residential segregation and preventing interracial social contact. But it also regulated relations in the commercial world. Businesses were required to locate in and limit their trade to people in the "group area of a member's racial classification." Indian, Coloured, and Chinese traders were allowed to trade in each other's non-White group areas, but only African-owned businesses were allowed in the designated Black areas: "They were restricted as limits were placed upon the size of the stores (initially 150 then 350 square metres) and the range of goods (only daily convenience goods)."[20] African businesses were strictly forbidden to operate in White areas. The state further intervened in the labor market by means of laws meant to "uphold civilized standards for European workers." Millions of unskilled Afrikaners feared the loss of their livelihood should the Black majority be able to enter the same sectors and hence pressured the apartheid state to ensure it didn't happen. Even before the National Party came to power, the introduction of the color bar limited employment opportunities to certain racial categories, reserving particular occupations in the mining and manufacturing industries specifically for White workers. Whites were afforded protected employment in public services such as the railways.[21] Menial and semi-skilled positions were reserved for non-Whites only, with no access to managerial positions and higher, more stable incomes.[22] The 1953 Industrial Conciliation Act had banned African workers from participating in the trade unions, leaving African workers largely voiceless in national labor negotiations.[23]

Finally, differential treatment in the educational system that grew out of the apartheid years introduced profound inequality that has left a deep imprint on South African society, creating skill gaps that remain a serious problem today. From the 1950s to the fall of the old regime, White children were the beneficiaries of massive investments in public education, which translated directly into the cultivation of skills for Whites and the loss of opportunities for people of color. Dr. H. F. Verwoerd, then minister of Native Affairs, introduced the Bantu Education Bill in 1953:

> Racial relations cannot improve if the wrong type of education is given to the natives. They cannot improve if the result of Native education is the creation of frustrated people who, as a result of the education they received, have expectations in life which circumstances in South Africa do not allow to be fulfilled immediately, when it creates people who are trained for professions not open for them.

The skills gap produced by Verwoerd's policy became so profound that it rendered the color bar and enforced wage differentials almost unnecessary. No one other than White workers had the background appropriate to highly skilled occupations after forty years of this kind of educational inequality.[24]
A separate Department of Native Affairs was created to take care of the distinct system of "Bantu" education. The educational system was further segregated, with White schools separated into Afrikaans, English, and (where communities could support them) German schools. Far fewer resources went into Black schools. Consequently, teachers in Black areas had the lowest salaries and hence were often not fully qualified. Thirty percent of all Black schools did not have electricity, only 25 percent had running water, and less than half had plumbing.[25] Conversely, education for White or "European" children in affluent urban and suburban schools aimed to meet European standards. University education was separated as well. Black universities were created in the homelands in 1959, alongside a number of Coloured and Indian ones in urban areas. None of the latter had permission to enroll Black students.

THE STRUGGLE

Boycotts, strikes, and civil disobedience grew as total apartheid descended on South African society.[26] It was not until the 1950s, however, that the first riots broke out, mainly protesting the separate educational system, the pass laws, and the large-scale forced removals. Two strong opposition parties formed—the African National Congress (ANC) and the Pan Africanist Congress (PAC)—and took the lead in organizing mass demonstrations. On March 21, 1960, sixty-nine Black people were killed by police in what has become known as the Sharpeville Massacre; more were killed that same day in the African township of Langa near Cape Town. The government arrested, imprisoned, and exiled the leaders of the opposition parties, effectively crushing their political organizations for the next few years. But the protests returned in force in the 1970s and 1980s.

The new regulations that imposed the inferior "Bantu" education and made Afrikaans compulsory as the language of instruction in mathematics, geography, and physical science in secondary schools led to angry protests organized by the South African students' movement.[27] Young children joined the protest marches, which placed them in the line of fire. Many died at the hands of the police in a protest in June 1976, which sparked riots all over the country in the days and months that followed.

Zondwa, Amanda's mother, remembers the riots. Her voice breaks when she describes the terror, the fear of the police, and the killings:

> 1976? I was already working. When it started that day, I was still staying at home in Mendi. We saw a group of school kids . . . a mob, in fact. We didn't know what was taking place. We saw buildings burning, that post office. And they were coming towards this bottle store. . . . It was . . . on fire within no time. As from then, things never were the same. Helicopters were here, police were here, caspers (those police vans, those funny-looking ones). People were there being shot, people were dying there in front us.
>
> At night in Mendi it was a no-go zone because the White police would sit there and camouflage. Whoever would pass there, I'm telling you they would get shot at, they would shoot. It was . . . *Yhoyhoyho.* . . . At night while we're sleeping we would hear footsteps walking in the yard. It would be the police. Hey, it was not happy times, man. It was just death everywhere, death everywhere. We were so scared, we were so scared. We couldn't move, man. . . .
>
> Then there [were] the funerals of the people that were shot by the police. And they didn't want people to attend those funerals. It used to be a battlefield whenever there was a funeral of one of those people that were shot. They were shooting people like birds.
>
> And if you were shot you were not supposed to be taken to any doctor. They would take you and throw you, literally to throw you, in the van. People . . . had to be sneaked out to be taken to private doctors, and private doctors were scared to attend to these people because if the police could get those people at their surgeries, that doctor is in big trouble. That's why people were dying.

These "troubles" became known around the globe and transformed South Africa into a pariah state. Exiles—Black and White—spread the word about the appalling conditions and organized, state-sanctioned human rights violations. University students in Europe and the United States joined hands with the exile community to launch a sanctions movement with economic teeth. Contested by conservatives including Margaret Thatcher and Ronald Reagan, economic punishments directed at the South African government and the country's banks and industries were nonetheless supported by the United Nations.

In 1983, a tricameral constitution was unveiled that effectively excluded African people from the decision-making processes of South Africa altogether. It provided for White, Coloured, and Indian houses of Parliament that previously had no authority within the apartheid state. Black people remained excluded. This, combined with the hated "Bantu" education system, dire poverty in the townships, the lack of housing, and an economy unable to provide more employment, led to a sustained surge in mass riots, mainly in the Black townships but also in some Coloured townships. The state began to crack.[28]

Domestic protests and international pressure on the government to end the system of racial discrimination would eventually lead the National Party to lift the ban on the African National Congress in 1990, to release Nelson Mandela, and to start negotiations over the process of democratization. Between 1990 and 1994, violent protests continued, but most of the discriminatory, racist regulations were abolished.[29]

The first national, democratic election in South Africa took place in April 1994. Organized hastily, the move was in response to the consensus among negotiating parties that an election was needed immediately to ensure legitimacy for the new democracy. The atmosphere in the run-up to the elections was a heady fusion of excitement, anticipation, anxiety, and fear over the possibility of violence. The day of the election itself is often remembered as a big festival, with South Africans of all races queuing together to cast their votes, embracing one another in the streets. Nearly twenty million ballots were cast in peace.[30]

The election raised the hopes and expectations of millions for a social and economic revolution to follow. Township communities immediately made demands for electricity, sanitation, and government-built housing. The cost of righting the wrongs of apartheid soared into almost countless billions. The vast majority of Black and Coloured people were desperately poor and lacked skill and education; the wealth of the country was in the hands of the defeated White minority. With the dismal example of Zimbabwe before them, in which White farmers had been dispossessed and the flight of capital was nearly universal, South Africa pledged itself to a multiracial democracy from which the White population would have little to fear.

Dramatic change was expected, if not overnight, then surely soon. What actually transpired during the two decades that have followed the historic presidential election of Nelson Mandela in 1994 was an uneven, halting, and politically complicated transition that left the communities that are home to the people of this book in wildly divergent positions.

THE LONG REACH OF APARTHEID

The inequality set in place by the apartheid system shaped the options for those who have grown up in democratic South Africa. In 1996, two years after the first free election, the gulf between Black and White in educational attainment was enormous. The majority of White young adults had graduated from high school or enrolled in higher education, while only 18 percent of African young adults and 24 percent of Coloured young adults had these credentials. In rural areas, only 12 percent of young adults had completed high school and 7 percent of Africans aged 16–25 had no formal education whatsoever, compared to less than 1 percent of White young adults with no formal education. Eight years later, in 2004, White adults had an average of 12.3 years of schooling, Coloured people had an average of 8.5 years, and Africans had an average of 7.9 years.

This educational deficit translated into dramatic inequalities in the labor market that continue today. While tiny proportions of White and Indian South Africans are unemployed, nearly a quarter of Black African people are out of work, as are 10 percent of Coloured South Africans. In 2000, White people still earned on average double what Indians earned; Coloured and Black people earned far less. In 2000, 37 percent of all households in the country lived on less than R1000 per month (approximately US$100).[31] Twenty-five percent of households still do not live in a permanent, formal dwelling. One-third have no access to clean water in their homes.[32] This poverty is shaped by race: the majority of those who are poor are Black.[33] White South Africans meanwhile continue to hold disproportionate wealth. Although inequality plays out along racial lines, contemporary South Africa has seen the growth of a Black middle class and elite, and some White families have fallen into a spiral of downward social mobility.[34] Accordingly, the landscape of inequality is more complex than it was in the past. Class matters—not as much as race does, but far more than it once did.

Nearly all of Anna's relatives have some form of higher education. That Anna too would attend university was assumed. Brandon passed his matriculation exam and decided not to continue studying but to concentrate on his entrepreneurial activities, much as his father had suggested. Daniel's mother did not complete high school, but his father did. Daniel has seen dramatic upward mobility because of the educational opportunities he has had post-apartheid.[35]

Amanda's story makes clear the importance of the transformation that began toward the end of apartheid, when fault lines in the system of racial separation began to emerge. As a young child, she was not allowed to attend a "Whites only" school, nor could she play with the children of other races. But in the 1980s, following the example of several Catholic churches that had taken a stance against the apartheid regime, some public schools too started to open their doors to a limited number of non-White children. Later, in the 1990s, more schools chose to open up to children of all races, and became "Model C schools," a term that is still used to refer to schools that offer a better quality education than most.[36] With the passing of the 1996 South African Schools Act, all schools were obliged to open up their doors to all children, without discrimination. Schools in wealthier areas would, however, continue to charge higher fees than those in poorer areas. As soon as the opportunity arose, Amanda's grandmother sent her and her older sister, Alison, to a previously "all White" school. That decision—which was a costly investment—created a path of opportunity for Amanda, not unlike Daniel's, although Amanda landed in a much more precarious middle-class position than Daniel.

Ambrose and Thandiswa were and remain among the most disadvantaged of South Africans. Their parents had little education and even less money, and they lived in some of the most peripheral and troubled areas of Cape Town at the time of the transition. Ambrose dropped out of high school in ninth grade and Manenberg offered few options for him other than to slide into drug use and petty crime. He was completely isolated from the broader process of democratization. Thandiswa completed her matric exams but her marks were not high enough for further schooling. For her to succeed would have meant studying and rewriting her matric exam, an unlikely scenario considering that she needed to support both herself and her two small children. The occasional jobs she does manage to get remain limited to semi-skilled or unskilled positions.

The pathways of these men and women were influenced in powerful ways by the life chances their parents were stuck with under apartheid. When the time of transition came, legal restrictions on education and labor were relaxed or abolished, and they could seek their fortunes, but they did so with unequal skills. As a consequence, their divergent destinies reflect both race and class.

CHAPTER THREE

Thandiswa's Struggles

MINIBUS TAXIS BUILT TO HOLD seven or eight people are crammed with fifteen as the mid-afternoon commute back to Khayelitsha gets underway. Heavy mamas with billowing dresses and hair wrapped in colorful turbans, tired workers fighting their way home from a long day on the job, school children lugging backpacks, and young mothers weighed down by a monthly haul of groceries are packed into one of the few modes of transportation that link the city of Cape Town to this township of 400,000 people.

Some have been waiting for more than an hour to get moving. While there is a rough schedule for these minibuses, drivers will not leave until their vehicles are full. Unless it is peak travel time, this can mean waits of an hour or more; no one can count on an arrival time. This helps to account for the universal presence of cell phones, even among the poorest riders, and people's mastery of text-messaging. There is no other way to let family members know when one might finally show up.

In Khayelitsha, the taxis disgorge passengers and pick up ones heading back to the city or the next township. Riders wait in whatever shade they can find, standing in clumps, passing the time. Every so often, a child begs his mother for some change and runs off to a tuck shop, a shack that sells drinks, snacks, and diapers. Often owned by immigrants from Somalia, these shops tend to congregate around bus stops.

Three people are wedged into the front seat of our taxi. The middle passenger, in this case a woman of about twenty-five, is responsible for collecting the fare, and she stretches around to the three rows behind her as riders dig into pockets, purses, and sacks and hand over crumpled rand notes. For some, the ride will cost as much as a third of their day's pay.

Breakdowns happen all the time. When a taxi breaks down, passengers get out and wait, or they push or walk, hoping they can hail another car or catch a bus.

Our driver is not a professional working for a municipal transport company. He is most likely a hired hand, commissioned by the owner of the van, who hopes he will cram as many payers in as possible so he can turn a handsome profit for the boss. Occasionally a Golden Arrow bus, the main competitor to the taxi fleet, pulls up at the same stop. Golden Arrow runs an organized service, with proper schedules. The buses charge less than the taxis but go less frequently between the city and the townships, have a less extensive network of routes, and maneuver more slowly through heavy traffic than the minibuses. A thin Xhosa-speaking man with a cigarette dangling from his mouth, the taxi driver keeps an eye on his fare collector. He will be expected to turn that money over to the van's owner.

Today the driver is in the mood for music, and he flips between channels that blare gospel or *mbhaqanga*, a popular style of South African music that dates to the early 1960s. Every time his eyes leave the road for the radio dial, the van swerves a bit, edging a little too close to the oncoming traffic. Still, the music makes the ride go by faster and takes everyone's mind off the discomforts that come with being packed in so tightly, with grocery bags tearing apart, bodies that are a bit ripe after a long day.

It is January and the South African summer is hot and dry. There are no clouds and little shade for the hundreds of people waiting on sides of streets for taxis to slow and drivers to call out their destinations. Fanning themselves with paper, stray ads found on the ground, or their hands, their faces glisten with sweat and mirror impatience, especially with children who, by late afternoon, are cranky. When the occasional breeze blows by, it is laden with dust and sand. Grit settles into the hair and mouth, irritating the eyes and skin.

Out of the taxi's back window, Table Mountain is receding from view. Majestic against an azure sky, it is the iconic image of Cape Town. When the sun sets and the air begins to cool, fog spills over the top, cascading down its sides in a white veil, flowing down the mountain. From the taxi, the windows of mansions glint in the sunlight on the mountainside. Up there, brilliant yellow, red, and pink flowers border perfect lawns and trimmed shrubs. Bougainvillea vines of deep magenta climb to the edge of red roofs. Clinging to the slopes, these homes sport stunning views of the City Bowl and the shimmering waters of Table Bay. The natural harbor once beckoned to English and Portuguese explorers who first rounded the Cape of Good Hope. Today it calls to tourists from Europe who come to South Africa in the dead of their northern winter to bask in the Southern Hemisphere's summer warmth.

Entering Khayelitsha, our taxi slows as it passes through the main intersection. Our driver calls out to the passengers, "Ukhona oya koo R?" (Is anyone getting out at Section R?)—he will stop only if someone responds. The taxi passes informal settlements on the outskirts of Khayelitsha. Shacks here are jammed next to one another and spill out to the edge of the road.

A sea of shacks. Informal houses in the townships are built of zinc panels and wood scraps. Roofing material made of plastic sheets is held down by big rocks.

The ground in between them is sandy and dusty, with no asphalt. The roofs of many shacks are draped in black plastic sheets, held down by old tires. In ninety-degree heat, the iron walls and black tarps create an inferno on the inside. The temperature is so high it makes everyone listless and irritated. The sound of babies wailing in their beds rises with the heat.

Yellow posters of African National Congress and the United Democratic Movement hang from the electrical poles that line the street. "*Xa simbambe singeeza lukhula*" ("We can do a lot if we work together"), notes the first. "Now is the time for all South Africans," claims the second. The Democratic Alliance, the strongest opposition party, has also been campaigning in Khayelitsha, hoping to win more of the Black African vote in the province.

At the four-way stop, cars pull up to take advantage of the informal businesses that line the road. Shopkeepers sell fruit to passersby. Fridges, wooden cupboards, and freestanding wardrobes are all on offer. Mechanics are bending over the open hoods of two taxies in a car repair shack. In another spot, workers are hammering and cutting pieces of iron for shack walls. As traffic slows, two young men move along in the middle of road, carrying water bottles, stopping to wash car windshields whether drivers want them to or not.

Some of the shacks in this area are more spacious than others; some are in "site and service areas" where electricity is available and communal water taps and toilets have been installed. From a distance, some of the colorful dwellings look attractive and cheerful. Up close, the scene is disturbing. People peer out from doors and cracks in walls—many have no windows. Children play in the rubble until their mothers pull them back inside. Families know to be cautious about anyone they don't know—robbery and burglary happen all the time. No one ventures out after dark if they can help it, but it is necessary in order to use a toilet (in these areas, nothing more than a portable latrine set some distance from the dwellings). Women are particularly afraid of using them at night since they are especially vulnerable to attack, and they try to protect themselves by going in pairs.

This is not a safe place, nor is it a healthy one. Khayelitsha's children are at the mercy of disease vectors, made worse by the damp in winter, lack of sanitation, and poor diets. The fortunate ones suffer only from skin problems and coughs. The less lucky fall victim to epidemics the developed world—and economically advantaged South Africans—left behind generations ago. Tuberculosis, pneumonia, dysentery: these killers of the nineteenth century are ever-present in Khayelitsha.[1] Even worse, this is ground zero of the HIV/AIDS pandemic.[2] No less than 30 percent of women aged twenty-five to

Families improve shacks by adding on new layers, wooden fences, and proper windows. The interiors are often decorated with colorful sheets of newspaper.

twenty-nine are HIV positive, and one in every ten young men are estimated to carry HIV.[3] Millions of children in the country are orphaned, many as a consequence of AIDS. Relatives take them in but often struggle to keep their heads above water.[4] An extra mouth to feed is not a small matter. Despite the valiant efforts of dozens of NGOs operating in the townships, extreme poverty and crowding ensure that many will not see adulthood here.

The community does not take these conditions lightly. In January 2009, residents of one of the informal areas organized protests, demanding services, mainly electricity and sanitation, from the government. Tires were set afire on the roads into the township and garbage was tossed into the streets. People lit containers and used them to erect roadblocks. They threw stones at buses and hammered at the asphalt on the main road. Politicians began pointing fingers. The Democratic Alliance (DA), which had only recently come to power in the province argued that the ANC was fomenting trouble in order to make the Western Cape ungovernable, while the ANC professed to have had no role in the riots. Why, they asked, didn't the DA do its job and deliver services anyway? The fact that electricity and sanitation had steadily improved over the previous few years made little difference to those stuck in the poorest of the informal settlements. For them, the aftermath has meant the same as in the past: no change.

Off the main road, in a warren of small, sandy pathways, we find a *spaza* shop or convenience store, iron on the outside, with wooden walls inside. The goods for sale are walled off from the waiting area by metal grating, with a small hole through which one can pay for and receive a single diaper, piece of bread, a can of soda. A woman with a small baby tied to her back is in front of us, and an older man leaning against the wall, clearly drunk, is waiting for nothing in particular.

Inside the shebeen next door to the spaza shop, billiard balls knock against each other, music plays loudly through a pair of old speakers, and the patrons are a little glassy-eyed. It is a bit before 11:00 a.m., but the drinking is advanced. People living nearby pass outside, some turning their heads to have a look at the unusual sight of White people who have somehow found their way to this spot.

Nearby, some kids play in the sand, and others are walking home in their school uniforms. A woman washes clothes in a bucket in front of her shack. Three young men walk out of the shebeen, each holding two empty one-liter beer bottles. The woman with the baby on her back comes out of the shop with two diapers. She stops to chat, and we ask her how this area fares when the rains come. The shacks flood every year, she says, several times over. "How do you manage?" we ask. She shrugs. Flooding is not the worst thing to befall her family. "You use buckets, everything you can get your hands on to get the water out." She shows us the interior of her shack and points to a table in the middle of the room where they pile everything to protect what they can from floodwaters. The furniture, all made of wood, has seen many seasons of the rains. The wood soaks up the water, expands, and then rots. The food gets damp, clothes get wet. "Everything, everything," she laments, but "you go on."

Thandiswa is all too familiar with these frustrations. One day she was looking at a photo she had taken of a stagnant pool of water outside the communal toilets. It brought back memories she recorded in her diary:

This is how the poor people of South Africa live, always jumping over dirty stinking water near their houses. It's always been like this. I remember when I was living in Crossroads in the 1980s. It looked just like this. When it rained, heavy water would get inside our zinc house. Everything was wet, even the blankets. If it rained for days, the house would be filled with more water.

We had [outhouse] toilets like these and the dirt from the toilets would be inside our house. It was horrible; the water was stinking. After the rain stopped and the sun was out, we would help my mother clean the house, wash the blankets, our clothes. We did all that every time it rained.

The "informal areas" or "shacklands" on the exterior rings of Khayelit-sha have grown uncontrollably over the years, but they are only one part of the sprawling settlement. In the interior of Khayelitsha we find tiny houses made of makeshift materials but laid out in recognizable zones, planned areas known to the residents as Site C, Section G, and the like.

Closer to the center of the township, in the oldest parts of Khayelitsha, are formal neighborhoods built under the apartheid regime. Most of the streets are paved in these more middle-class zones and they are wider, with space to safely walk along the edge. The larger roads have sidewalks and stop signs, and the busy intersections have traffic lights. Khayelitsha feels more organized here and the houses have small yards, fences, and plaster walls.

This is J section, where Thandiswa lives. The walls of her house are white stucco and the wrought iron gate swings on rusty hinges. Inside, the tiny sit-ting room, painted ochre, has two couches arranged in an L. The walls have holes where they meet the ceiling, and a sheet of corrugated iron pokes out of the plaster. There are no pictures on the walls, but Thandiswa proudly shows us a framed photo of Andile, her six-year-old son, who is now living in the Eastern Cape with one of her sisters.

Down the corridor, which is completely dark even in daytime, there is a TV on at the back of the house, and the other people in her family who are home during the day are watching a cops-and-robbers show.

Besides Thandiswa, who was twenty-eight when we met her, we find her two-year-old son, Akhona; her mother, Mam'Cethe (known by her Xhosa clan name, Cethe); Thembinkosi, her older brother; and Zoliswa, her young-est sister, who has a baby of her own. Zikhona, a middle sister with twin two-year-olds, Mbulelo (a boy) and Nombulelo (a girl) live there as well. Lulama, Thandiswa's ex-boyfriend and Andile's father, has been staying there for some time too, since he has no other place to go. Her parents would like the two of them to reconcile as they like him better than the father of Thandiswa's two-year-old, but she will have none of it. Thandiswa and Lulama tend to ignore one another, which is not a simple matter in such a small place.

Thandiswa's father, Tata Boya, does not really live here. He stays on the farm where he works, returning to his home in Khayelitsha only on Fridays and just for that one night. He is one of only two people with a regular income in Thandiswa's house, but he provides faithfully for all of them by turning over his salary to Mam'Cethe. Once in a while, various members of the family go to stay with him and help out with weeding the plant beds on the farm, where he is a long-term laborer. For the most part, though, they just see him one day a week. He is seventy-five now and one wonders how long he can keep up a physically demanding job and what will happen to this household when he cannot work. To get back to his workplace, he must take three taxis and then walk an hour from the closest drop-off point.

On the day we first visited Thandiswa's home, Nomonde, another sister, who lives in the nearby Black township of Mfuleni, was visiting with her seven-year-old son, Thamsanqa. Nomonde has more education than most members of her family, having completed high school and recently gone on to complete a teaching credential. Today she works for an NGO that delivers public health services and HIV/AIDS education. Nomonde herself is HIV-positive but keeps a close eye on her health and treatment, and manages a full working life just fine. Indeed, in addition to taking care of Thamsanqa, she invited yet another sister, Zizipho, to live in the small shack behind her house. Nomonde is a quiet woman, somewhat reserved like Thandiswa. But she is worldlier, reads more widely, and has learned to navigate middle-class environments more readily than her sisters.

As with many others in their situation, Thandiswa's family remains closely tied to the Eastern Cape, from whence they migrated some thirty years ago.[5] The oldest siblings were born there, but everyone who followed has been back and forth, and some, like Thandiswa—during her cow-minding assignment—have lived in the region, off and on, for many years. Another sister, Zakithi (Abbie), is living there now in the town of Seymour, where she has been caring for her daughter, nicknamed "Beyoncé," her son who is eight, and Thandiswa's son, Andile. Andile was sent to live with his aunt because of his terrible eczema, a skin condition exacerbated by the dust and grit in the air in Khayelitsha. Thandiswa explains that it is also less of a financial strain on her when Andile is away because she can't afford to take him to the doctor and buy the special cream he needs for his skin. She speaks to her son every week by cell phone, but he is growing distant and sometimes complains that she is really only Akhona's mother, not his.

Now thirty-nine, Abbie has one other child, seventeen-year-old Thumeka, who spends some of her time in Khayelitsha and some in Mfuleni. Thandiswa confides that she and Abbie spent hours trying to convince Thumeka to stay in school, knowing full well how hard life becomes for those who drop out. Only a fool would have risky sex in this day and age, they told her. Their warnings had little impact. The underserviced schools in the townships were never happy places for Thumeka, and today, at seventeen, she is the mother of a one-year-old girl and has dropped out of high school. She had been living in Thandiswa's house when we met, but a year or so later she and her daughter moved to the Eastern Cape to be near her mother.

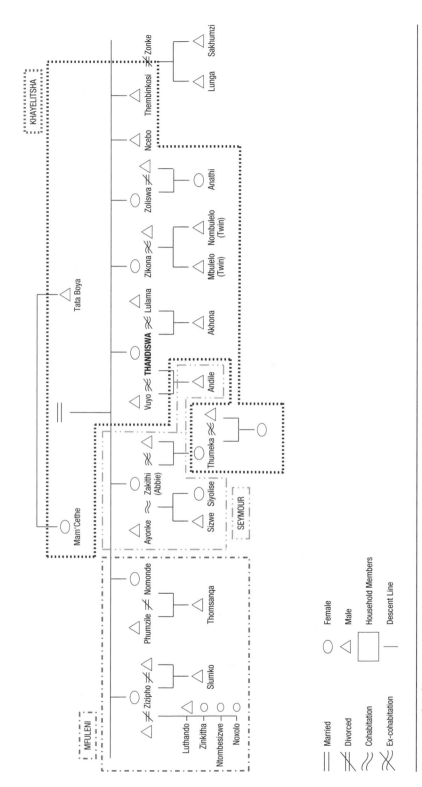

Figure 1 *Thandiswa Boya's Family*

Together, then, there are ten people—six adults and four children—in this four-room Khayelitsha house, not counting the father, Tata Boya.[6] There are no doors between the bedrooms and the ceiling is not complete. They have only four proper beds—two doubles and two singles. The two oldest men, Lulama and Thandiswa's brother, Thembinkosi, sleep on the floor. They have only a few cupboards in which they store their clothes. There is no quiet place for a child to do homework. Everyone feels crowded. No one can find a private space.

Within ten minutes of our first arrival at the house, a neighbor, curious to see White visitors in the area, walked in unannounced and sat down on the couch next to Thandiswa. Thick burn scars covered one side of her face and one ear was mangled, the consequence, she explained, of a terrible car accident for which she received inadequate treatment. Talkative and inquisitive, this neighbor must be tolerated, Thandiswa later explained, because if you asked her to leave, you would seem disrespectful and she might start spreading gossip.

Maintaining good relations outside of the family is essential for survival in the townships. It pays to know people and to remember the connections you have to them because if those links are recognized, even tangentially, strangers will be less likely to threaten your safety. Thandiswa recounted a time when she had been attacked. She had shouted her brother's name, hoping he could come to help her. Her attackers recognized the name, realized they knew him, and let her go. They even handed her back the phone they had been trying to take from her. Had her assailants been strangers, totally unrelated by friendship or blood, the situation could have been very dangerous. Instead, these men were distant parts of Thandiswa's network, and hence they thought twice about endangering their relations. They backed away.

These rules of engagement illustrate the uneasy atmosphere that pervades much of Khayelitsha. Thandiswa practices the policy of remaining as inconspicuous as possible. Attracting attention by wearing anything valuable, she says, is an invitation to robbers. She has often instructed us to shed watches, earrings, necklaces, and anything else of visible value before coming to see her.

During the day, except when heated demonstrations flare in the streets, people go about their business. Entrepreneurs sell their services and run small shops. Children find their way to school while mothers wash clothes or cook food. As night falls, the tension level rises. It becomes riskier to be outside, especially in the most "informal" areas of Khayelitsha. Many feel a knot in the stomach when they have to venture out for any reason. Burglar bars on windows and doors accentuate the feeling of being behind barricades. A pervasive sense of risk, uneasiness, and threat of violence settles over the township.

Thandiswa has adapted to these surroundings by turning inward. In the first few months we met with her, it seemed clear that she was clinically depressed. Her energy level was low, apathy settled permanently on her shoulders. Her diary records the enervation that was her constant companion:

> *The tasks that I did today are the daily routines. These include washing my face, brushing my teeth, and making myself a cup of coffee. This is the way I start my days. . . . My mother went to the clinic at 10 o'clock. I did the normal cleaning of the house, feeding the kids and washing them. At 11 o'clock I forced them to sleep, because I was so tired of talking to them. They give me a headache!*
>
> *After that I wash the [diapers] and hang them. At 13:13 I slept, to let my mind rest. I was woken up by one of my [sisters'] child[ren] at 14:30 pm. I woke up, gave him food, and changed his nappy. After I finished, the other twin (the fat one) woke up; I also changed his nappy. Others were still asleep and I was also feeling tired because I had not rested well. I went to sleep again for a few minutes. I left the two watching TV, chatting in their own language, I cannot even figure out what they were talking about.*

Often at her wits' end, stuck in an overcrowded house without any adults to talk to and too many children for the space, Thandiswa feels simultaneously listless and overwhelmed:

> *There is nothing new other than the same routine as yesterday. Except that these kids make me tired. There is too much of them and they cause me headaches. I have to talk to them every minute; they do not want to listen. When I talk to this one, another one would be doing something wrong. Like yesterday, this one of mine [Akhona] fell and hit the corner of the table with his head, as a result he was bleeding. I understand that they are kids, but sometimes they are too much.*

No one ever asks Thandiswa how she feels or what she wants in life. She thinks she has been taken for granted by her family as a source of labor. The time she spent in the Eastern Cape—seven long years of isolation, looking after the family's "savings account," those eight cows—was only the beginning. Back in Khayelitsha, without a job to contribute to the household's income, she is expected to look after her own child and those of her sisters. Does her family know that she resents her situation, wishes she had been able to do more for herself, more to prepare for a better life? How would they know, she wonders in her diary, when she rarely speaks up for herself?

> *I am just sitting and thinking about my own issues. I was thinking how far I would have been if I did not go to the Eastern Cape. Maybe I would have got a job and be working by now. But by then I was still too young; at that time I knew nothing about life, except to stay at home and watch television. All I wanted was to further up my studies. Sometimes I think if I was a wise and outgoing person (not a shy person) I would have stood up, gone and look for a bursary to further my studies. Even the ants are [more] alive than me. They are always busy collecting food in preparing for tough times. I am so lazy; I am just like a statue.*

Thandiswa is tall, slender, and lithe. Her cheekbones are high, her eyes a deep brown. Today her hair is straightened and pushed back from her face, framing a stunning smile, which she rarely showed in the first few months of our acquaintance, although when she did let it flash she was beautiful. She attracts notice in Khayelitsha, where women are often heavy and lumber under loads that make them appear stooped and exhausted. Few have had good dental care and it shows: many adults have broken or missing teeth. Thandiswa has managed to survive her environment with a special kind of physical grace.

Fully bilingual, she is able to both read and write in Xhosa and English, which she speaks with a soft accent. She complains that when she is under pressure her English crumbles, but in the two years we have spent with her, we have never heard her falter. It is remarkable that she has this skill, given her educational history. As a young child, she lived in different townships, starting out in Crossroads, which was then an informal settlement plagued by violent political protests. Later the family moved to different parts of Khayelitsha. As was typical in the apartheid-era school system and its "Bantu" education for Black children, Thandiswa attended an overcrowded, underserviced elementary school not far from her home in the late 1980s.

She found it painful to talk about the corporal punishment she endured in the classroom, but her more voluble sister, Zizipho, was full of stories. "We were beaten up," she remembered, "especially the boys."

> They were beaten on their buttocks . . . with pipes. You see the red [rubber] pipe that is used for plumbing [she points to one on the ground]?

They used that. . . . The girls were beaten on the hands. The hands would get swollen up; after school, you couldn't even wash your socks [it hurt so much].

Zizipho is tough, and while she grew visibly angry when remembering what school was like, it seems she did not retreat in fear as a child. Indeed, in time (and with a less punitive system to compare her experience with), she had come to appreciate some of the side benefits of strict expectations. "I think it was better then [under apartheid]," she argued, "because now people do what they please at school. The students . . . are not serious. They under-mine . . . there is no respect."

Zizipho is older than Thandiswa and was a student at the time of the school boycotts organized in resistance to the apartheid state. The infamous Soweto marches of 1976, in which young kids were gunned down, setting off waves of violent reprisals, were in the international news every night. The crackdown that followed hit the Black townships with full force. Mandatory curfews were imposed; everyone had to be indoors when the street lights were cut out around 6:00 p.m. Big yellow security vans, locally called *iihaug*, the Xhosa word for pigs, began roaming through the townships. Zizipho remembers it as a period of tense excitement, laced with real terror, as the Afrikaner police would go around the township looking for people who were protesting. She says,

> People burnt tires on the roads and put big rocks on the streets so that the Boers' cars would not be able to pass. As the cars slowed, people inside the shacks would hurl stones at their windshields.

It became increasingly risky for White people to travel anywhere near the townships, lest their cars be hijacked. Police sprayed the streets with tear gas. One time, a man running from the police broke in through an open bathroom window in the Boya house.

For Thandiswa's generation—especially that of her older siblings—those were years of interruption and turmoil. Already enrolled in weak schools, their attendance was disrupted, often for weeks on end by the protests. Black students participated in demonstrations, some feeling forced to, on pain of violence at the hands of their own people.[7] These disruptions left their mark on members of the Freedom Generation, who came into their teen years miss-ing some essential academic building blocks.

More disruption arose because the Boyas were so often on the move between different townships. The family left the violent, informal area of

Crossroads for a shack in Khayelitsha, and then they finally settled in their current house in Section J. A sensitive child, Thandiswa found the moving from one area to another, and from one school to another, bewildering. She felt lost and lacked the ability to pilot her way through the maze. To make matters worse, she associated school not with learning but with physical punishment and authoritarian control. To her it was a place where no one was ever helpful. Hoping to do better, Thandiswa later transferred to Mfuleni High in the township near where her sister Nomonde now lives. There she had to start again in standard six (the equivalent of eighth grade) because she had failed the previous year. She stayed for a year and then finished her remaining schooling in Masiyile High School in Khayelitsha.

The rapid succession of schools did not improve Thandiswa's education. She was forever facing the need to start and stop, to move and regroup. Her motivation started to drop. Even so, she learned seven subjects, including physics and math. Unusual among many of her acquaintances in Khayelitsha at the time, she completed her final high school year, a milestone that only 30 percent of young people in lower-income households manage to pass.

Given the extraordinary significance of the anti-apartheid movement and the revolution it promised, particularly in education for the country's majority, it is striking how discouraged Thandiswa and her sisters sometimes were about the post-apartheid years. Zizipho acknowledges that the old regime was evil, but she argues that it was more stable and that a vast inequality has since erupted between Black South Africans who have done well and those who are still mired in poverty. Most of all, Zizipho remembers that the sense of order and predictability was greater. "People were struggling," she remembered, "but the government provided everything":

> Things like books, pens, rulers, and everything. What you had to buy was the book cover. Even the school fees [were covered] . . . if you were a family, you only paid one amount for the whole family. . . .
>
> We even ate at school. The food that they cook now for students is . . . not [good]. During the apartheid government, they brought good things. Like when it was cold, they brought soup and bread and then in other days they would bring milk and bread. We also had milkshake!
>
> Doctors came to the school . . . to look for deaf children and maybe children who had eye problems. They also looked for students that wanted to have their tooth taken out. Dentists came to the school.
>
> We did not struggle like this.

This was neither the first nor the last time we heard a Black South African look back on the apartheid years with nostalgia. To our ears, it was a shock. Nonetheless, we had to credit their perceptions and understand that the challenges faced by the ANC, to speak to the aspirations of people so long denied, were daunting—there were insufficient funds to do it all. Many dreams have been deferred, and frustration has grown in their place.

THANDISWA'S WORK WORLD

Having completed final high school exams, and given her mastery of English, Thandiswa should have been more fortunate in her search for employment than she has been.[8] Her schooling, sadly, has not helped Thandiswa very much. She has never held a long-term job, and the intervals between her short-term jobs grow longer and longer. None of the positions she has landed have made use of her intelligence. Hired to pump gas for a few months when she was seventeen, that job ended when she was sent to the Eastern Cape. Pregnancy interrupted her efforts to find work when she made her way back to Khayelitsha. After that, she found it hard to figure out how to launch a search for work. Today she is often at a loss, unable to figure out how one learns about job opportunities. Since so many people in her community are unemployed, including most of the adults in her own household, there are few people to whom she can turn for leads.[9]

Instead, she has to think up places that might be hiring. During our fieldwork, she landed on the idea of going to stores she shops in and leaving her résumé. Earnestly, she sat down to write a CV and she caught buses and taxis to stores she knew, leaving the paperwork with the clerks she found behind the cash register. No one ever called. She was puzzled and upset that her efforts seemed to lead nowhere.

After several failed expeditions of this kind, she heard about an opportunity that sounded perfect: selling medicine door-to-door. She bubbled with enthusiasm about the chance to earn real money. It was a chance to be her own boss, get back on her feet, pay her own bills, and be a respectable adult for the first time. All she had to do was borrow enough money to pay the company, True Health, for boxes of medicine.

After nagging Mam'Cethe for a week or two, Thandiswa had R1,900 in hand, and another 1,000 promised by her new supervisor, another "sales representative" in the township. Proudly, she showed us a box of medicine in small plastic containers and the glossy magazines she was told to show her customers. One would help people stop drinking alcohol. Another was for stomach problems. Yet another would help those with skin diseases or problems with pregnancy.

Thandiswa was under pressure to repay the loans, but she was excited about the earnings that were sure to come her way. "In one of the presentations, a member told us about how much money she gets," she said. "She showed us her pay slip, which showed a salary of R16,000. She told us about all the positions you can go up to when you work for True Health."

"Level one" of the True Health sales force was Thandiswa's starting point: after paying the entry fee of R2,900, the box of medicine was hers to sell. Reaching the second level would mean becoming a supervisor, something that has never been a remote possibility in any other job she has held. To her ears, "level two" sounded lucrative and important. Yet to get that far Thandiswa would have to find two other people—like her sisters—and get them to sign up. For that, she would receive R160 a month and take responsibility for supervising these two "reports." Above this rank are the higher reaches of the True Health organization: each of the "reports" recruits two more entry-level people, and the highest person in the chain of command now pockets R2,100 a month. The pyramid is supposed to grow without end. Someday, Thandiswa was told, she could look forward to earning R25,000 a month or more, enough to possess fancy cars and houses.

Thandiswa is tailor-made for what True Health was selling, because it offered her more than money. It showed a way out of her psychological inertia. True Health was capturing the imagination and longing of township residents with the prospect of entrepreneurship, action, and independence. Her enthusiasm was further stoked by a celebration sponsored by True Health. A great hall, the largest she had ever seen, was booked for the occasion. Every participant had to purchase a ten-rand ticket. Three speakers took to the front and spoke with conviction about True Health's medicines. Each one in turn told the crowd about the limitless future in front of them once their sales grew. They led the audience in song and urged them to clap their hands. "Ekugqibelini ude wabonwa nandim!" (Eventually I have found you!) "You will no longer have a boss!" the attendees were told. "You will be rich."

Some of the speakers called volunteers from the audience to witness how their lives had been changed by the medicine. One testified that her child had suffered terrible stomach pains, but because of the True Health products they had disappeared. Another proclaimed that her mother had had lumps on her head and had always been tired, but after she took the medicine, the bumps disappeared and she felt young again. The mother, an elderly woman, stood up, and the crowd stomped and clapped. Someone began ringing bells and singing a True Health slogan: "Life is about choices, therefore choose True Health. Go for what makes you successful." "Asoze aphele amandla, u True Health ngowethus sonke" (The strength will never end, True Health belongs to all of us). Another man faced the audience and announced, "Ndenziwe ugqirha ngu True Health, ndinkwe isdanga" (I have been made a doctor by True Health, I have been honored with a degree). This brought thunderous applause from a crowd now riled to a fever pitch of the kind usually reserved for a religious revival.

Thandiswa was determined, excited, and ready to get started on her new life. Diligently she contacted everyone she knew in the township, explaining how these medicines were wonderful. "You must try this," she admonished. "It will take care of your problems."

A few weeks after the gathering in the great hall, we asked Thandiswa how the new business was doing. She no longer looked hopeful. She sighed and nodded, "It is okay." But the True Health job was not as easy as she thought it would be, going from house to house to try to sell the medicine. Were people buying? Some were, she explained, but then "they always have stories." They didn't pay her immediately. She would give them bottles of medicine and then have to go back time and again to collect the money owed to her. Some of her customers would tell her that they didn't have any money yet and that she would have to come back at the end of the month when they would be paid or receive child allowances from the government. Or they would tell her that the medicine didn't work and begin to back away from the promise to pay.

"I don't understand," Thandiswa complained. "If they get sick today and they have to go to the doctor, then they have money. But they say they don't have money for the medicine?" The True Health management team exhorted its sales force to sell only to people they know will pay them. "How do you know that?" Thandiswa fretted.

In the first three weeks of her new job, she discovered just how hard it would be to make a living at selling True Health medicine. She told us then, "So far I have only three potential clients: my two sisters in Mfuleni township and a cousin here in Khayelitsha." Nomonde and Zizipho were eager to get into the business, at least at first, and thought their neighbors in Mfuleni could be good customers.

So four family members became enmeshed in a system that pushed them to collect money from neighbors, while under more or less constant surveillance from the True Health organization. One Saturday night, the "level two" leader who had recruited Thandiswa paid a visit to her home on the pretext of checking on how she was coping. What the supervisor really wanted to know was how many people Thandiswa had managed to recruit—she needed that number in order to get paid from Thandiswa's sales work. Thandiswa discovered from this conversation that the only way to secure those promised big sums of money was to ensure that new people were entering the system. If you don't recruit more sales workers, you would not get paid. This did not go down well with Thandiswa. She said she would never be able to get used to being paid R30,000 a month, and then, all of a sudden, when she failed to bring in new recruits, watch this salary go away. Less than two months after being inducted into True Health, Thandiswa and her sisters quit the medicine-selling business. "The whole thing is too much stress," she explained to us at the time. "This kind of work is not for me."

Fortunately, within two months, another possibility came her way, this time through a safer route: a nonprofit, church-based organization that receives used clothing from rich countries and refurbishes them for resale. She was hired by Renew and Reward, an NGO that had received a grant from a corporate social investment program and had started a secondhand clothing business that employed township residents deemed in need of training. While most of its employees were under contract for manual labor, some were put to work learning the basics of computers, office administration, and sewing.

Renew and Reward opened a warehouse in Epping, an industrial zone outside of Cape Town. The bus that leads to Thandiswa's new workplace winds through a cluster of factories. Plascon (a paint company) has opened here, as has a bed and lounge factory. Another warehouse contains a clothing manufacturer that makes workers' overalls and yet another, Maxidor, makes home-security gates, a booming industry in Cape Town.

Thandiswa's warehouse looks like a big storage garage. It is surrounded by a fence, with a gate opened manually by a security guard posted at the entrance. Workers are searched when they leave the building, even for their lunch period. Cameras track the movements of employees coming and going. On her way out, Thandiswa is motioned inside a little room with a blue cotton curtain to be examined by a female security guard.

Metal shelves packed with clothes line the entryway. Just beyond is a row of forklifts and machines used to check for faults in material. Posters on the walls of the break room remind trainees of the kind of "team building" they are there to realize: "Moving African business." "World class business." "Packaging for Africa." There are pictures of fashion models, cricket teams, and truck fleets. The felt board on the wall has a black-and-white photocopy of Michael Jackson and Eddie Murphy pinned to it.

With a radio blaring in the background, Thandiswa settles down to sort through a mountain of boxes filled with used clothes. Most of them are women's jackets, skirts, tops, and pants. Those that need repairs go one way, clothes that show no obvious signs of damage, but are just dirty, go another. Items that need no attention are folded and packed. Thandiswa is remarkably strong for such a slender woman. She lifts heavy boxes by herself with no help from her male coworkers and refuses help if anyone offers.

Renew and Reward aims to make enough money on clothing resale to cover the costs of running the organization, leaving enough profit to sustain their charitable mission. Along with giving people jobs, the nonprofit wants to see its employees in church. "We are a Christian organization," Thandiswa's boss, Michael, explains, "so we believe in catering for the person in a holistic way." He adds, "If there is a spiritual need, then we would like to see if we can maybe play a role satisfying that need, then maybe showing that person towards God, and this is where we have these classes."

THANDISWA RARELY TOOK Michael up on attending religious classes, but she was pleased to have regular work, even if it did pay only a training allowance: R400 a week. Apart from her natural desire for privacy, she had come to understand that there were limits to the organization's trust in and care for its workers. Michael suspected the workers of stealing clothes to sell on their own and insisted that they put all bags in lockers he closed with padlocks. Some months later, Thandiswa realized that Michael himself was spiriting boxes of clothes out of the warehouse, presumably to sell. In fact, everyone was on the take. It was part of the deal, she reasoned, especially since they were paid such a low amount. Despite the limitations, especially a fixed contract that could not be renewed, Thandiswa genuinely liked this job and was happier during the time she held it than at any other time during our fieldwork. The light banter of her workmates, having a place to go every day that took her away from the children, and most of all the money in her pocket gave her the sense of autonomy she had thought might never come her way. "This is what it feels like to be a true adult," she mused.

Then Renew and Reward came to an end. Six months for Thandiswa and it was all over. Once again, she had nowhere to spend her days except at home looking after the little ones, cleaning up after them and the other people in the house, and shrugging off the catcalls of the men next door.

The doldrums were punctuated by the occasional high of a new opportunity that seemed to come out of the blue. A worker from her days in the clothing business let her know that the same NGO was operating a furniture refinishing workshop and if she was lucky, she might be able to sign on to a training scheme that would give her skills she could use to find a good job. Flush with enthusiasm, she came home later that day to report her success. "I have the job!" she told her family.

Two weeks later, her excitement was gone. There was no training program. Thandiswa had been placed in a factory and told to sand tabletops for a ten-hour shift. The boss had complained that the quality of the new recruits' work was not up to standard since an order that should have been finished was not. Thus the "trainees" would have to stay and do unpaid overtime. Thandiswa arrived home exhausted around ten in the evening. She knew immediately that she needed to get out of this scheme, but having taken a training bursary, she was stuck for three months or would have to pay the money back.

This is the rhythm of Thandiswa's work life. Pyramid schemes that entice and exploit her. Training schemes that lead nowhere. Real employers that never call. Long periods of nothing in between, leading to boredom, apathy, and self-disdain. This corrosive combination does not make her feel like a good mother either, as she senses that she cannot provide, financially or emotionally, for her children.

It is not as though she has many positive or successful models to emulate. In her house, Thandiswa explains, people talk about starting something but never follow through. Her father had the idea of selling sheep entrails in a nearby market in Khayelitsha. He bought all the meat and then took Zizipho and her son Slumko to run the business. Zizipho lasted one day and never went back to the market again. She complained about the work, saying that she did not want to sit the whole day dealing with smelly meat from the inside of sheep.

Thandiswa is not sure what happened to all of the meat, but she says that in the end it was a waste of money. Had Zizipho not decided to quit, the business might have been a booming venture by now. It might have been possible to employ someone else to take care of the smelly part of the job. The family could perhaps have expanded the business to selling meat that was not so smelly. All of this might have meant an alternate pool of money to support the household.

What does Zizipho do instead? Nothing much, Thandiswa remarks. She occasionally gets jobs as a domestic worker, but they are few and far in between. When she was married, she helped manage a shebeen that her husband was responsible for in the evening, after his regular workday was done. Thandiswa points to her older sister to illustrate her conviction that nothing much is likely to change in her life or the lives of those she lives with. They are all stuck.

DOES THE PAST MATTER?

Does Thandiswa believe that her condition is connected to her color? To the long arm of apartheid? She does not think in these terms. It is not that she doesn't see the shape of South African society, at least the part that surrounds her. She does. But these social facts—her unemployment, the thousands of jobless around her, the obvious privileges of Whites living in the City Bowl— are simply givens, within which she makes choices. But how those choices got to be so limited, and why she had so much trouble getting through school or finding employers that would take her seriously, are questions that she doesn't connect to the larger political economy—unless pushed. Thandiswa is more likely to look to what she sees as her own faults.

She does not lack opinions about the past or about the implications of apartheid for the future. She will give them if asked, if one can push through the initial shrug that is her usual response to questions about politics. Does she think it fair, we ask, for the ANC to install policies that depend on racial preferences in hiring?

> T: It's fair because we are now being given the chance. You see what was happening in the apartheid [era] and we could not access certain things [but] it is our time now, for us to [be] part of things.
>
> *What about the White child who can't get work?*
> T: Tough luck because we were also once there. It's still a small thing for them because they are a minority. For us it's a big majority, thousands and thousands experiencing that.

Apartheid may be over officially, but Thandiswa believes that it lingers in the form of poverty, inequality, and the unwillingness of employers to teach their Black workers any skills that will matter. She has seen it on the shop floor. Training schemes she has gone along with for a while have promised a lot, but they have not left her with any skills she can use, nor have they done so for anyone else she can see. When she worked at Renew and Reward she told us, "Emmanuel is the only Black person working on the side of the machines. . . . Our floor manager, when he talks to Emmanuel, he speaks to him like he is stupid. Like, sometimes he shouts at him and tells him that he is doing shit.

And he'll shout at him and tell him to stop using the machine." Why couldn't the floor manager teach Emmanuel how to do his job properly? Thandiswa thought it all came down to what that boss thought Emmanuel capable of: not much. He came from the wrong group.

Assumptions about who is worthy, who is teachable, who deserves to be educated, explain why Black people remain at the bottom of the economic ladder today, twenty years after the end of apartheid, she argues. "If we treated each other as equals," Thandiswa says, "people [in authority] would not . . . feel as if they are seeing a monkey.

> We would also have been able to reach the same levels as they are in. Like, for example, if you work at some factory and you learn [skills] over the years, your experience increases and your rise up the ranks. You have to be promoted and be on another level, until you become a foreman.

Is there any real prospect of a "rainbow nation," of the country Nelson Mandela imagined when he was liberated from prison, a country in which everyone prospers? Thandiswa is not sure. On the one hand, she thinks that equal treatment is a luxury given to those who are already successful, the people she sees on TV, who are treated with respect and assumed to be worthy because they are already rich or beautiful. She says that they are the people who have *ubuntu*.[10] These are the fortunate ones who have "reached a point where they realize that it is bullshit to hate someone who is just like you. We bleed the same blood . . . we breathe the same air."

For the country to adopt this perspective, and truly mean it, will take a long time, in Thandiswa's opinion. A new generation needs to come of age that has grown up together, attended the same schools, rubbed shoulders in integrated communities, seen one another in store aisles and on the rugby pitch.

For her generation there is still too much bad blood. "[We] parents still have apartheid," she reminds us. All groups in society still battle the old thinking. "While there are still people who think [like the old regime], they might pass it on to their children, who will grow up . . . to be the same. But I don't think [prejudice] will be there as much. Now these children can go to school with White kids and go to their [child care]. So then their children are getting used to our children." More interracial contact will bring people closer together, Thandiswa believes, and begin to wipe out the stain of apartheid. "It may still be there [in the future]," she says, "but not as it has been in our time."

If the old racial order were the only thing that needed to change, Thandiswa would see progress ahead, if not for herself, then for Akhona and

Andile. Instead, there is a more complex form of inequality: the kind that divides Thandiswa from Black African women (like Amanda) who grew up in slightly better circumstances, graduated from more-integrated high schools, and found their way into the urban white-collar world. Intra-racial divisions based on class have opened like chasms across South Africa. When Thandiswa sees successful Black people on television, local pop stars and actors who now travel the world, she feels the gap in ways that she didn't experience when the country was under the heel of the Boers. But how much that gap matters depends entirely on how she is doing in her own search for stability. If she is in a good period, she can ward off envy. If she is depressed, it eats at her.

When she focuses on the question of why someone in her situation has so much trouble finding work, she tends to ignore the consequences that follow decades of discrimination, the patently unfair ways in which opportunities to "Renew and Reward" are distributed. It does not come naturally to Thandiswa to think like a social scientist. Hence, when her "luck" runs out, she wonders why the movie stars she sees on television have such cool clothes and she cannot buy a simple T-shirt.

Under apartheid, this question did not surface as often as it does now. When the color line was rigidly enforced, the answer to why someone in Thandiswa's position was poor and unemployed always came back to the regime. Once freedom was in the air, the answers were not so simple. People like Thandiswa started to oscillate between the old account and a new one: I am not worthy.[11] The problem is me.[12]

Who do you think holds the wealth in this country? Who would be at the top of the pyramid?
T: [Everyone] has their own gift; [some] are gifted to use their hands, others sing, others act. Everything is in your hands.

So, getting yourself out of the situation you're in now is dependent on you?
T: Yes, it's up to me. It's me that's going lift herself up. Mandela is not going to come and give me one million and say here, go get yourself a nice life in Jo'burg.

What about freedom? Do you feel we have it here in South Africa?
T: Yes, we have it. [It] depends on how you accept it.

And how do you accept it?
T: Well, I'm free now to go wherever I want to and do anything that I want. I could live anywhere I want to. No one is going to say, "Hey, kaffir, you don't belong here." If I have a lot of money and I want to buy land I can just go there and buy it.

Except, of course, that Thandiswa has no money, no land, and for most of the time we have known her, no job either.

Where, then, does she fit in the new South Africa? What can she expect for her own life and, looking ahead, for her children? In the past, the answers would have been bleak and consistent from one generation to the next: expect nothing, hope for even less. Now there is a more complicated landscape. It is possible for Black people to experience the mobility that Amanda Sophotele has had, and hence race is not the absolute barrier that it was in the dark days of apartheid. Yet the fortunate ones are not simply Black, they are educated Black South Africans who—more often than not—come from more advantaged families than Thandiswa's.

There are other cleavages in the country that have complicated the identities of the people of this book. Traditions that once held groups together are withering, recombining, and surfacing where we least expect them. Families like Thandiswa's straddle several cultural worlds. She is a member of the middle generation in a migration process that is not complete. Her parents were born and raised in the Eastern Cape, as were some of her older siblings. They are steeped in religious and tribal traditions that carry deep meaning and implicate them in a web of obligations for an extended family that is strung along a migration route of thousands of miles. Those cattle in the highlands near the outpost of Seymour are a bank account that they cannot conceive of abandoning.

Yet Thandiswa was raised mainly in the Western Cape, and she is largely divorced from the customs that form her heritage. She knows about the rituals that her parents hold sacred, but she cannot see herself in them. Her father, in particular, observes customs that come from his tribal origins. "If someone is sick, or something is not going right, or someone has a [bad] dream," she explains, "we have to do all those cultural [rituals]." But for herself, she is not entirely sure whether she believes in them anymore.

"It is very difficult . . . because I don't know if I am like [that]. . . . When I am in trouble and I am asking for help, I don't know who answers first; is it God or the ancestors?"

Her children, who were born in Khayelitsha, know even less of this tradition. Thandiswa does not see the relevance of her ancestral culture for her life and has not transmitted what she barely knew to her children. She can locate herself in the clan structure that organized her family and their ancestors from time immemorial, but beyond that she doesn't know what the clan has meant to her father's generation. She doesn't particularly care either. "I'm Thandiswa Miranda Boya," she explained on the day we met. "I'm a Xhosa and belong to the Qwathi Clan. On what the history of the clan is, I don't know and I don't care." Why is that? we asked. "It doesn't help to know that, it won't do anything for me."

For first-generation internal migrants, the traditions that shaped their families remain important sources of identity and belonging. Thandiswa, however, is disengaged from her heritage, though she can recite her clan lineage, and in this she is not unlike many of the other second-generation migrants, who live in the townships and are bilingual, but whose poverty seems to weaken the connections that mattered in the past.

This leaves Thandiswa largely without a cultural anchor. She has no alternative identity that might rescue her from the punishing consequences of poverty and the extreme inequality that plagues South Africa. She cannot take pleasure or shelter in a proud ethnic heritage; it does not mean much to her. Instead, she thinks of herself as "just an ordinary person," someone who isn't quite modern but who no longer belongs the rural ways of her parents' generation. To be modern, she explains, she would have to "live a fancy life, live in town in those nice houses, drive nice cars." For her, modernity is equivalent to a promotion in class, to live in a place where people are educated and hence know how to behave. People who went to what used to be called "Model C schools," which became more racially integrated and far more elegant, those people are truly modern, she says, and have nothing to be ashamed of.

> You will never find Model C's in a shebeen that is dirty and where you find all kinds of people drinking there. People like Model C's will never be found in places where there is also people smoking marijuana and just drinking everywhere.
>
> [Schools] like the ones here in the township, they are not as good as the ones in town. People who are modern are those who live in the schools that are in town. Live in town and then you'll be modern. That's what I want too. That's what modern means to me, to be there.

In the new South Africa, Thandiswa can look up at the television and see soap opera stars, popular singers, and politicians who are Xhosa or Zulu. For that matter, she can look at her sister Nomonde and see someone, her own flesh and blood, who has managed to get a college degree, claim a white-collar job, and live in a better house. An entire legislative apparatus now exists, whose purpose is to ensure that the kind of blind prejudice that ruled the day under apartheid cannot prevail now. Whether it works or not, the ozone of racism is not the same.

For millions of South Africans like Thandiswa, the new order has meant better housing, NGOs dedicated to making a positive difference, and options for children that may in time pay off in the kind of nonracial nation Mandela imagined. But for Thandiswa, those improvements have done little to provide momentum, at least not of the kind the majority dreamed of when the new South Africa was born.

Thandiswa sees herself "at the bottom, bottom" of post-apartheid society. But she is not actually at the very bottom. The real bottom is nearby, however, and visible from her house: the informal shack lands of Khayelitsha and the people there who endure floods in the winter, punishing heat in the summer, epidemic disease, and fear for their safety if they need to go out at night.[13] Shack dwellers look upon someone in Section J as fortunate. Rural poor people in deserted areas like Seymour are even farther down the ladder. From Thandiswa's vantage point, the gulf between what she is and what she ought to be by now is immense. But race alone no longer explains why she sits: waiting, stuck, frustrated, and filled with self-doubt.

Thandiswa's children witness their mother's despair as well as her occasional periods of hope and confidence. They circulate between the various urban and rural houses of the different family members, depending on their mother's available income, her search for employment, or simply her need to be close to them. When we met Thandiswa, her youngest was growing up amid the hustle of Khayelitsha, one of many little ones careening around the family's house. Her oldest, six-year-old Andile, was living with his aunt Zakithi (who goes by her Christian name, Abbie) and two cousins in the Eastern Cape.

Andile had not seen his mother in many months when we decided, as a group, to take a trip to visit him. Seymour, the desolate settlement where he lives, is a thirty-minute drive (for those who have cars) from the nearest real town, Fort Beaufort, which was established by the British in the early twentieth century, a remote outpost for colonial troops during the Anglo-Boer War. After it came to power, the African National Congress, determined to bring services to the most impoverished rural areas, began a campaign of building houses right next to the old town of Seymour, one-room structures with basic utilities, as part of its Reconstruction and Development Programme (RDP). It became a modest community of small homes painted in many colors, with real glass windows and little yards surrounded by chicken-wire fences.

With little economic opportunity nearby, however, many of Seymour's residents migrated away to other parts of the country in search of work. Others absconded with the windows and aluminum frames of the abandoned

RDP houses built by the African National Congress on the edge of Seymour have been stripped of aluminum, doors, and anything else of value when their owners migrate out of the region in search of work. This area now has electricity and roads, but the commercial farms that employed the residents have largely collapsed.

Fort Beaufort, but without a car that is not easily done. Thanks to the post-apartheid reforms of the ANC, Abbie receives a child support grant for each of her two kids and they subsist on that, and the extra her boyfriend can bring home, for most of the month. We arrived in the third week of January and food was scarce by then. No one in the house, save the baby (fed on porridge—"pap"), had eaten anything at all for several days. This is not an uncommon occurrence, Abbie explained, since the grant of R290 per child rarely lasts through a whole month.

It was the weekend when we arrived, which was one reason the children were hungry. On school days they are fed by their teachers, who are dedicated but underfunded. Children in Seymour, including Abbie's son and Thandiswa's Andile, attend an Afrikaans-speaking elementary school in the center of the hamlet. Dressed in green uniforms, forty children to a classroom sit in orderly rows of wooden desks, completing worksheets and reciting their multiplication tables. At the end of the sixth form, eighth grade, they will leave the area for high school.

The main advantage to living in Seymour, as Abbie sees it, is safety. There are no gunshots at night and she can walk outside without fear of violence. In Khayelitsha, she was always worried about being attacked. Here she is at a loss without the support of her kin, but her kids can play outside. It is a meager existence, though, and one that left us worried about the children's health. Just next door to Abbie was a young woman with three siblings to feed, whose mother, Thandiswa confided, had run away with whatever money they had. Three young men of dubious appearance were sitting in her yard, waiting. We surmised she was selling herself for money to feed the family, a terrible dilemma in the age of HIV and AIDS.

One might assume that the sight of her hungry son would motivate Thandiswa to do something for Andile, Abbie, and Abbie's children. After all, whatever the problems of her household in Khayelitsha, no one is going without food. Strangely, though, Thandiswa's face was blank. Her reaction was not for lack of caring. Inside, she explained, she was happy to see her son and worried about how thin he had become. On the outside, though, she greeted Andile, whom she had not seen in months, with detachment, and she seemed unmoved by Abbie's dire straits. Perhaps feeling unable to make a significant difference, Thandiswa shielded herself from feeling too much. The sight of baby Beyoncé's orange-tinged hair, a sure sign of malnutrition, was deeply disturbing to Thandiswa and to the rest of us.

Once we had finished a shopping trip that would supply the household for a couple of months, Thandiswa sat down on the couch and watched the real Beyoncé strut her stuff on television, powered by an illegal electric line. It seemed to be a refuge from the distressing condition of her sister's family. When we finally packed up to leave Seymour, Thandiswa said good-bye to Andile, but she did not look back to watch him disappear in the distance.

CHAPTER FOUR

The Coconut Dilemma

CAPPELO'S BAR AND RESTAURANT ON trendy Long Street in downtown Cape Town caters to an upscale crowd. Waiters in black shirts, red suspenders, and tight black pants weave expertly through the crowd, balancing trays of cocktails aloft. Twentysomething Black women who work in the banks and brokerage houses of the Cape Town financial district are out in force tonight, sporting high heels, matching faux designer bags and eye-catching dresses. They nurse their drinks while clustering around small tables, hoping to connect with a well-dressed young man who might cover their drinks. White girls with pencil skirts mingle too, drinking and laughing with their workmates after a long day at the office. Men of all skin colors in sharp suits, their ties loosened, iPhones at the ready, are looking over the ladies, hoping something will click for the evening.

We could easily be in midtown Manhattan but it is Friday night in the new South Africa, prime time for Khanyiswa Sophotele, known to her family and most of her Black friends as Khanyo and to her non-Black friends by her Christian name, Amanda.[1] Amanda is sporting her favorite green outfit: a form-fitting dress that shows off her figure and perfectly coordinated jacket, shoes, and handbag. She has been to the salon this week and the blond-brown extensions fitted to her natural black hair cascade down her back. Her big brown eyes are framed in dramatic eyeliner and shimmering silver eye shadow. Her skin takes on a warm hue when the candlelight on the table plays off her face. The effect is exactly as she planned: Amanda looks like a star fresh off a movie set.

Four or five different languages are swirling through the air. Amanda herself shifts from Xhosa to English to seSotho in a single sentence, choosing the words that best fit what she is trying to get across. While some White South Africans are able to switch from Afrikaans to English, many remain clueless when it comes to the African languages of the country.

Amanda is hoping to find a nice young man who will spend a week's wages ensuring that she has a good time—those cocktails are expensive—and who will give her a lift home to Sea Point when she decides to call it a night. There is a kind of tournament underway, with Amanda competing with her girlfriends at finding Mr. Wonderful. She hopes he will be tall, broad-shouldered, worldly, and Black, but there are people from all of the ethnic groups in the Western Cape at Cappelo's tonight, so who knows?

Individuals in this cosmopolitan mix of young people have a lot more money and infinitely more polish than Thandiswa. Poorer Khayelitsha residents do not come to nightclubs on Long Street. The closest Thandiswa has ever been to a trendy spot like Cappelo's is a shebeen in her township where she goes only rarely because she doesn't like the drunks who weave in and out. These City Bowl people seem to be a new breed altogether: the lucky ones who managed to ride the waves of change, to find their way to former "Whites only" schools, followed by at least some college education and a white-collar job. They are the new middle class of the Black South African majority.

Amanda owes her good fortune to the wisdom and background of her grandmother, who is now eighty years old. We listened to Grandmother Nosiphiwe tell her life story from the comfort of a padded rocking chair in her living room in New Brighton, a well-kept Black neighborhood of the Eastern Cape city of Port Elizabeth. Houses are small here, but they are houses and not shacks as one finds in the informal settlements of the townships. Nosiphiwe has four modest rooms, including a kitchen, with running water and electricity. Her tiny forecourt is surrounded by a low wall that fronts the street. Her front door and all of her windows are covered in decorative white burglar bars, a reminder of the security problems that beset most neighborhoods in Port Elizabeth as they do in Cape Town.

"I was born and bred in Kimberley," Nosiphiwe begins. The year was 1932, the height of the Great Depression. "My father died when I was six years old. My mother was pregnant with my sister, my younger sister [who has since passed away as well]. My mother's name was Andrea, but I was raised by my grandmother and grandfather. Amanda—my grandmother's name was Amanda."

That Amanda, Amanda Yelesi, also born in Kimberley, lived with her husband, Nosiphiwe's grandfather, who worked as a laborer in the Bantu Gallery, a museum holding the photographic and ethnographic works of Alfred Martin Duggan-Cronin, a photographer especially interested in the "original tribes" in South Africa. Amanda Yelesi, who would live to the age of 102, worked as a laundress in the Kimberley hospital, a job that many Black Africans would have given anything to have in the 1920s and 1930s but not all that unusual in Kimberley. The city was the initial center of South Africa's industrialization, following the discovery of diamonds and gold there in the second half of the nineteenth century. Mining attracted large numbers of migrant workers, and it became one of the first cities to see the formation of a Black working class. By the early twentieth century, Kimberley was a place of opportunity, with more employment and better chances for education for Black South Africans. With the increasing mechanization of labor, they began leaving the city around 1915, but many of those who stayed—like the Yelesi family—became tradespeople, artisans, or office workers. These opportunities placed Amanda and her husband and the generations that followed ahead of Thandiswa's family economically.

Amanda Yelesi could take good care of her granddaughter, Nosiphiwe, while Nosiphiwe's mother, Andrea, migrated to Johannesburg to look for better work. "There was plenty of money and better-paying jobs there," Nosiphiwe explained. As a consequence, Nosiphiwe did not know her biological mother very well. During the years she was growing up, Andrea came home only on holidays. But Nosiphiwe knew that Andrea cared about her, because as like many economic migrants, she sent her wages home to pay for her daughter's clothes and her education. "She took care of me from a long way away."

Kimberley had not only been a hub of industrialization, it also housed the St. Cyprian's Mission Schools[2] that, despite segregation, allowed "African" and "EurAfrican" (an older label for Coloured) children to attend.[3] Nosiphiwe's family valued education, and in the early 1940s, with the support of her grandmother, Nosiphiwe was able to go farther in school than the vast majority of African women of her generation. "I went to Greenpoint Primary School," she explained, up to standard five (seventh grade).[4] She then completed her education with a standard eighth (tenth-grade) diploma from an English-speaking high school that she explained was staffed by White missionaries, with a British principal in charge, almost certainly one of the St. Cyprian schools.[5]

It was Nosiphiwe's ambition as a young woman to put her schooling to use as a nurse, a profession she could enter having finished standard eight, but her grandparents were opposed to the idea. Nursing was hard and dirty work they told her, and Nosiphiwe couldn't defy them. She stayed home and helped her grandparents with their small coal-delivery business and also sold vegetables grown in their garden.

In 1950, at the age of eighteen, Nosiphiwe finally persuaded her grandparents to let her leave Kimberley and follow her uncle (their son) to Port Elizabeth, where he was a teacher. She told the family she wanted to finish her "junior certificate."[6] That is how she ended up in the community where she lives now, although her ambitions for a higher degree did not come to pass. Instead, she met and married Albert Sophotele, a handsome young man working as a truck driver for South African breweries. Sophotele came from a large clan of Xhosa speakers in the Port Elizabeth region. With his wages, the family was able to buy a small house just down the road from where Nosiphiwe lives today.

Nosiphiwe and Albert raised their children, Zondwa and her older brother Joseph, in New Brighton, home to the working-class Africans of Port Elizabeth. When Zondwa had children—all out of wedlock—they all took the Sophotele name, not the surnames of their fathers, an indication of the strength of the maternal line the family would choose to follow. Nosiphiwe took up the mantle her own grandmother had held before her and became the "mama" of Zondwa's daughter, Amanda Sophotele and her half-sister, Alison.

Today, Zondwa and Nosiphiwe's great-grandchildren, including Amanda's daughter, Lindiwe, are in and out of the house all day, to look in on the matriarch. They want to be sure Nosiphiwe is taking care of herself. She has now raised three generations of Sophoteles, starting with her own children, and continues today at the age of eighty. "I think in our culture, when our children have children out of wedlock they are ours," she explains.[7] "We take them to us, you see. We make them ours. I love children . . . so that's why I raised [them]. I've always been with them. They don't want to live with their mother. Amanda does not want to live with Zondwa. Even Alison too. Even when they visit [now] they stay here. They don't . . . live with her."

Nosiphiwe finds it harder to play the matriarchal role these days. She takes medications for high blood pressure; her waking hours are spent in the easy chair in her living room, watching television. Even so, she has responsibilities. "Yhuuuuuuu, yhoo, I am tired," she sighs.

THE APARTHEID YEARS

Nosiphiwe's husband, Albert, died in 1981, the year before Amanda was born. Nosiphiwe had Alison, Amanda's older sister, to look after, while her own son Joseph and daughter Zondwa were moving around in search of work. She was beginning to think about the best way to provide for the education of her grandchildren and landed on the idea that she might be able to maneuver them into one of the few "Whites only" schools that were beginning to open their doors to children of color, if she volunteered to be a "lunch lady" in one of them. Surrounded by beautiful grounds, with state-of-the-art facilities and first-rate teachers, these schools had been bastions of the minority White elite. From such a launch pad, university admission was virtually guaranteed in an era when less than 10 percent of South African high school graduates went on to college.

By the early 1980s, the pressures that ultimately cracked apartheid wide open were mounting with relentless force, and much of the attention focused on educational inequality. Township schools and "White schools" both received state support, but much more state support flowed to the White schools that could also bring in substantial additional funds through school fees paid by the families of their pupils. The glaring differences took on powerful political significance, and as the Nationalist Party tried to squirm away from the mounting anger toward apartheid, it also responded by allowing the first tentative attempts at racial integration. In practice, this meant a tiny number of Black children started to make their way into the previously "Whites only" schools.

Working in the Sunridge primary school, it was not lost on Nosiphiwe that getting her own grandchildren onto that very short list for admission would be the opportunity of a lifetime. They were bilingual speakers of English and Xhosa, which made a difference, and part of the solid working class of New Brighton, raised by an English-speaking, educated grandmother. Nosiphiwe herself had a good reputation with the school administration since she was a hard worker. It was a great day for Nosiphiwe's household when the oldest Sophotele sister, Alison, was admitted to the school.

In the long aftermath of the 1976 student uprisings, riots and strikes were spreading throughout the townships around Port Elizabeth and in the city itself. Many ANC supporters boycotted businesses in the center of the city, resisted police, and refused to send their children to school at all. The state responded with brutal force: midnight raids in the townships, secret police swooping in to pick up militants who were never seen again. "As a Black person, in the evening, by nine o'clock, you couldn't been seen in town," Nosiphiwe remembered with a shudder.

Lukhanyo, a Kimberley cousin of Nosiphiwe's who frequented her home in Port Elizabeth, took to the streets to protest the regime and paid with his life. It was 1977, and Nosiphiwe recalls:

> He was here for the holidays and went back home. . . . Two days later, I got a call in the morning saying that he was dead. He promised me he was coming back to see us again because he didn't stay for long. He was a nomad from Durban, and would be going back to his home in Cape Town, but he promised he would come and see me after a few days. That morning, when he was preparing to come back, the Special Branch arrived and

took him to the Transvaal. My mom and my granny said that after about four hours, they brought him home and then searched the house, pulling drawers out.

There was nothing [incriminating]. They were old and knew only that there was something going on but didn't know what [it was.]. When he got back to our home, the Special Branch stopped him and said, "Say good-bye to your parents and grandparents." They could not understand why. At about one o'clock a telegram came: "Lukhanyo Yelesi is dead." . . .

A cousin to my mother was working in the [detention building]. She saw all that happened. "They threw him out of the window." But they lied, they said he was trying to escape. But he couldn't, because he was so beaten.

He was such a good man, a Christian. He was a teacher.

Apartheid strangled the lives of families like the Sophoteles, so much so that even those who were relatively well off—as Nosiphiwe and her husband were during his truck-driving days—were desperate for the revolution against it to succeed. Indeed, Luvuyo, Amanda's father, a prominent jazz musician who had played most of the major venues in the big cities, joined the struggle, played for ANC rallies, and later performed for sympathetic audiences in places like Harlem, New York City, where support for the movement was strong. Luvuyo's concert appearances alongside world-renowned artists like Hugh Masekela and Miriam Makeba took on an increasingly political tone. Why Amanda's father was saved from the same deadly fate as cousin Lukhanyo is a mystery.

What is clear is that Nosiphiwe and her family were supporters of the struggle. They were eager to see the ANC take down the apartheid state, even as they did not always adhere to the party's demands to demonstrate in the streets and boycott the schools. The movement aimed to shut down the major institutions of apartheid, taking their inspiration initially from the nonviolent methods of the American civil rights movement that had in turn been shaped by the anticolonial struggles in Gandhi's South Africa and India. Yet the extraordinary opportunity for Alison to enter a previously "Whites only" school was too important for Nosiphiwe to let it go. Nothing was going to stop Alison from taking advantage of this chance.

It was not a popular decision. Neighbors surrounded their New Brighton home under the cloak of night and heaved stones at the roof. "Alison Sophotele, you will not go to school tomorrow," they yelled into the dark. Theirs were not idle threats in the days of the struggle. Turncoats who broke boycotts in the townships often paid with their lives, in a string of infamous incidents involving people who were forced to don "necklaces" of burning tires.[8] In New Brighton, the Sophoteles did not face this level of intimidation, but they were scared just the same. In order to get Alison to school, they spirited her out of the house before the sun came up and drove to another part of Port Elizabeth where she could catch a bus that took her within walking distance of her school.

Though the politics of the situation were complex, with hindsight it is clear that Nosiphiwe's insistence that Alison (and later Amanda) seize the opportunity to attend a previously all-White school played a powerful role in their subsequent upward mobility. During the apartheid years, it was a rare Black child who had the chance to enjoy schools with a rich array of classes, immaculate rooms, computers, and language instruction in Afrikaans and English, linguistic tools that gave the Sophotele girls the capacity to operate anywhere in South Africa.

Today that educational advantage has turned into a class line that separates Alison and Amanda from many of their cousins and neighbors as well as their own parents. Few others in their community have the kind of jobs they have. When the post-apartheid ANC government began to promote the mobility of the majority through labor legislation that insisted on preferential hiring in professional employment and business ownership for Black people, Alison and Amanda were in the wings with the kind of human capital and educational credentials needed for those jobs. It is the tool kit that Thandiswa never had.

Amanda was born in 1982. She remembers, in a very distant way, the climate of fear and intimidation that was apartheid, though it is hard to disentangle what she knows from experience from the stories she has been told. When asked about what it was like for her, she mentions the murder of Lukhanyo, with a sense of pride that one of her relatives was one of the many martyrs for the cause. Though she did not grow up with her father, she is proud that he was a prominent musician who was involved in the struggle, and she arranged for us to visit him in Port Elizabeth, where he showed us scrapbooks full of his album covers and photos with all of the legendary figures of the anti-apartheid movement. But Amanda was only eight years old when Nelson Mandela was released from prison.

In Amanda's early years, then, she was the beneficiary of the same begrudging reforms that had made it possible for Alison to go to a school that had taken the first steps toward integration.[9] She learned the language of the Boer people in elementary school, which grated against Nosiphiwe, since

Afrikaans is associated with oppression at the hands of Whites and accommodation in the hands of Coloured people, for whom it is also a native tongue.
"My [grand]mother took me out of that school," Amanda explained," because
she hated the fact that I had developed that Afrikaans accent. She wanted me
to sound more English . . . So I went to Sydenham Primary School and then
Strelizia High School, which taught in both Afrikaans and English."

Strelizia, located in the Eastern Cape city of Uitenhage, was, and remains,
a school that prides itself in offering top-quality education. Academics come
first in this elite preserve with its extensive grounds, spacious classrooms and
dormitories, computer and science labs, and elaborate sports facilities. Boarding fees for this school sapped a good deal of Nosiphiwe's pension money in
addition to modest contributions from Zondwa, who was by then making a
living selling clothes and taking in boarders.

While Amanda would never call herself poor, and many in her community would say that she comes from a middle-class household, it seems clear
that sending her to a primarily White boarding school was a major commitment for her family and out of the question for her circle of friends. "Among
my [childhood] friends, the ones I still know now, I think I was the only one
to go to a multiracial school," she explains. To this day, Amanda is not sure
how Nosiphiwe managed to find the money. "I don't know how she did it . . .
I promise you, I really don't know. But she sent me."

By the time Amanda was in high school, Alison was enrolled in Dame-
lin, a tertiary business and technical school in Port Elizabeth. The cost for
both girls turned out to be more than Nosiphiwe could manage, so Alison
dropped out in her third year and started to look for options elsewhere in the
country. It was common knowledge that there were more jobs in the Cape
Town region than there were in the Eastern Cape Province. Alison's father—
one of Zondwa's partners from the past—had already made this trek and was
living in Nyanga, one of the Black townships outside of Cape Town. In fairly
short order, Alison moved into her father's house and set about building a
new life for herself. With her educational background, she had good prospects and eventually found a job in the telecommunications industry, where
she was working when we met. Her job paid well enough for her to build an
extension to her father's house, for privacy. From the outside, it looks like a
metal shack. On the inside, though, it is a cozy retreat, complete with a TV
and a small fridge.

Alison's white-collar wages were good enough that she was able to send
money back to Port Elizabeth to help with Amanda's high school fees. It took
the combined efforts of Nosiphiwe, Alison, and Zondwa to give Amanda the

gift of her education, and she was happy enough to pack her bags for Strelizia. Amanda liked the idea of getting out of Port Elizabeth, away from the social networks and local gossip that were part of her early adolescent years. Always something of a party girl, she had some reputational baggage to jettison and Strelizia gave her that chance to start over.

In retrospect, Amanda confesses, she did not fully appreciate the opportunity her kin were giving her. Too many of her school days were spent in the headmaster's office for having misbehaved in class or forgotten to do her homework. None of these troubles were major infractions, but she admits sheepishly today that she could have done better and learned more rather than spend her time embellishing her social life. Her grasp of math was weak and her interest in science limited. To the extent that she cared about her classes, it was the humanities and the arts that mattered. To this day, she thinks of herself as a creative, expressive soul, something of a chip off her musician-father's block. In the humanities and arts she did well, but all in all, the academic side of what she now calls the "Model C experience" was not high on her list of priorities at the time.[10]

Yet Amanda is very conscious of what her time at Strelizia did for her. It bequeathed to her a certain worldly panache, the capacity to move easily in multiracial and multilingual circles, a sense of what is possible in the world beyond the close confines of New Brighton. It is this cultural capital—and her fluency in multiple languages—that has made Amanda's upward mobility possible. This is the "Model C" advantage: ease in the new multicolored middle-class world, and knowledge about how people make connections, find out about opportunities, and present themselves as actors who belong in the firms they want to join. Amanda's schooling gave her a polish that Thandiswa could not acquire in the malfunctioning and disrupted township school environment she experienced.

The road between Strelizia and Cape Town was not entirely smooth for Amanda. She did not do well enough on her national exams to pursue a true university degree. She headed, instead, for a technical college that offered a more vocational track, and by the time she arrived at the Cape Town Technikon she was pregnant with Lindiwe. A high school boyfriend, also from Port Elizabeth, was the reluctant father.

This is not the fate Nosiphiwe had in mind when she emptied her retirement savings into Amanda's tuition account. Zondwa was not pleased either, but as the mother of three out-of-wedlock children herself, including Amanda, there was no point in getting on a high horse. Instead, the extended family set about deciding what was to be done with little Lindiwe.

When a young woman has a baby without the benefit of marriage, an understanding prevails between her relatives and those of her partner that it is time for grownups to step in and provide a "stable home" for the child.[11] When Amanda fell pregnant with Lindiwe, her boyfriend (who would not stay in the romantic picture much longer) notified his father and uncle, and Amanda did the same. A meeting followed, with the male relatives in negotiation mode and the women of the two families standing to one side, acting as advisors.

Two options were presented, both of which are acceptable in Xhosa culture. In the presence of the families of both the young mother and the father, the young man must make a public pronouncement that he is responsible and offer to pay a fee—*ukuhlawula isisu*—that will help to cover the expenses of nurturing the newborn.[12] Amanda's relatives debated whether to let the father do this for Lindiwe and decided, ultimately, that to do so would be a mistake. They wanted the young man to acknowledge his child, which his male relatives agreed he needed to do, but they did not want to give up any control over the baby's future. Hence, they took the second option, which was to accept the boyfriend's declaration but refuse the fee. That is how it was left. Amanda gave birth, the father owned up to his responsibilities, and Lindiwe was enfolded into the arms of her matrilineal kin.[13] Zondwa soon ascended to the same role that her mother, Nosiphiwe, had played for generations. Zondwa became a true mother to her granddaughter.

In this pattern of "skipped generation" parenting, Amanda is following the example laid down across the generations in her family: able-bodied adults migrate, leaving their children to be raised by grandmothers, and one day take up the same responsibility for their descendants. It is what Amanda herself expects to do when Lindiwe has children.

As their family tree shows, Nosiphiwe was raised by her grandmother—this was because her own mother had migrated to Johannesburg from Pretoria in search of work. Amanda was raised by Nosiphiwe. Lindiwe is being reared by Zondwa. Such a pattern ensures that a young Black woman as upwardly mobile and modern as Amanda can pursue her occupational aspirations without taking responsibility for the daily care of their children.

Readers of anthropologist Carol Stack's *All Our Kin* (1974) will recognize these practices instantly. Stack described exactly the same structure for multigenerational, female-headed families in the Flats, an African American community on the rail line to Chicago, where migrants from the rural South established themselves in the years between World War I and World War II. Stack explains that when a young woman in the community has a

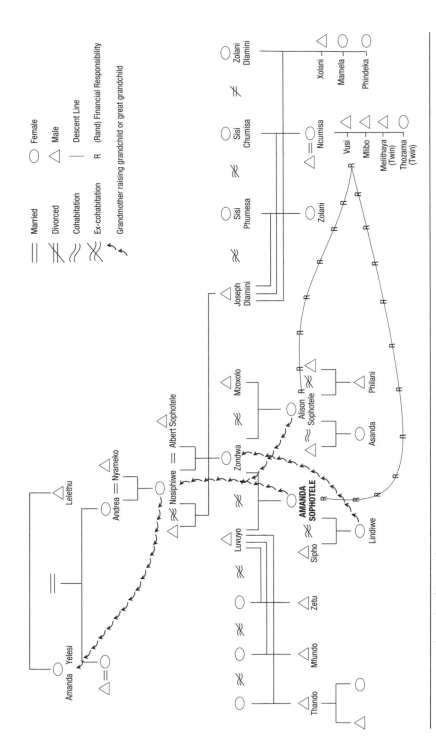

Figure 2 *Amanda Sophotele's Family*

child, her mother becomes the "mama" and the biological mother is something closer to a sibling, in part because the community around her does not define her as capable at her age of being a responsible parent. Children are swapped with extended relatives to underscore the bonds that extend beyond the immediate household. Families in the Flats, Stack explains, are units that collaborate to raise children, and only occasionally do they map onto the nuclear structure in a single household that we have come to think of as the normative family.

The system works, if by this we mean that everyone is raised by someone who feels responsible for the caregiving. But it also imposes a distance—social and geographic—between biological mothers and their children, and it means that children look to their grandmothers as the emotional center of their lives, relegating their actual mothers to a more peripheral role. This can be something of heartbreak since many migratory parents have sacrificed their own emotional health to the task of sending much-needed money home. For decades under apartheid, men moved to mining regions to earn enough so that their families back in the homelands could eat. Even after the fall of apartheid, economic necessity often requires people to leave loved ones behind, and recent trends indicate that maternal migration is on the rise.[14] When Amanda finds her way back to Port Elizabeth, there are two people she really wants to see: Nosiphiwe and Lindiwe. Her own mother, Zondwa, is not that important to her. They don't get along all that well anyway and have never really lived together as mother and daughter. Lindiwe may come to feel the same way about Amanda someday.

This fluid family structure does also allow someone like Amanda to be able to enjoy what she herself calls "the high life." When we met her, she admitted that she hates planning her social calendar. She wants to be "modern," "cool," and spontaneous, rather than traditional and rigid. She lives on her cell phone, stays out late whenever possible, and makes sure she frequents the right night spots, ones that signal her status in the "in crowd." She strives to ensure that she never has to pay for her own drinks, that she is desirable enough to make suave young men fork over enough money to keep her entertained. This is part of what upward mobility has meant in her life: the capacity to approximate the lifestyle she sees in magazines and on television. In this, Amanda is like millions of other young women around the globe.

Amanda admits that taking full-time care of little Lindiwe would not fit well into her lifestyle. Because Lindiwe is growing up back in Port Elizabeth, Amanda does not have to think about child care, find housing that can accommodate a family, or rush home to attend to her child's flu. Someone else is doing all of that work and that frees Amanda to organize her world almost as any childless young woman might do. At the same time, she is actively engaged in Lindiwe's schooling and hence looking out for her daughter's future. During the time of our fieldwork, Amanda decreed that the extended family should speak English in Lindiwe's presence to strengthen her prospects for entry into selective schools. She traveled back to Port Elizabeth specifically to meet with the headmaster of her old school in an effort to smooth the way for her daughter. In this sense, she is acting in the best interests of her child's long-term mobility, even if she is not a daily presence.

Lindiwe is one of the millions of South African children born to single mothers who are able to rely on what the extraordinary strength of intergenerational bonds can do to put a solid foundation underneath them.[15] Surveys cannot capture what Amanda Yelesi and her husband did for Nosiphiwe when her own mother, Andrea, could not care for her. They cannot adequately represent what Nosiphiwe, in turn, means to Amanda and to Alison. Parenting by grandparents is the foundation that migratory families rely on when the middle generation must move to find work. For Amanda and Alison, this is the reason why single parenthood did not compromise their mobility in the labor market.

Single mothers who lack this support and cannot afford or find reliable child care almost inevitably end up at the bottom of the job ladder. If they can find work in the first place, they often lose it because they have to leave when their children need care. This is as true in Harlem, as it is in Cape Town.[16] Fortunately Amanda never had to face this problem. She left one-year-old Lindiwe in the care of Zondwa and struck out for Cape Town to position herself in the white-collar labor market without having to worry about her daughter's care. It is a tradition that has been going on as long as anyone in her family can remember. "We Africans," Nosiphiwe explains, "it is a necessary thing that we have to raise our grandchildren. If I hadn't wanted to raise Zondwa's children, I wouldn't have. But I did it. I'm still doing it now." And will this custom continue into future generations? Will Amanda raise Lindiwe's children? Nosiphiwe thinks so. "I don't think it will change. Our grandmothers have been doing it, our mothers have been doing it, we are doing it. I think [the next generation] will be doing it too."

While her daughter is in Zondwa's care, Amanda and her sister, Alison, have begun taking financial care of their "cousin," Vusi, the son of one of the many partners of their maternal uncle. Vusi is nearly eighteen and about to undergo the ritual ceremony of initiation into manhood back in the Eastern Cape. A traditional Xhosa initiation process involves young men—who are until then considered boys—to separate themselves from their usual environment and undergo, among other things, circumcision in their transition to manhood. After the initiation ritual they will be considered adult men, with the right to get married and start their own families. It is an expensive occasion, especially because the community and family welcome the young men back into their midst with feasts fit to celebrate their new status as men.

> *Although she is not sure how much everything will cost, Amanda has budgeted R5,000 (approximately $500) to contribute toward the process. Alison is contributing the same amount. Zondwa will take care of the costs of paying the man responsible for the surgery, but she will give this money to her brother, who does not work because he got laid off, so it will seem that the money comes from him.*

Following Vusi's initiation, Amanda explains, he will no longer be able to stay in his childhood room. A man who has just been through the initiation process needs to show his new status to the community by means of new clothes and even a new place to live. Of course, few eighteen-year-old South Africans can afford to live on their own. The compromise between tradition and pragmatism has often been to build an extension onto the back of a house where the young man will now sleep, or simply to provide a separate room in the family's house.[17]

Alison and Amanda clearly feel responsible to find Vusi a new dwelling and to pay for it. Exactly how they will afford this is not yet clear. Amanda is rarely depressed—it is not in her nature—but she looks genuinely upset when she thinks about how she will meet all these obligations. "This initiation thing coming up," she says shaking her head. "You don't even know the half of it." She is thinking about using a room in Zondwa's house for him to stay for now, but doesn't really seem to believe that this would be the "proper" way to do things.

Vusi is also graduating from high school and will attend his "matric ball," an event as important to South African teens as the senior prom for many of his American counterparts. Given her penchant for high style, Amanda is focused like a laser on making sure he looks just right, and once again she and Alison will empty their wallets. In all these ways, Amanda and Alison are taking on the role of caring for a relative who is not their own child, while other women in the family are raising their children. This shows the intricate strength of kinship care and the sisters' commitment to remain part of that tradition.

Amanda frets about how she misses Lindiwe and sometimes thinks about bringing her to Cape Town, but it is not clear whether she is serious about it. In the long run, she may well raise children of her own. When she fantasizes about the future she would most love to have, it involves marriage to a good-looking, high-earning Black man—the kind she sees every night on the long-running and wildly popular TV soap operas—who will settle down with her. Together they will raise the children who will come thereafter.

It is a measure of the dramatic change in the fortunes of the most advantaged Black people in South Africa that she thinks of herself in this league. Yet Amanda's very mobility subjects her—if not openly, then behind the scenes—to questions about just how Black she is. The same challenges are often heard in the United States, where middle-class black people often have to defend themselves against the charge that they are "Oreos," black on the outside but white on the inside. Are they assimilating to a world in which they cannot be truly black? Or have they created a new form of middle-class life, one that is true to a racially inflected set of values or priorities? The problem is often raised by college graduates in the US black middle class who are often uneasy about their relationship with poor blacks stuck in segregated communities with high rates of violence. The stereotypes and journalistic sensationalism that equate all blacks with pregnancy outside of marriage, high rates of divorce or never-married relationships, and educational failure—characteristics that have actually spread to many in the white working class—lead whites to pity, fear, or condemn African Americans whom they may barely know.[18] But they also place a burden on middle-class black families that desire neither to be confused with these pernicious images nor to be criticized as somehow distant from their culture.

It is a dilemma highlighted by the contrast with the happy, healthy, romantic image of President Obama and his family, a portrait much closer to what many middle-class black families experience or aspire to in the United States. But because black popular culture, especially the hip-hop movement, celebrates "street culture," there is a battle for the cultural symbols of racial authenticity.[19] Mobility is one of those tests. Can you be a lawyer or doctor, with two kids and a suburban house, and still be authentically black?[20]

Amanda faces a similar critique, or at least she thinks she does. Xhosa people from the townships around Cape Town are suspicious of her, she says. She has more education and a better job, and the more her work draws her to the townships—where the organization she works for promotes public health—the more she comes in contact with people working at the local level who see her as a threat to their jobs. They counter by questioning her right to speak on behalf of all Xhosa people and the legitimacy of her self-promotion as a Black woman in modern South Africa. "I know who I am," she insists.

> I come from a Xhosa clan and my beliefs are structured according to Xhosa beliefs. I am a Black person . . . that came from teachings. We should respect our elders. Respect seems to be at the forefront of our belief that we are proud of. So I am respectful and I'm a proud Xhosa woman. . . . We are strong. This is not a world for the weak. If something is pulling you down, shake the dust off and just carry on. . . . What doesn't break you basically only make you stronger. These are values that were instilled in me by my grandmother. So . . . my definition of Xhosa-ness comes from what [she] taught me at home.

If Amanda is so integrated into her native culture, her imagined *and* real critics want to know, why does she live in Sea Point, an integrated, gentrifying neighborhood of beachfront walks and yuppie gyms? Some call her a coconut—Black on the outside but White on the inside. She speaks posh "Model C" English and doesn't always behave like others in the townships do. Sometimes she wonders whether perhaps "they are right." When she moved into an office in a busy part of Khayelitsha, right next to a market where radios blurred loud music all day, she called us and laughingly wondered, "Maybe I am a Coconut. I cannot deal with all this noise!"[21] But she is adamant that the fact that she acts differently, speaks differently, and enjoys her middle-class lifestyle does not make her less Black. Her Black heritage is something she is proud of and wants to deepen. She does not reject her origins.

Meanwhile she looks with suspicion on Black people who eclipse her in the class hierarchy. Africans with even more education and more prestigious jobs are, in her eyes, a bit dodgy when they claim—either out loud or by default—to be Black. They have to prove themselves to her, just as she must prove herself to those in the townships, including her own sister who has never lived in the city but sticks to Crossroads.

A member of our fieldwork team, Nwabisa, took her bachelor's degree at the University of Cape Town. The daughter of teachers, Nwabisa grew up in Gugulethu, a township near the city, where she and her family still live. Amanda kept her distance from Nwabisa for months after our research began and put her through many tests of authenticity, mostly involving her skill on the dance floor. She resisted Nwabisa's attempts to organize their fieldwork together and worried quietly about whether Nwabisa would prove to

Sea Point, which was a "Whites only" area under apartheid, is now a thriving mixed-income, multiracial neighborhood overlooking the ocean. It was home to Amanda for the first several years we knew her.

be high-handed. Most of this suspicion revolved around Amanda's concern that Nwabisa would "judge" her and find her lacking. Knowing that she has no university education, Amanda is wary of being defined as a lesser being.

This behind-the-scenes tug of war, waged over pecking orders within the same racial and ethnic group, reflects the intrusion of class-based hierarchies that have grown as a result of intra-racial inequality. Under apartheid, there were Xhosa people—Nelson Mandela among them—who were university-trained professionals. But few ordinary people expected to equal the status of a tribal chief, which is what Mandela was born to. Today, however, thousands of Black Africans have been able to move into the professional middle class. The beneficiaries of efforts by the nation's universities to incorporate the formerly excluded, they have reaped the rewards of higher education as investment capital has been eager to embrace the new elites, support Black Economic Empowerment, and meet hiring quotas.[22]

The South African Black middle class remains a tidal pool in the ocean of poverty that is the lot of most Xhosa, Zulu, seSotho, and other Black ethnic groups, not to mention the poorest Coloured people, who are also among those left behind in the scramble for upward mobility. Nonetheless, relative to the old regime, a Black woman in her thirties is more likely to be a professional with a university degree than in the past. This social fact leads someone like Amanda, who is clearly upwardly mobile but less accomplished than Nwabisa, to feel defensive and in need of proof—in advance—that she will not be judged and found deficient.

Ironically, Nwabisa is attuned to rituals and traditions that define parts of Xhosa life that Amanda's family had not engaged with. Living in Gugulethu, with parents who are embedded in the customs of the community, Nwabisa has seen and experienced more of these cultural traditions than Amanda, who was raised by a Christian grandmother and estranged from her father, who would have had to play an important role in any rituals that matter in a patrilineal society. This has left Amanda looking on from the outside at times, and she has scrambled to catch up, mainly by learning about "Xhosa traditions" from the Internet.

When Amanda tries to explain why she knows so little about her heritage, she ascribes the situation to the impact of apartheid, to the repression that made it impossible for members of the older generation to live in a way that was true to themselves. "They kept their inner beings very subsided," she says. "They kept their true selves underneath, kept it hidden. I don't think they had enough room in that generation to just be given the freedom to just go and discover themselves." This reasoning leads Amanda back to an ambivalent view of tradition. Since she wasn't raised according to Xhosa customs as Nwabisa was, Amanda isn't sure whether she is entitled to claim them as her own or whether she has the right to insert herself into something that is, in essence, foreign to her:

> I didn't grow up in a household where we do rituals. So I don't see their significance. I don't connect with it. It's something I don't understand. . . . It would be like I'm faking it. . . . Those [traditions] you have to grow up with while still young and be cultivated . . . so that it's in your veins, so it becomes part of you. It's not something you just pick up along the way and get excited about because we're more accepting of tradition and we just want to be African to prove a point to people. No.

Amanda has a desire to learn this heritage but wants to be careful that she doesn't exaggerate its role in her life or cheapen its value by embracing something she has no authentic claim to. She realizes that her lack of knowledge also derives from her separation from her father's side of the family, which was embedded in Xhosa tradition. He is more of a cultural nationalist and regards his daughter's ignorance of their heritage as a consequence of modernism, a path he warns her against. "He has the notion that I am too Westernized," Amanda explains.

> Just because I went to White schools, went to boarding school, and now I am in Cape Town [rather than the Black neighborhood of Port Elizabeth where she grew up], he has just put me in this box and [believes] that I am not accepting of amaTshawe [royal Xhosa clan] traditions. But I want to learn!

From the Web, Amanda has learned about the ritual slaughter of animals for initiations and weddings and the appropriate way to clean tools when a person dies. She plans to be entirely conversant with these customs by the time her grandmother—who never practiced them because she was a devout Christian—dies. "I do want to honor my [grand]mother," Amanda says.

> If I were to be told that by doing this [ritual] you are honoring your grandmother and her spirit . . . then I would do it for those reasons. The motivation behind that is genuine . . . [since] she is the person who gave me life and I . . . would want to give back in return.

Amanda also learned, belatedly, that she has been assigning herself to the wrong clan all these years, that she should have been claiming descent from her father's line, while she thought she belonged to her grandmother's clan. These are sensitive matters in the family because they go to the heart of how she aligns herself among competing customs and identities, not to mention the sore subject of the circumstances surrounding her own out-of-wedlock birth. What her father did or did not do to address his obligations when Amanda was born goes to the heart of her clan affiliation. He is clear that he paid "damages"—an appropriate fine to be paid when an unmarried woman gets pregnant—in order to properly acknowledge her as his own daughter, and this should set to rest any question of her descent. Amanda is not up to speed on these matters, given her lack of knowledge of Xhosa traditions and her understandable desire not to stir up an emotional hornet's nest. Accordingly, one day she just adopted her father's clan name and let it go at that.

Thousands of Xhosa men and women who have experienced the kind of mobility that Amanda has been through must wrestle with competing options for their identity. Are they fully Black? Do they know their ethnic customs? Can you be Xhosa, for real, if you no longer live in the townships where thousands of "your people" live, in conditions that you have never really experienced? As you move up the class ladder and come into social contact with people from different groups—including those who once pinioned millions of Africans just like you under their heel—how close can you get to them? The "rainbow nation" that Nelson Mandela gave birth to has had to contend with these complexities since its birth, but the spectacular growth of the Black middle class, to which Amanda belongs, and its open embrace of modernity has created new social questions. Her very mobility has exposed her to doubts about her authenticity, her loyalty, and her political commitment to the fate of those less fortunate.

People like Amanda have to defend the privileges they have enjoyed—a "Model C" education, a white-collar job, a home in the city—even as they confront what may actually be a rather tenuous hold on privilege. She does not own her home—she is a tenant, and often a rather precarious one at that. In the short time we have known her, financial exigency has forced Amanda to move three times. Amanda loves her job and would love to ascend the management ladder. Yet for the first eighteen months of our fieldwork, she lived in fear of unemployment. Nonprofit organizations like hers are at the mercy of donors and foundations, and as the recession of 2009 began to bear down on South Africa, the money for public health outreach began to dry up. Without much of a safety net, she was on a roller coaster ride of hope and anxiety.

Unlike the truly wealthy and richly connected classes, the newly anointed Black middle class is often perched on a razor's edge. Many are among the most accomplished in their families and are expected to provide liberally for others who have less. When the ground shifts under their feet, however, they are not likely to have family with a big margin to lend to them or space to absorb them. For Amanda, the prospect of being unable to live the life she has worked for is troubling precisely because she is so much higher up the ladder than the people she grew up with and has a lot invested in the idea of success.

Some would argue that the mere fact that Amanda worries about the future is testimony to just how much mobility some Africans have experienced since the first free election in 1994. Compared to millions of destitute township residents, after all, she is privileged. But those skeptics do not live inside Amanda's head, and they haven't had to watch her fret while packing her bags in a hurry because she has lost her housing again. For Amanda, the possibility of a downward slide is the flip side of her upward mobility. She has not reached a safe plateau.

How much easier would it be if Amanda had a husband to share these burdens? Infinitely. Here the complexities of gender relations in the contemporary African middle class assert themselves. Her kinship tree shows very few married couples who have made a go of life together. Amanda's mother was unmarried. Her aunts and uncles have multiple partners. Amanda is a single mother herself, and the father of her child did not remain in the picture for long. These family configurations are not unusual; they are common in the world where she grew up. Even so, the more Amanda moves up the class ladder and absorbs the norms around the world for people in the professions, the more she has come to see the model of the durable, loving couple as her personal desiderata. "Women are born to care," Amanda explains, "but we want to receive it back."

Modern women, she believes, are not content with the idea that love is ephemeral. They have seen how relationships between men and women are supposed to develop and want that model for themselves. Every night on the wildly popular South African soap operas, broadcast in prime time, she sees how love is supposed to blossom. Amanda wants a dreamy wedding on a beach with flowers. "I am such a romantic," she sighs. "But there are no romantic men. It is as if all they want is to pick you up, have [sex], and drop you back home again. Where is the love there?" She wants a Black man who is willing to be publicly affectionate, not a guy who stakes his masculinity on how cold and distant he can appear to others. She wants someone who will stick with her, remain monogamous, and raise a family with her. What kind of man is this likely to be? Says Amanda,

> You'd need a grown-up "coconut" guy, who has been exposed to how relationships can be in the White people's environments, but who, at the same time, has realized his culture is also still important to him. "Coconuts" who have been to "Model C schools" will have seen how interaction between men and women can be more romantic. He will have tried out all that White stuff—skateboarding and wearing loose trousers and going to pop and rock concerts. But when he grows out of the teenage stage, he will realize that he also needs to relate to his culture in order not to get lost. He realizes he is still Xhosa or Zulu, and that defines who he is. But he understands how interaction [between men and women] can be better than what he has seen at home.

For Amanda, this is part of what being both modern and a "proud Xhosa woman" requires. She must express solidarity with her people, defined by race and ethnic heritage, while not being bound by what she sees as sexist practices that run counter to her own budding feminism. That contemporary fusion represents her attempt to marry some sense of solidarity to the kind of life that she sees increasingly close up in the work place, where her colleagues are well-educated and multiracial.

Yet these aspirations for a secure life of white-collar professional jobs, a cushion of savings, and housing in a nice neighborhood, are far from assured. Amanda's short-circuited education is likely to limit her. The sector in which she is employed right now is almost inherently unstable and it is very vulnerable in the maw of a recession. Her responsibilities to her kin draw down her reserves, and she currently has no one in her life with whom she could build a future. Cresting into her thirties, a woman like Amanda has a lot to be proud of, but she also has a lot to lose if any elements of her current strategy begin to falter.

She could, at times, turn to the state for some help, especially with the cost of raising her daughter. The extended child allowance system, an important achievement of the ANC in the post-apartheid period, could make a real difference. But when asked whether she had applied for the child grant when she was unemployed, she took offense. How could she put herself through the wait in long queues? Her grandmother had helped her, so her mother can help Lindiwe. The grant is for people who need it most, those who come from the informal settlements and are desperate people without support structures, she told us. The grant is for people from a different class, and class is an integral part of how Amanda thinks about her own social location.

How, then, might Amanda work her way toward the life she really wants? In the time we have known her, she has attempted to hatch four or five different entrepreneurial schemes that held out the promise of a more glamorous life as a businesswoman. She has worked on one business plan for a spa that would sell clothing and makeup and another for a cleaning service that would operate in the downtown business district. Nothing has come of these plans, but they express a longing she has to take control over her economic destiny and add a splash of glamour to her life. Amanda has thought about going into television and of going back to school to further a career in the media. Yet she holds back from taking the plunge on any of these plans because she has neither the money to start a business nor the credentials to enter the field of communications or public relations. What she has is energy, a vivacious personality, a sense of style, and the capacity to project herself even when she knows she may not succeed. Her high expectations mix with continuing insecurity. The combination often feels overwhelming to her.

When it all comes crashing down, she retreats to Nyanga to spend time with her sister, Alison, or takes the bus to Port Elizabeth to see her grandmother and her daughter, or she commandeers one of her many friends in

Cape Town who are largely in the same predicament. She knows dozens of Black women who, like her, migrated from the Eastern Cape and who have found work in the burgeoning office culture of the city. Her girlfriends are a solace to her. Their wild nights spent in clubs remind her that she is a modern girl, able to move around with ease in worlds that people like her would not have dared to dream about only one generation ago. In these places, she can see that the sky is the limit, and if she feels weighted down by the distance between her aspirations and her reality, it is in Amanda Sophotele's DNA to shake off the doubts. She never wallows in worry but turns instead to another scheme for an entrepreneurial breakthrough.

CHAPTER FIVE

Forgotten

"THE FIRST GENERATION OF GANGSTERS didn't fight over drugs," says Patrick Arendse, Ambrose's father, "it was just about protecting your turf and looking after your fellow gang members. We beat each other with machetes and other knives. But now it is about the smuggling of drugs into Manenberg. This generation of gangsters is fighting for the control of drugs and now they are using guns."

Patrick Arendse came to know Manenberg, where he has lived since his early twenties, as a young man. He was part of the founding generation in the township. The Arendses moved into this unforgiving place in the late 1960s, when Coloured families who were living in overcrowded houses in other areas of Cape Town were given houses by the city council.[1] Many of his Manenberg neighbors, however, were forcibly removed from communities that had all of a sudden become "Whites only" territories. They were exiled to this peripheral, underserviced Coloured township as a consequence of the 1950 Group Areas Act, ending up far away from their extended families.[2]

Kensington, where Patrick was born, was closer to the Cape Town city center, with all its bustle, shops, street markets, and jobs. Patrick lived in a household of twelve people, surrounded by a web of ties to his extended kin. "Old people taught the young kids about respect," he recalled, "or else . . . they would give you a hiding."

Speakers of Afrikaans and believers in Islam and Christianity, the Coloured community of Kensington was wedged between White South Africans, whose language they shared, and the Xhosa-speaking Black Africans. Many would join ranks with their Black neighbors when the struggle to break the back of apartheid gained ground.

More affluent "Cape Coloureds" lived in comfortable, multistory houses with yards and fruit trees. Those down at the heel had small houses or flats. Patrick's family was not well off, but they were far from desperate since those who were old enough to work had jobs and could bring home paychecks to pool toward the living expenses of the extended family. They had enough to eat and clothes on their backs but there was nothing extra, and the wage labor of every able-bodied person, teens included, was needed, even at the expense of schooling.

With all this hard work, a family like the Arendses could manage in the urban community of Kensington. Not too far from the city and with easy access to major roads, working adults commuted to their jobs on foot or on the back of a labor truck and left the little ones in the care of older relatives who were done with the formal work world.

Kensington had its problems as well. The politics of race and the deep resentment it created, even before the Group Areas Act, led to skirmishes at the border between Kensington and neighboring communities, but most people stuck to their own kind and that was enough to manage in the world.

Back then, Kensington was full of men and women who—if they were educated—took the low-level jobs in bureaucracies, foremen positions on the factory floor, entry-grade work for the postal service. Patrick's mother finished a high school course in nursing and qualified for one of the better jobs a Coloured woman could hope for in the 1960s.[3] The less educated—like Patrick—were stuck with blue-collar options: the docks, the assembly line, or transportation. Long before mechanization became common (container ships with mechanized lifts, and the like), blue-collar work in South Africa's shipyards was physically demanding, exhausting, and dangerous.

Patrick learned this the hard way: on the job. He began as a teenager, helping his parents to provide for the twelve people in their household. "I worked for a large roofing company, started at fifteen," he recalled. "We made various types of tiles, small ones and big ones. The Cape Town train station was built with those tiles. I worked there for about three years. But the work was difficult. . . . I went to the . . . foreman, who was an Italian guy, and asked for an increase. They said, 'Kid, there's no point you get an increase. You are still young in this work.' I told him I was fifteen years old. But they take you when you are young and they think you are stupid. They thought I wouldn't speak out and ask for things like increases."

By the time he was twenty, Patrick was a seasoned laborer with a steady track record. Though proud of what he did to support the Arendses, Patrick has only the harshest memories of the work itself, backbreaking and simply oppressive. He learned at a tender age that Coloured people were, as he puts it, "slaves." "In my young days," Patrick recalled, "the Boer[s] were rough."

[They would say], "Hey you, Hotnot, come here!" . . . You could not look at the Boer because then he will say, "Hey, why are you looking at me,

Hotnot?" . . . We were like slaves. . . . We worked for these people, we got nothing from them.

What we were given at the end of the year was just a little for some groceries and bonus for some small change. We were getting R11 a week. I worked for six years; we never received an increase. For years I went on with this work . . . then we found out they wanted to retrench us. . . .

They took on new people, removed us from the workplace because we were becoming smart. [The boss] would just say to us: "Take your jacket and go." I wasn't even twenty years old.

When I was about twenty-three, I looked for other work and . . . the Boer[s] were all the same. They spoke the same. We couldn't speak back to them. If you act smart at work they won't like you. We used to tell them, "How [can] we get a piece of bread with the money [you] gave us? How can you look after your wife and kids with that money?"

Working under these conditions nurtured Patrick's ability to grit his teeth and bury outward signs of resentment. Years later, when the riots and strikes that brought down the apartheid state began to roll across the country, many men like Patrick stood shoulder to shoulder with their Black African brothers. But for most of his young adult years, Patrick could not show even a hint of defiance.

Within the confines of Kensington, at least, Patrick and his family could lead a meager but reasonably stable existence. In 1969, Patrick's family moved into the hostile and underdeveloped place that was Manenberg. Like so many other families used to being in one place, they were now scattered, thrown together with strangers, and not easily able to visit with one another, much less depend on the kinship network that had been the core of their lives in Kensington.

Manenberg is only a twenty-minute drive from the center of Cape Town, but for many of its residents it may as well be hundreds of miles. Even with a bus or taxi, given all the waiting, it can easily take over an hour to get from the city to the township or vice versa. Few of Patrick's neighbors can afford cars even now. In Manenberg's early years, virtually none had wheels. "At that time," Patrick remembered, "there were no shops in the neighborhood, there were no real streets. Manenberg Lane [now a main street] was a dust road." Accustomed to living within easy reach of work, stores, and extended family, Patrick's immediate family found themselves isolated. There was a flat field that boasted some green, an opportunity for a pickup football game, but for the most part Manenberg was gray and brown, dusty and bleak. For Patrick it was a whole new and entirely unwelcoming world.

At least his family avoided the trauma of forced removal. Thousands of other Coloured families had no choice. A teacher at the local high school, Mr. Yus, provided us a vivid account of the culture shock and sense of shame that so many took to heart as they were ejected from their homes to the township of Athlone on the outskirts of the city. "I grew up in Newlands, which we all know now as Bishops Court [today one of the wealthiest enclaves in Cape Town]," Mr. Yus recalled.

> It was upper Newlands. Basically it was two houses that my father bought; we combined it into one, because we were a big family. There were lots of fields and open spaces running up into the mountain, running down to the river. Those kinds of environments I spent my childhood in. Then, obviously, with the Group Areas Act, all this came to a stop.
>
> We were moved to an area called Bridgetown. We got a little council house that was obviously too small for us. My father refused to take occupation of the house and built us a service quarters [an informal dwelling] of a kind, off Thornton Road. At the time Repulse Road was still a sand road. Now I am mentioning this because this had a direct impact on all our lives, my family's lives, my brothers' and sisters' lives . . . Moving from this almost idyllic situation and growing up at the foot of the mountain and now being moved to the Cape Flats, with all its gangsterism involved. As I said, I come from a big family, so there were lots of sisters involved, so we had to almost create a protective shield around my sisters growing up in the Cape Flats. My father was obviously broken by all of this, because his idea of raising a family under those conditions, living in Newlands, was obviously ideal and now he had to fend for himself.

The Yus family had been middle class in Newlands, hence the forced removal meant more than just a change in the quality of their home life. It was a powerful push down the ladder and an end to dreams of an independent business and a prosperous life. "[My father's] businesses started to go down," Mr. Yus says. "He was a builder in the building trade, it went into a slump. So he really . . . [became] a broken man . . . [but] the one thing he concentrated on [with] his children was education, because he felt his building business was taken away from him."

Middle-class families who had been displaced tried desperately to regain their footing, if not for the parental generation, then at least for the children. For families like that of Mr. Yus, this translated into a strong culture of educational ambition. While Black Africans were left to swallow an inferior "Bantu" education, Coloured people were relatively more privileged. They had more and better houses, access to better schools, and jobs that paid more and were more plentiful. Pushing their children to grab what they could get out of the education system, the Yus family looked for a way to preserve the options for the next generation. "I can still remember the words my father said," Mr. Yus recalled.

> "There is one thing they can't take away from you: it is education, education, education!" So it meant that we would go into education because that was subliminally imprinted into our minds at night, the big family sitting at the supper table. So those were the kind of thoughts that he projected. Very religious man, but he obviously had to rear his children and that was that. He built a double garage and added some bedrooms in there and many meals were [eaten] in this double garage, because that was the only room big enough for us [all] to be able to sit in.

Mr. Yus's pathway through higher education, to the position he holds now as a teacher in Manenberg, wound through the most violent years of anti-apartheid strikes, protests, boycotts, and mass demonstrations. The upheaval interrupted his schooling and put him—and thousands of other Coloured youths—on a collision course with the South African state. Standing alongside his Black brothers, Mr. Yus temporarily gave up on his goal of becoming a teacher, recovering it only years later as the country came into its liberty.

> My matric year was 1976 . . . and we all know what happened in 1976. Being on the student representative council and stuff like that, your whole life galvanizes into this [protest movement], where all the years spent with [our high school teacher], who gave his students a political education in the racial politics of the country, [education that] almost comes to fruition.
>
> Here we are, young sixteen to seventeen years old . . . making all kinds of excuses at home, wanting to attend meetings in Johannesburg [he laughs] and Port Elizabeth and all these kinds of things. So it was kind of good in a sense, but also I now realize that it took a lot of my youth. We weren't allowed to be seventeen-year-olds and eighteen-year-olds in 1976. So my matric year . . . I wrote my matric [but] didn't get my matric certificate until five years later, because we were blacklisted. Fortunately there was a rector who was involved in the Unity Movement at the time, he accepted some of us with no matric certificate.

As the upheaval subsided, Mr. Yus was able to return to the mission his father had set out for him years earlier: becoming a teacher by attending a training college. But the struggle formed the backdrop for his aspirations. He looked for a chance to use his skills to do something positive for Coloured kids in troubled areas and landed in Manenberg.

> I had a social inclination to be involved by becoming a teacher. So after two years at Hewat [teacher training college], I decided I [would] come to an area . . . well known for its violence, even in the late 1970s, early 1980s. So I decided I [would] teach in Manenberg, see what that was all about.
>
> [I thought I would] come here and see what I [could] contribute. I started off at a primary school and then, when Phoenix, the high school, opened, I was requested among others to join the staff. . . . The principal at the time was a very progressive man, and I felt this was a place I could actually nurture myself.

In common with other middle-class Coloured people, Mr. Yus had not grown up in the worst parts of the Cape Flats: Athlone was a more middle-class township than the apartment blocks of Manenberg, something closer to a segregated suburb. Yet when he began searching for his adult profession, he turned to the township world, which he felt was his calling. "Older teachers . . . didn't experience 1976 like we did, because we were students," he says. "So I think that drew me nearer to the learners at Phoenix Secondary School because I had that experience, I [had been] a student not so long ago. I could relate to learners. I could relate to teachers. I could even relate to parents, because they now saw me as a teacher and not as a deviant student."

But what set him on his heels were the conditions of life in Manenberg. It had already begun to develop the gang culture that Patrick Arendse found upon his arrival and that lives on today. "Manenberg is a strange type of place," Mr. Yus remarked. "They have this demon called 'the gangsterism issue.' Many times as teachers and especially principals we are called in to intervene in the kind of gangster activity that takes place. I want to shield my learners from the gangsters and whatever else takes place. I mean Manenberg is known for . . . its violence." Within a few years of its establishment, Manenberg had gained a reputation for being one of the most deadly townships in all of the Western Cape. The solid social structure of places like Kensington, where Patrick Arendse and his family had been surrounded by their extended kin, did not survive the transplant.

Manenberg consists of a number of different areas: freestanding houses on relatively large plots along the outsides of the township, semidetached or row houses, and then the actual flats.[4] It was especially in this cell block structure of the township that gangsterism started to take shape.[5] Each "court" or street became its own little community. Territorial defense was the main purpose of the groups that formed around the apartment buildings, Mr. Yus explains.[6]

> The flats are built in squares, so you have fifty- to sixty-odd families, living in a square. And fifty-odd families for their own protection would live quite closely together, because that is their area, that is their turf . . . and now I am already going into gangster language, because gangsters talk about their turf.
>
> But if you look at the different flats, they are situated in a square and the doors come open into that square. The kids growing up in that little perimeter of under one hundred meters would almost be forced to protect each other. So [all the local gangs], the Hard Livings would be in a little area, and the Americans would be in a little area, Rich Kids would be in an area and so on.
>
> We have had competitions at school . . . and [when forming teams] the kids would say: "Let's play according to the roads in which we live." Like the Irving Street Kids would gang up and start their own soccer club and so on. As a school we wanted to move away from this, so we gave them names like Green Dolphin and Phoenix, to have another type of identity away from the closeness of their abodes. Because those types of things give rise to gangsterism.

One reason why the gangs took hold so quickly was that Manenberg had become, almost overnight, a township ruled by adolescents. Many of the adults had to make their way back into Cape Town in order to keep hold of their jobs. Patrick's mother, who worked as a nurse, was gone from early morning to late at night. Other mothers and fathers too left the township during working hours and suffered a long commute into and out of the city. They were often nowhere to be seen from 6:00 a.m. to 7:00 p.m. or later. Adults did have a hand in the community, of course, and some of that engagement was as violent as the youth's.[7] "The first year I was in Manenberg," Patrick remembered, "they almost stabbed me to death."

> One Friday evening . . . I just walked past a man and he tried to stab me with a very long knife. It went through my new jacket. He didn't say a

word to me. He just tried to stab me. Then I saw another man come out of the dark and then I ran for my life. When I got home and locked the door behind me, I looked at the back of my jacket, which had a huge hole in it. That knife could have gone into my spine and I would have been crippled.

Walking through the township became an exercise in defensive feints, glances cast back to see who was skulking in the shadows, moving through gang territories as quickly as possible so as not to give wary observers much opportunity to attack.

Until he was twenty-six, Patrick worked for roofing companies. On the side he began to pick up odd jobs on the docks, including on Russian ships. The work was brutal. It paid better than the roofing companies because it was so harsh, but it took a toll that is visible today in Patrick's worn, bent frame and his arthritic hands. "We worked on the coldwater tankers," he recalled. "It is very cold underneath those ships. You have to lie on your back to work or you must sit on your knees. You can't stand and work. That is how I got arthritis. I can't walk properly anymore. I didn't know the cold would do to that to me." He worked on the docks for nearly twenty years, until his legs gave out. Even then, Patrick tried to find casual work so that he could pay his children's school fees.

The flats of Manenberg, the Coloured township where Ambrose was born and his family lives now. The apartments are very close together and, hence, privacy is scarce.

Married at thirty, Patrick and his wife, Felicity, found each other in Manenberg, moved into one of the flats, and set about starting a family. Though they divorced later, they had three children and supported them on the strength of Patrick's blue-collar jobs and Felicity's on-and-off jobs as a nurse and later running a small construction company. Today Felicity employs her oldest son, Edwin, in the family business. Edwin is lucky that this opportunity is available because he would have a hard time finding an equivalent job outside the family network. A veteran of several prison bouts, including one that was occasioned by his conviction for armed robbery on the eve of his matric exams, Edwin has had to make up for his criminal record, but he has done so successfully. He completed his matric behind bars and convinced his mother that he could be trusted; he had passed through the volatile adolescent years and was more stable and sober when he came out.

Nadia, Felicity and Patrick's oldest daughter, lives in a flat of her own, not far from her mother. Among the children, she keeps the closest contact with her father, who drops by to see her and to borrow money when she has it to give. Now that he is no longer employed, Patrick often needs his daughter's help. He asks for the loan of R100 (the equivalent of $10), but she says, "No, it's just too much." She doesn't earn a lot and cannot afford to be quite this helpful. Nadia inherited her apartment from her parents; it was the place where her younger brother, Ambrose, was born and where he lived until their mother bought the modest house where she lives now, on a nearby street in Manenberg.

At the age of twenty-nine, Nadia is the mother of a three-year-old girl, whose father no longer lives with her. While Ambrose and Edwin have very dark skin, Nadia is lighter in appearance, with exquisite features: pretty brown eyes, gleaming white teeth with some gold pieces in the gaps, and a stud in her tongue.

While older brother Edwin ran into trouble with the law, Nadia was the more conventional, straitlaced sister. She attended Sonderend Primary School and then completed her matric year at Silver Stream High School. Since only 25 percent of Coloured students complete their high school education, Nadia was ahead of the average, and she remembers her school years with pleasure.[8] She enjoyed geography, Afrikaans, and needlework in high school, which she finished in 1998, a post-apartheid time of ferocious gang fights in Manenberg. Nadia recalls with a shudder that she rarely left the house during that time except to attend school; it was simply too scary to travel the streets of the township. Edwin's criminal career attracted unwanted attention from local toughs, leaving Nadia and her family feeling exposed. Nowadays, as long as she is mindful of the tik (crystal methamphetamine) addicts on the streets, people who will steal to support their habit, she feels reasonably safe.

In 2003 Nadia started working in a local factory. Her formal job title is "operator," which fundamentally means assembly-line work. Nadia is expected to be available around the clock over three different shifts and gets little warning of changes. When she works the morning shift, which starts at seven thirty, she drops her daughter at Felicity's place at six thirty and takes a crowded taxi to work. She finishes at three thirty, and then it takes her until nearly five to fetch her daughter, get home, and settle down for the evening meal. If she gets a new shift assignment, she has to rearrange all of her domestic arrangements. Even so, she feels fortunate to have a steady weekly paycheck.

Ambrose is the third sibling and the real problem child of the family. Even Edwin, with his criminal record, is respected for having turned himself around. Ambrose has never managed to make anything of himself, and his failures are constantly thrown in his face by his mother and by Ambrose himself. He is tall and slender, but hunched over, as if he is trying to make his frame fade into the surroundings. His persistent stutter makes it hard for Ambrose to speak his mind, but he seems to have grown accustomed to having little to say, at least in the presence of people in Manenberg. With outsiders, like ourselves, he talks at length about his disappointments and offers keen observations of the people around him. He is troubled by Manenberg's decay, by the ways in which its young children go astray, and by adults who cannot or will not look after them. Ambrose is often quite moralistic about these failures, but he doesn't exempt himself from the same withering disapproval. The moral fabric of his community has weakened to the point of no return, he argues. And he often feels no better than the drunks and addicts he points to in the streets.

To her credit, Ambrose's mother saw potential in him and tried for many years to nurture it. Felicity paid for two different trade courses after Ambrose was expelled from high school. She bailed him out of jail on several occasions. She scolded him, prodded him, and tried to cajole his father, Patrick, to get him out into the blue-collar labor force. Today, though, Felicity has largely given up. She puts a roof over Ambrose's head reluctantly and expresses unremitting exasperation regarding his inability to pull his life together even when handed an opportunity "on a platter."

Once Ambrose stole equipment from her company and she called the police to come and arrest him. Felicity took no pleasure in this but was desperate. She had reached her tolerance limit with her son's "screw-ups" and felt he needed to be taught a lesson. She had expected him to be kept in a holding cell at the Athlone police station but instead he ended up in Pollsmoor, a notorious prison with a history of torture and extrajudicial detention during apartheid, today a war zone of gang violence.[9]

It was not his first time in prison, and hence by then Ambrose had learned how to keep his head down and survive in a frightening environment. He says,

> Prison is not a place for people, but sometimes you can simply land in there without asking for it. You must use your head. . . . There are very dangerous men in there. If you know yourself, then nothing will make you angry and nothing dangerous will happen to you, like the things people hear about in prison. I have seen very strange things with my own two eyes that have happened to men in jail who do not know themselves or love themselves.

It would be tempting for Ambrose to react to his mother's frustration over his behavior with his own anger. He could blame Felicity for not doing more to help him. To his credit, Ambrose never does that. He acknowledges without prompting, with a matter-of-fact attitude, that his mother has reason for not trusting him, not seeing any real future for him. Stuttering, as he often does when he is nervous, Ambrose confesses that he is at a loss and says he understands why his mother is as well. He doesn't know where to turn, how to rectify his mistakes, who would ever help him now, or what kind of life he could have in the future that is different from the monotonous, stuck-in-a-rut present.

Ambrose spends his days hanging around one of the Manenberg community centers, hoping for an odd job or two. Whenever there is one, Ambrose fairly leaps into action. He is so bored most of the time that the very idea of a purpose or task that needs attention is like a tonic. He has painted the walls and courtyard of the community center; he has planted flowers in pots. If classrooms need sweeping, Ambrose is there. He is never paid for these "jobs," though Graham, the director of the place, sometimes gives him something to eat. And Ambrose is always hungry because he fears asking his mother for food, especially during the day, when she wants him out of her house. The real reason that Ambrose helps Graham is that he is desperate for something to do, for structure or purpose, even if it only lasts a short time. Working at the community center without pay is a decent day for this young man of Manenberg.

At twenty-seven, with no matric and few skills and with a criminal record, Ambrose is likely to spend most of his life scrambling for the odd rand. He fears losing his hold on his lifeline—a place to stay in his mother's house—and tries to stay out of everyone's way to avoid being turned out. This is one reason why Ambrose has adopted a kind of modus operandi that might best be described as skulking around, trying to avoid attracting attention. His presence in the house is suffered, endured, especially since his mother remarried and his stepfather, a foreign African we have never met, is not keen on Ambrose's presence. He also lies as low as he can because his daily life in Manenberg is constantly under pressure from random violence that seems to come out of nowhere.

Throughout our time in the township, it was shocking how often assaults, ranging from the mundane to the deadly, descended without warning. In this, Manenberg seems considerably more threatening than Khayelitsha, which has its own problems with crime and threats to personal safety. In Manenberg, the atmosphere itself seems unpredictably violent. One day, Seraj, our research assistant, was visiting with Nadia, Ambrose's sister. Sitting on the stairs, waiting to talk with Patrick, their father, Seraj witnessed the kind of attack that happens distressingly often in Manenberg:

> Suddenly a young man, probably eighteen years old, came up to Ambrose in a very quick, aggressive manner and started shouting at him about something or other. At first, I did not know if the guy was joking with Ambrose or not. At this stage I could see Patrick sitting on the top step of the concrete staircase, just outside Nadia's place, reading a book with his spectacles on—enjoying the sun and the stillness of the time. I was almost halfway up the stairs, then I started hearing more commotion from this young man, who then picked up half a brick and flung it toward Ambrose.
>
> Ambrose just stood there and told the guy to take it easy. At this point, other guys from the neighboring flats started throwing big stones and bricks at Ambrose. . . . Some were aimed at his midriff and others for his head. All you could hear was the bricks and stones bouncing off the concrete floors and the metal laundry lines in between the building. Ambrose had a few rocks near his feet though and immediately retaliated by throwing rocks back at these guys.
>
> The women in the flats were starting to shout at the boys and told them not to throw the stones . . . not because someone would get hurt. They were more concerned that these misfits would shatter the windowpanes of the houses.
>
> While all this was happening, Patrick stood up and started shouting at the young men. . . . He told them to leave his son alone and go somewhere else. . . . Ambrose walked away.

Episodes like this happen to Ambrose all the time and they take their toll. Living on the edge, in a perpetual state of hyper-vigilance, always on the lookout for the next attack, distorts his nervous system.[10] Ambrose is jumpy, anxious, and enervated all at once. There are few—if any—moments of peace in his life.

Ambrose's downward spiral began in high school. Before that, particularly as a young child, he remembers, his life was fairly happy. His optimistic attitude began to darken in the middle of high school when he started hanging out with people who were taking another path. "When I got to tenth grade," he recalls, "I made different friends."[11]

> I began to smoke cigarettes, marijuana, and [take] Mandrax [methaqualone], and I used it even more when I got to grade eleven. I used to drink wine a lot too, sometimes two or three times a day. . . . Every morning before school, my friends and I got together and smoked until we were high. . . . I started losing interest in school.

Ambrose's conduct went from bad to worse. His reputation at school cycled down, while his new circle of friends grew tighter.[12] Teachers and administrators tried to intervene, called on his family, issued punishments. None of it changed Ambrose's path. Together with his friends, he participated in various acts of mayhem that got them into trouble.

Eventually the parents of his clique filed in front of the school's governing body for what can only be described as a tribunal. They listened as the violations of school rules and riotous behavior of the previous year were recounted. Felicity heard for the first time that Ambrose had "bunked" (cut) most of his classes, turned up stoned, disrupted gatherings, and damaged school property. She was stunned. Ambrose had managed to hide most of his misbehavior, knowing that his mother would be furious if she knew. Here it was out in the open. When the trial ended, Ambrose and his five friends were expelled from school and told they could not apply elsewhere. They were done.

With no institutional connections to put structure into his day, Ambrose drifted into the arms of the gangs that were by then a force to be reckoned with in the Coloured townships. He started with a petty group, no match for the serious gangsters. "I joined the Bad Boys," he explained, "because it was a start. They were not as big as the other gangs in our area. This was the wrong choice. People started seeing the types of people I was hanging out with. I started walking through different paths to get to shops for my parents, because the Bad Boys were [a target]. The police stations started to hear rumblings of the name, 'Bad Boy.'"

The gang was divided into two groups. The first was more of a turf-protection operation: they "fought for the name of the Bad Boys." The second "smoked, stole and were into fraudulent activities." The latter proved more attractive because its members "always had money from their [illegal] ways." Ambrose recalls:

> We used to hang out in front of the shops. We used to steal and do other crooked things. People were afraid of us and now knew who we were. . . .
>
> I hid all [of this] from my parents. . . . They found out through other people that I was part of the gang. No one ever came to our house to complain about me. However, one day I was coming home from the swimming pool, [and] two friends and I saw a drinks van stop outside a shop. We thought no one could see us. Each one of us took a crate of drinks and ran off. We found a buyer and sold them.
>
> That night I was quite high from marijuana; I was also hungry, so on my way home I got something to eat. . . . In the middle of the night, through my sleep, I heard someone knock very hard on our front door. My mother opened the door and it was too late for me to flee. The police rushed in the house and asked for me. . . . She asked what I had done wrong and they answer[ed] that they [were] looking for me because of a theft and that my two friends had also been picked up.
>
> They told my mother I wouldn't be back; I was taken to the police station and saw my friends there too. They were hit black and blue by the police. At 8:00 a.m., they took us in a police van to court. We were put in a holding cell. At 11:00 a.m., our names were called to come and stand in front of the judge.

Ambrose pleaded not guilty but was convicted and bundled off to Pollsmoor. At the age of seventeen, he was about to get his first taste of prison. Terrified, he tried to stick with his two friends and fellow Bad Boys. He had heard that the only people who come out unscathed were those with enough money to buy privileges. Even those who work at Pollsmoor are at risk for violent assault.

Three notorious gangs that got their start during the apartheid period continue today to control both the internal hierarchy of the prison system and the drug trade in the townships. One of their most famous leaders, Magadien Wentzel, the subject of a best-selling biography, lives in Manenberg now, the community to which he retreated after twenty-six years behind bars.[13]

Magadien was a young man when he entered prison. A law student at the University of the Western Cape, which was the main university for Coloured students in the 1970s, he was arrested in the midst of a protest march. Sentenced to two years, he was moved around to four prisons during this time, a policy the apartheid state used to confuse families about the location of inmates and to prevent power blocs from forming. The policy had the opposite impact. Gangs formed and their influence spread throughout the prison system.

A bright man, Magadien speaks Afrikaans and English, but prefers the former, his native tongue. Slight and thin-faced, he is covered with tattoos from his neck to his waist, signatures of prison gangs. While many of the prison thugs he knew were tall, muscular, and threatening, Magadien is a reed by comparison and an aging one at that. We took him for seventy the day we met him to hear about the role of the prison gangs in the townships today, but when we tallied the years he spent behind bars, we realized he was in his fifties. Wearing a faded Manchester United jersey, black jeans, and battered tennis shoes, with a blue cap pulled down low over his eyes, Magadien neither looked nor sounded like a notorious gangster. Amid the sounds from the street outside, where people were yelling, he could barely be heard. He coughed incessantly, so hard that he doubled over in an effort to stop it. He was clearly not well, the consequence of years of smoking, drinking, and assaults.

When Magadien talked about his early years, it became less hard to imagine how he could become such an atomistic loner. "I hated my mother," he explained. "She left me when I was very young. She went to look after a White family, to cook and clean for them and live in their house. I tried to kill her three times, but never succeeded."

Ambrose's eyes opened wide as Magadien described his murderous impulses of his past. In his worst moments, Ambrose fears he might be headed in the same direction: an alienated, disconnected man, alone in the world. But Ambrose is not a violent person and cannot imagine doing the things that became second nature to Magadien in the penitentiary. Ambrose is not a leader either. He lacks Magadien's strategic intelligence and cannot draw on the kind of education that made him a formidable figure in the gang world.

The 26s, 27s, and 28s—known as "the numbers gangs"—are feared by inmates, guards, and the public at large, which has come to know their terror since they spill outside the boundaries of the prison system into the back alleys of the townships. The subject of documentaries, investigations, hearings, newspaper exposes, films and biographies, the numbers gangs have worked their way into the country's lexicon as a synonym for uncontrolled violence and intimidation. They are not unlike the drug networks gaining control on the streets of Mexico, the favelas in Brazil, or the shantytowns of Haiti and Kenya.

The 28 gang had an eye on Magadien and he had reason to welcome their attention. No one is safe without a gang backup in a South African prison. He soon learned that admission to the gang's ranks required a display of bravado and loyalty. In his case, this meant stabbing a prison guard with a knife designed less to kill than to draw blood. With this mayhem behind him, Magadien found himself initiated into the 28s, with a twenty-five-year prison term added to his initial two years. By far better educated and smarter than many of the street thugs, Magadien put his cunning to good use organizing contraband networks. Willing to be as ruthless as his fellow gang members, he rose through the ranks to the leadership of the 28s.

He was not the only one behind bars originally as a political prisoner, and some of that identity remained, at least among leaders of the numbers gangs. When Nelson Mandela was released from prison in 1990, Magadien explained, the gangs on the inside declared a truce with the wardens and between each other. Having fought for freedom against an oppressive White government, it seemed time to lay down their arms rather than contest the authority of the new Black leadership. It was a short-lived arrangement, however, for the prisons refilled after the apartheid regime came apart, this time with nonpolitical criminals spilling out of the increasingly violent townships and urban centers.

After twenty-seven years behind bars, Magadien was done with that life. As his release date neared, rumors began to fly that he would be offered lucrative opportunities in the drug trade back in Manenberg. With no other visible means of support, this guaranteed "job" had its advantages. For Magadien, though, a religious conversion led him to refuse. "I only follow God now," he explained. "I struggle financially, but I believe the Lord will save me." He lives in a small house and gets by on the fees he earns when he gives talks about his life, an opportunity that comes his way fairly often since his biography has been on the best-seller list for nearly a decade.

Magadien is no longer in the trade, but he is in the minority. Thousands of ex-convicts are operating the drug networks that are now linked to township street gangs, much like the Crips and the Bloods who bridge California's prison system and the poor neighborhoods of Los Angeles.[14] Ironically, it is the freedom of post-apartheid society that makes the expanse of the drug trade possible. In the old days, when movement was restricted, it was hard to smuggle Mandrax, tik, heroin, or any other controlled substance from one part of the country to another. Once the notorious pass laws were demolished, with their bureaucratic paper trails that stopped Black Africans, Coloured people, and Indians from moving about freely—the freedom to move throughout the country opened up a river of illegal goods that flowed into the poverty-stricken regions. With that flow came menacing street gangs and a relentless wave of assaults, shotgun murders, and rapes that terrorized townships like Manenberg.

Control of the lucrative drug trade is at stake. Just as Mexico has succumbed to virulent, almost epidemic lawlessness, so too have the townships of South Africa become the victims of this scourge. With little else to take its place as a conventional alternative—given record high unemployment, social isolation, and a failing educational system—the economy of large parts of Manenberg has descended into illegal drug profiteering.

Not everyone who is affected by gang violence ends up walking the same path. Sometimes the exposure to that life sends Manenberg youths looking for an exit strategy in the form of a conventional career. Liam Petersen is such an example. He is about Ambrose's age, and if it can be said that Ambrose has any friends, Liam is one of them. Liam has grown up in Manenberg and never lived anywhere else. Unlike Ambrose, who lives in a fairly meager but

Young men in the "American gang" hang out behind the flats where "backyard dwellers" live.

nonetheless conventional flat, Liam's home is a "Wendy House," a prefabricated two-room place with a corrugated iron roof. Liam's father and grandfather were both fishermen who worked in the off season first on a plantation that grew rooibos tea, a favorite of South Africans for its aroma and supposed medicinal qualities, and then for AVP, a national air conditioning and refrigeration company.

Out on the water, the world is peaceful. There are no menacing people to deal with, no depressing, dusty streets. Liam fell in love with the sea during the fishing season when he was given the chance to do odd jobs on the boats where his father and grandfather worked. It was his father's first love as well, but it didn't pay well enough to take care of the family. Bouts of unemployment are common in Coloured fishing communities that dot the coast.[15] Before AVP emerged as an off-season possibility for him, Liam's father was out of work for several years at a time.

Fortunately for his family, the man had an aptitude for mechanics and he attracted the attention of the management at AVP as a result. Finding the resources for vocational training was difficult for a Coloured man during apartheid, but AVP stepped in and paid for a correspondence course in refrigeration repair. Liam remembers his dad bent over books and drawings, trying to get through the training course, and this example of dedication stuck with him.

Liam's uncle, his mother's brother, was another story, one with consequences for the Petersen family, who, during the years his father was without work, moved into the tiny Wendy house:

> When I was small, we just used to hang out, fighting with stones, having fun. I remember . . . growing up in the shack, in the summer you could [lie] on the [metal] roof. They used to wet the roof because it was hot and the Wendy house was getting warm. We used to play on the roof, eat on it. But when my uncle came from prison, we couldn't do that anymore because there was conflict. He was a big attraction for violence.
>
> We couldn't go out of the house. We had to [lie] flat in our Wendy house because there would be a gun raid. Sometimes we had to run out of our house to protect ourselves because guys were stabbing each other in the house. [Finally] my uncle went [back] to prison and we moved out of that house because it had [belonged to him].

Liam's uncle, nicknamed Phil, had been imprisoned the first time for six years on a robbery conviction. The second stint was twenty-five years for murder. Liam says, "There was a factory shop in Cape Town that sold elephant skins.

[Phil] and his mates robbed that place and they shot five policemen. I don't believe he had a scared hair on his body. When he used to look at me I used to get scared. If he just put on his angry face, I would get scared."

Phil was thrown into the toughest penitentiary and moved frequently from Cape Town to Johannesburg to Paarl and then back. Liam and his mother used to visit him every two weeks, a routine that left an impression on Liam. Many young men in Manenberg grow up admiring outlaws and consider a couple of years in prison an initiation into manhood. The drug lords have money, they have power, and they inspire respect and sometimes outright admiration. Liam came to the opposite conclusion after living with a man who seemed to have a target on his back. "Growing up with my uncle was very hard," he reflected.

> But it also helped me not to grow up as he did. He used to tell me, even when he was intoxicated . . . "Don't live *my* life. Live your own life." And those were words I would never forget. And now he's been in prison for twenty-five years. He's been in prison since I was twelve. So I think it's because of my uncle that I became a stronger person in my community, and because of my surroundings I could see that I'm not going to do this same thing . . . I want to be the opposite of him.

By the time Liam was in high school, his family had emerged from the poverty and unemployment that had consigned them to the Wendy house. His father had a steady job and they were able to move to the Flats. Their new-found stability gave Liam the peace of mind he needed to focus on schoolwork, and he moved steadily toward the matric exam, setting his sights on a career in the South African navy. He remembered:

> I always had a liking for the sea. Being a fisherman is not for me. I was good at fishing, but no, because it is a seasonal trade and the navy had a feel-good thing to it. In grade three there was a guy who did our assembly, a naval officer. I was, like, "Wow, that's cool!" I was sitting in the assembly and I thought: "Yes, I'm going to wear that [white] suit some day." . . . From that day onwards I was bragging to my mom, now I'm going to the navy.

In grade seven, Liam was offered admission to Simon's Town School, a naval school. But this was during a rough patch in his father's job history, so he had to turn it down. The family could not afford the fees that were (and still are) assessed even for public schools.

Instead, he enrolled in the South African Sea Cadets, a less expensive alternative, and attended Silverstream Secondary, an ordinary—largely Coloured—high school in Manenberg and hoped to qualify for the navy by examination. It was not to be. He says,

> I applied to the Naval Institute at grade eleven. I think my report [card] was excellent. It had four A's in it, so I thought I had to get in. In grade twelve I started to become despondent because I hadn't heard anything from the navy, not even a letter or a phone call. So I applied again, with my June matric that was also a great report, even better than grade eleven. . . . Still no response. I went for another opportunity in the navy, a post to be a clerk. . . . I still didn't get anything back.

Liam had put all of his ambitions into the dream of becoming a naval officer and it was going nowhere. "I was crushed," he admitted. He had two applications going, one through the Sea Cadets and one on his own, and neither of them yielded so much as a reply. The blow was all the more difficult to absorb because other people—none of them Coloured—were accepted, even though Liam had outperformed them in the Sea Cadet program and in high school.

> The guy who had the weakest report . . . this African guy . . . made it. I was like, "Wow, what did I do wrong? I have more certificates than him; I have more skill than him; and I have more onboard experience." But they never gave me a reason. There was this naval and cadet meeting led by the first African admiral . . . at the Simon's Town naval base. He read out the new naval requirements . . . "80 percent Blacks (Africans), 10 percent Indians, 5 percent Coloured, and 5 percent Whites." I was standing there, dead still, and I looked at the majority of the naval citizens. I am not racist, but they were mostly Xhosa- and Zulu-speaking people.

Liam applied seven times. He enlisted the help of his mentor, a Coloured warrant officer whose time in the Navy dates back to the time when it was mainly Coloured and partially White. Together they appealed to a board of review. "I told them, 'I'm really eager to work here. I have all the work skills and don't have a criminal record.' They couldn't even give me an answer."

The emergence of affirmative-action legislation under the ANC was intended to redress decades of exclusion suffered by the Black majority. It was meant to ensure that they would at last be able to claim their rightful place in integrated, well-provisioned schools, including universities, and in public- and private-sector employment. For Coloured South Africans, who came out of apartheid better educated than their African counterparts and speaking Afrikaans, the imposition of these quotas went down badly. For Liam, it led to questions about whether he has a place in the new order at all:

> Where do I fit in as a young Coloured man? Where do the White people fit in? I don't think Mr. Nelson Mandela had a plan of electing anyone from any race or culture, but to boost everyone, to give everyone a fair opportunity. So [how] does this BEE [Black Economic Empowerment] legislation fit that?

He considered going overseas, to join the navy of another country. It was a sensible plan, his mentor told him. "Go apply to the American Seals. Canada has a great naval crew [too]."

> But why must I work there? I'm South African! I was to be part of the South African navy, not another country's navy. I felt like shit and just got up from my seat and walked out because these guys couldn't say a word to me and I felt undignified. I felt, 'Why must they be in charge of my life? Why must I submit to their authority, when I have more skills than some of them? I don't know why they are sitting there.' This one White guy stood up and said, 'You won't get work here. Go somewhere else, to another land, because you won't get work here at all.' My heart was broken. I did not want to apply after that.

Racial politics in post-apartheid South Africa put a block right in the middle of the road Liam thought he was on, and his experience illustrates the contradictions of the "forgotten ones." The Coloured population has lost the favored status, relative to Black South Africans, that they enjoyed under the old regime. While most Coloured people were stranded in lower-middle-class occupations, their lives were still a significant step up from the abject poverty and total oppression that was the lot of most Black people. That middle ground left Coloured people like Liam with ambitions for upward mobility.

Sense of purpose is foundering among Coloured members of Liam's generation who live in townships like Manenberg. From their perspective, the advantages they had were jettisoned by a ruling party that does not care about their future. Policies designed to improve the lot of the majority have passed them by and left them without a foothold in institutions like the navy. Living conditions in Manenberg are clearly better than they are in many parts of Khayelitsha, but the disappointment Coloured people have experienced has created a community that is in many ways more damaged.

If someone who has worked as hard as Liam has comes to feel this way, what hope is there for someone like Ambrose? Or his friend Rashid Jackson? Rashid was born in Athlone but moved to Manenberg when he was only a few months old. There were seven children in the family, but they had different fathers, none of whom were in the picture. He recalled:

> It was just Mother, my sister, myself and my five brothers. We got a house with three rooms, a lounge area, our bedroom, and a kitchen and toilet. . . . We sometimes slept three or four in a bed. My mother's bed had four people in it and the other people slept where they could, just to survive.

Although Rashid went to school, he missed long stretches because his family didn't have the money for fees. When Rashid was fourteen, one of his brothers was shot before his eyes. This propelled Rashid into the small-time gang life, mostly for protection and for the fun of hanging out with other boys who were, in the main, harmless. "Candy Cool Cats, that was our gang. It was friends . . . we weren't gangsters. We just loved the women and sports and so on." In 1994, though, he joined a more serious gang, the Hard Livings.

> I wormed myself in there for protection because I saw what happened with people . . . how they got shot and killed. To be safe, I had to be aligned with this gang. Later on, I had to prove myself to them. . . . They said, "Here's a gun, go and shoot." I didn't have a choice. So they shoved a gun in my hand and said, "If you want to be one of us, then you must show us." . . . Guys who didn't want to belong to the gang, then all of a sudden they shoot the guy dead.

Rashid's life careened between stretches in jail and periods on the street. He became a father at the age of fifteen, and now at twenty-nine he has five children, two with his wife, and three with other women whom he never sees any more. When her mother discovered she was pregnant, Rashid's wife was kicked out of her home. Together, Rashid and his wife took shelter in a madrassa [Muslim school], where he paid rent cobbled together from one of his meager jobs. When that job ran out, they had no money and no-where to live.

> There was a time when my wife and I . . . slept on the street. Then I left my kids with my mother or her mother, and my family accepted this. I never slept at their house and neither did my wife. If I didn't work . . . then I would take a large wooden board . . . a garage door, and leaned it against a wall, brought some blankets . . . and we slept there. That was 2005–6. For a period of three to four months, I hustled and slept under this thing, my wife and I. On rainy days and sunny days.
>
> There were days when my baby did not want to sleep at my mother's house because she was breast-fed. Then she would stay with us. So myself, my wife, and kids lived on the street. Sometimes I would sleep in my mother's yard . . . or in her mother's yard. Sometimes in the evening, the gates are locked and then I would knock on people's doors to ask if my wife could sleep at their place. Then the whole night, I would make a fire and would sit the whole night in front of it.

Rashid is hard-pressed to make an honest living given his criminal past, and says, "I need to make money every day, so I just hustle the things I can get my hands on. . . . If I get money, then I just keep it and then after a while . . . we decide (my wife and me) how we are going to spend the money and what we are going to eat. We just live for the day. We can't think of the next day . . . If we get money now, we need to think what we will buy to eat now."

Rashid finds broken cell phones he can fix and then sells them to people in other townships, especially Gugulethu, where he finds Black people who will pay cash for the things he brings them. Whenever possible, he hustles at the margins of the legal economy. But when things got desperate, in 2007, he turned to boosting small electronics and anything else he could get his hands on:

> I started robbing people and started breaking into cars. If I got the loader [the radio and CD player that comes out of the dashboard], then I would sell it in Gugulethu. When I got the money, then I first bought drugs, then the money I had left over I took home. I would pass people and hurt them. I would assault people in the evenings. We were always a gang of two or three who would do these things together, and whatever we did stayed between us. We made sure we always had money in our pockets. And not a single day went past that I did not use drugs.

With his life spinning out of control, Rashid finally decided that he could no longer go on that way. He resolved to leave the drugs and drinking behind and swears now that he has not touched either in the last four years.

Rashid's extended family is in the same leaky boat. His brother and sister-in-law and their two kids were living with him because they have nowhere else to go. Eight people reside in what Rashid says is a four-person house with one bedroom. Rashid's brother gets occasional jobs installing garage doors, and, when he can, he hires Rashid to help. A typical job might bring him R100, once or twice a month. Combining his meager earnings with the child allowance he and his wife receive of R150 a week, they just barely manage to feed the family. "When we get the [child allowance], we spend all of it on food," he confesses. "That food doesn't last us for two weeks. Then it's back to hustling.

Rashid's life reflects the dire circumstances of his youth—spent in substandard housing, dodging bullets—and the poor options he was left to face as he got older. Rashid's only protection lay in the threats his gangster uncle could issue from behind bars, evidently sufficient to ward off attackers he might have faced otherwise. Perhaps we should not be surprised, given this background, that Rashid descended into drug addiction, which in turn fueled a life of theft, assault, and under-the-radar hustling.

Rashid is at the very bottom of the Manenberg ladder. He has a weaker safety net under him than Ambrose and more people depending on him, especially his kids, whose lives are not likely to turn out well because of the chaos that has now dogged the heels of their family for generations. Rashid has made real efforts to find a job. The week before our interview, he had been in town knocking on doors and had put in an application to the council that manages the utilities in Manenberg. One of the community centers in the township lets him print his résumé there and they give him advice on ways he might fudge the truth about his education so as not to completely take himself out of the competition. "I always phone," he says, "but then I'm always unsuccessful. . . . Maybe it is because I come out of a Coloured community."

Whatever the reason, nothing is working for Rashid, and mostly likely that will continue to be the case for him or his neighbors who are among Manenberg's poorest residents. Like Ambrose, who also has little to offer an employer, Rashid is floundering without any clear sense of how to make a difference in his trajectory. Unlike Ambrose, he is trying to dedicate his energy to changing course. Ambrose has largely given up on himself.

Ambrose cringes, shrugs, shakes his head, kicks a rock, and stares into the distance when we ask him about what he could do to change the trajectory of his life. He says he cannot turn to his family, for they have tried in the past to help him and he has disappointed them so often that he simply cannot return to that well. His mother will never employ him or recommend him to anyone. Nadia, his sister, knows that Ambrose is unreliable and is too vulnerable to risk any of her reputational capital on him. She will not put his name in for a shift at the factory where she works. Patrick, Ambrose's father, is no longer employed and has never thought of Ambrose as someone willing to stick out the hard physical labor that was his life. He would not dissuade Ambrose from hustling for work on the docks, where Patrick spent the better part of thirty years working. But Ambrose has nothing to offer the shipyard and admits as much when asked why he wouldn't just try to do what his father did for a living.

Who remains to help Ambrose land a job if his family is out of the picture? The people he knows who have jobs are overwhelmed by requests from the unemployed in their social networks and deflect the vast majority of these appeals. The rest of Ambrose's contacts are out of work themselves. Rashid cannot help Ambrose find a job. He can't find anything for himself. Liam is scrambling. Graham, Ambrose's "main man" at the community center, throws Ambrose an opportunity here and there, paying him in food rather than money. But Graham is running a counseling center, not an employment agency, even though that is probably the one thing most needed by residents of Manenberg.

At some level, Ambrose knows all of these roadblocks are standing in his way. But he translates the barriers into an emotional stance that is pervasive in Manenberg: he doesn't trust anyone around him and they don't trust him. He is convinced that people right around him would steal him blind if he let down his guard; they would gossip about his faults if he confided in them. If something good was in the offing—a job, a grant, an opportunity of any kind—they would hoard it. The Manenberg flats are a survivalist camp, with everyone for themselves. "The people here!" Ambrose shakes his head in disgust.

> They are the ones you must worry about. The neighbor's son will steal from me. Here there is a different mind, Katherine. The people here steal everything they see. If I put my sneakers there on the roof or by the window . . . I must stand there the whole time till they dry. They will try to climb the roof to snatch them and sell them.

Graham understands Ambrose's point, but believes he is thinking about the symptoms without understanding the cause. Graham argues that the Coloured community of Manenberg has been robbed of its heritage and left with nothing to stand on as a culture or a community. He was born in

Manenberg—as were his parents and grandparents before him—and went to primary and high school here. Finishing his matric in 1990, when political conflict was high and jobs were scarce, Graham found a job working with his uncle in construction. For three years, he did the grunt work on one building site after another. With the help of a friend who worked as a taxi driver, Graham found a spot taking in fares for the group taxis that ferry workers from the townships to the City Bowl and the docks. For four years of twelve-hour days collecting cash, he was at ease except when the gangs came looking for their share. "I was a person that didn't give up money. The gangers would come and say, 'Give a rand [or] give twenty-one rand.' I would tell them, 'I don't have money.' But one day, four guys got into a taxi and threatened me with a gun because I was not respecting them by not giving them money."

It was time for a change. Graham had a child out of wedlock and had to support the kid. His mother was living alone and he needed to help her as well, but the risks in the taxi business were too great. After trying one blind alley after another, he ended up at the community center, where the director told him that the most she could do for him was to give him a volunteer job. Over the next thirteen years, he worked his way up to the rank of counselor, and then, finally, when the director's slot opened up, he was ready, willing, and able.

Given his long history in the township, Graham has come to a firm conclusion about how the community came to be so broken. The answer lies in its apartheid origins:

> When I was young, if you robbed a White business or you killed a White man . . . [it was understood as a strike at the oppressor]. There was a hatred towards White people, White companies . . . because a lot of people worked for White bosses in the clothing industry, furniture industry. . . . These businesses were robbed because people working at these places could give information to people in Manenberg and then these . . . gangsters would go and rob these people . . . sometimes killing people. . . . It is wrong to rob from your own people, but it was almost like right to rob the oppressors. Maybe it was just an excuse to rob and steal . . . but to justify it . . . because apartheid was also not right.

Graham grew up admiring the Robin Hoods of Manenberg who would rob a White vendor's meat truck and then sell a whole sheep on the street for next to nothing. It was a form of revenge. The streets were sullen, deadened, alive only on Thursdays after the council workers were paid and then they would drink themselves under the table. Graham had plenty of opportunities to see the wild side of Manenberg since his grandfather "was a very violent man. He drank a lot and he was truly violent." But then the grandfather "got saved and gave his heart to the Lord. From that time . . . he changed the family. 'You will walk the narrow path.' . . . He was very strict. 'Every Sunday you must be in church.' Coming from a life of doing wrong things, that was his stance and that was our family's way of operating."

Graham had the experience, unusual in working-class Manenberg, of growing up with two working parents. Surrounded by poorer neighbor kids who were hungry for bread, he had it easier. That strict grandfather insisted that his children and their partners would work, especially if they were married. It didn't matter if they did garden work or helped out in a shop, they were going to find a way to make an honest living. Graham got a taste of that medicine early: "I had a part time job. I worked at the bazaars, packing shelves with my uncle. I gave money to my mother, but I had extra money and I started to sell beer at a very young age. . . . I pulled neighbors from the streets to take me to Gugulethu to sell beer."

As he looks back at the winding road toward his current position as community center director, Graham credits his family and his own wisdom at recognizing a dead end when he saw one. He sees his work as a way of making amends for the wrongs he committed in his brief stint on the wrong side of the law. But he also bridles at the fact that there are so few options for a real career for people raised in Manenberg. "Looking back at high school friends, how many of them are dead through gang violence," he thinks, shaking his head.

In 2008, Graham had an opportunity rarely offered to Manenberg citizens, a chance to travel overseas. He was invited to visit Germany, where the sponsors of his organization are located. What he saw there opened his eyes to the toll that living in a poor, segregated township takes. "I was in Germany for two weeks," he says, "and I told myself: 'Wow, if I could grow up like this.' It is like people are naive. They don't think of crime. I asked them, 'Is there any crime here?' They told me that two months before, three boys had robbed another boy of earphones and his iPod and it was in the newspapers. I thought, 'You haven't experienced crime. You haven't been threatened. You haven't seen one person being drunk hitting another person. You haven't seen someone lying dead there.'"

Graham could attribute the brutish side of Manenberg life to the poverty of its people. He could blame them for having a callous attitude toward the lives and rights of others. Conservatives outside his community could, and do, suggest that the culture of the Coloured people somehow leads to the disaster that is gang culture in the township.

Some might point to the long reach of apartheid, with its disdain for Coloured people, as the root cause of broken lives. Having been told they did not deserve the quality of life that Whites could expect, and having been removed miles from the city center to reinforce the point, people on the left might argue that the broken culture of Manenberg today is a direct result of the deprivation imposed on its residents.

For Graham, there is an element of truth in each of these explanations, especially the one that emphasizes the oppression of Coloured people under the apartheid heel.

> Fifty to sixty years ago, people will tell you, we could walk late at night and nothing [would happen]. We [could] leave our windows open and . . . sleep with the doors open. There was respect for one another. But apartheid had an impact. [It] created that anger and that violence within people. . . . People are hurting themselves now and wanting to hurt other people. So if a person gets raped, they want to rape again.

But the explanations for Manenberg's dire straits are all missing one key ingredient: post-apartheid inequality. Where race was once the main dividing line, widening class differences—which were there in the past, but submerged under race—have added layers of complexity. "I think the biggest problem for me is post-apartheid," Graham says. "The enemy was clear [in the past]. I think Coloureds are now trying to project their anger towards Blacks who are rich. . . . The community is hurting itself, [people] killing each other. Drug dealing is an escape for people. We are at a point of inward killing or hurting, because the enemy is now people with money . . . it is not Whites anymore. It's about the haves and have-nots."

The ugliness of class is becoming more palpable in South Africa. It is more painful because the promise of democracy, the hope that followed from the largely peaceful transition after apartheid, is still very real in Graham's generation. The contrast between what was supposed to have happened and what has actually transpired is stark and breeds a despair that is reflected in the red-rimmed eyes of the alcoholics in Manenberg. Indeed, even in regions of the country where the ANC is working to bring people out of abject rural poverty—places with no roads, electricity, or water—the effort goes unrecognized because it is not enough. Deprivation remains too widespread, while the wealthy—especially the "new rich" among Black Africans—are too visible against this disappointing backdrop.

If anger was the main reaction to inequality, one might imagine that mobilization would follow. But Manenberg is not a place where people march in the streets or direct their frustration at a target. The township appears to be too enervated for a response. Mr. Jackson, the director of a rival community center to Graham's, tried to capture the plague of listlessness. "There is almost a permanent atmosphere of apathy in Coloured communities," he explained. "You must work double hard to motivate people, to get young people to come and get the opportunities."

Jackson's experience in Manenberg contrasts sharply with the community work he has done in the Black townships, like the one where Thandiswa lives, which is, if anything, poorer than Manenberg:

> In Khayelitsha, you only have twenty jobs left and you will have 5,000 people coming to you. . . . Here [in Manenberg], you have five job opportunities and you find no one. So there is a big contrast. I don't think education is important in this community. It needs almost an inspiration. If you drive through Manenberg, you will see the amount of young people just milling around, not at school at all. . . . Unemployment, poverty, and there are a lot of backyard dwellers. Everyone lives on top of each other.

Jackson's account accords with our own observations of the listless air around the township. Since neither we nor the people we have come to know ever hear of jobs on offer, it is hard to know what would happen if there were employment opportunities. But the contrast in energy levels is striking nonetheless.[16] In Khayelitsha or Gugulethu, people are bustling about. Not everyone, of course. Thandiswa herself often feels apathetic or lost, but when job opportunities have come up, she jumps for them, and during those periods when she is working, her demeanor is upbeat, even when the job is menial. And while her community also has a serious problem with crime and assault, the general conviction is that there are some bad guys plaguing the vast majority of people who are trying to get by.

In the Flats area of Manenberg, as Ambrose has explained to us often and Mr. Jackson confirmed, people complain that no one is trustworthy.[17] "Everyone is on the take," Jackson lamented, "and friendship doesn't prevent people from harming one another. It's every man for himself." No one we met in Khayelitsha ever spoke in these terms.

Ambrose lamented this ugly aspect of his community when he tried to tell us that he knew the people who were doing him harm. In some cases, he had known them all his life. That didn't mean he could count on them. "So these people who are assaulting and robbing," we asked, "these aren't strangers? You know these people?"

Ambrose responded: "I know these people. They rob a lot. They grab the people's earrings out. Every day, blood is running from the people."

"So, you can't trust the people that you know?"

"I trust big people, yes, like Graham, my mother, my sister . . . but I don't trust the others. . . . The people here, they are the ones you must worry about. The neighbors' son will steal from me. There is a different mind here, Katherine. The people here, they steal everything they see."

CHAPTER SIX

The Other Side of
the Coloured Divide

THE WINELANDS OF CAPE TOWN are among the most beautiful landscapes in southern Africa. Whitewashed Dutch colonial houses with their gray thatched roofs stand out against a brilliant blue sky. Acres of verdant vines stretch over the hillsides. The farmhouses that dot the vineyards date from the eighteenth century and are of grand proportions, though simple in style. The walls are thick stone, cool to the touch even on scorching summer days. The gentle gables that grace the front are reminders of their first residents, the Afrikaans-speaking Dutch or the French who built the industry into one of the world's great sources of fine wines, on par with the Napa Valley in Northern California or the Bordeaux region of France. On a warm summer day, visitors can enjoy the fare at the wineries in Paarl, which sport elegant outdoor restaurants where oenophiles can taste the estate's best and partake of local cuisine.

Nestled within the picture-perfect setting is Paarl Boys', one of the country's legendary elite high schools. The school is reminiscent of Eton and Harrow in Britain or Groton and Hotchkiss in New England. During the apartheid years, Paarl Boys' was exclusively White and patronized only by the sons of the wealthy.

The whitewashed buildings housing classrooms, theaters, laboratories, and lunchrooms are surrounded by lush greenery, brilliant flowers, and signs that announce that one is on "private property." Visitors are subject to search and trespassers can be prosecuted. The sense of security is reinforced by gates, which bear the school seal, but the school does not feel like a fortress as so many other institutions in contemporary South Africa do. There is no barbed wire or broken glass atop the perimeter wall, perhaps because guards are ever present but also because the area surrounding the school is so upscale that those who "don't belong" would stand out in an instant.

The centerpiece of Paarl Boys', a magnificent manicured rugby pitch, looks out toward Paarl Rock (or Pearl Mountain), which is so close that the lines in its granite surface are visible to the naked eye. From the tall trees that surround the base of the mountain to the hawks that circle above, it is a breathtaking setting. More than a playing field, the rugby pitch has long served as a proving ground for the ideal Afrikaner youth, who should be fit, full of endurance, and a bit rough.

Paarl Boys' was established in 1868, and hence is one of the oldest boarding schools in the country. Its graduates have become lawyers, surgeons, captains of industry, prominent politicians, owners of vast tracts of land, and the merchant leaders of South African trade. The school has contributed more than its fair share of Springboks, members of the national rugby team. It is ranked the third most prestigious rugby school in the country. Students today all wear a light-blue shirt, blue-and-white striped tie, and dark-blue blazer with the school's coat of arms emblazed on the chest pocket. As the boys ascend through the grades and distinguish themselves academically and on the playing fields, they acquire the right to wear special blazers and ties.

A great deal of store is put in tradition at Paarl Boys' precisely because admission to this special circle conveys so much privilege. Opening the insular fraternity to non-White boys was a dramatic change that came under duress. In the early 1990s, before the legal edifice of apartheid was dismantled, the school became "Model C" and began to accept a handful of Coloured and Black boys, but cracking the color barrier in such a venerable place was a special symbolic victory.[1]

It was not lost on anyone that the community that houses the school is near another institution of symbolic importance, Victor Verster Correctional Center, the last prison residence of Nelson Mandela. He spent three years living in a private house within the walls of the prison, the period of the most intense negotiations between the National Party and the ANC that led to his release and the beginning of the end of apartheid. Freed to walk the jubilant streets around the prison in February 1990, Mandela ended twenty-seven years behind bars, spent mostly on Robben Island, visible a short distance from the Cape Town harbor, on the road that leads to Paarl. A bronze statue of the national hero now stands outside the prison.

Paarl Boys' is a short walk from a ritzy downtown shopping district. Its windows sport elegant displays of Yves St. Laurent fashions, European furniture, specialty chocolates and cheeses, and fine linens. Built to accommodate shoppers with fortified credit cards, Paarl's main street is frequented by upscale South Africans who today include people of all skin colors, if mainly White. Who one doesn't see there are the residents of the "other Paarl"; they have their own shopping areas: Coloured people to the east of Berg River, in communities like New Orleans and Charleston Hill (known collectively as Paarl East), and Black people to the north, in Mbekweni.

Lady Grey, a neighborhood on the east side, comes into view just across the bridge that spans the river. Here telltale burglar bars cover most of the shop fronts. Down-market groceries advertising cheap goods mix with low-cost clothing shops, outlets for toys and videos, and liquor stores. Mothers pushing strollers take in the summer sun as they do their Saturday shopping. Occasionally they have to wind around a drunk splayed out on the sidewalk or beggar with cap outstretched.

Lady Grey is the heart of the Coloured area of Paarl, which came into being as a consequence of the Group Areas Act and the forced removals that gathered force in the mid-1950s. Up until that time, central Paarl was a mixed-race area, albeit one where Coloured and Black South Africans were confronted with evidence of their second-class citizenship on a daily basis. But when the evictions began in earnest, the Coloured families were sent packing to the east side of the river, where the most prosperous of them moved into sturdy houses and the children attended ordinary-looking schools well below the standards of Paarl Boys', with modest playgrounds.

The Drankenstein Municipality, of which Paarl is the largest settlement, boasts a population of about 251,200. About 130,000 live in Paarl proper, the third-oldest European settlement in South Africa (after Cape Town and Stellenbosch) and the largest town in the Cape Winelands region. As in the rest of the Western Cape, Coloured people make up most of the population: 62.4 percent; 24.1 percent of the municipality is Black, and 14.5 percent is White.[2] The White and Coloured communities speak Afrikaans, the area's dominant language. As is to be expected, huge income gaps separate these groups.

Charleston Hill is the neighborhood where Daniel Cornell and his sisters lived when they were young. A redbrick primary school stands at its center. Surrounded by a high metal fence, featuring one ordinary playing field, the school looks solid but unexceptional. This is a long way from Paarl Boys', with its manicured lawns and graceful walkways. But it is also a long way from Manenberg, home to a much poorer Coloured population, where school buildings are rundown, fences are topped with barbed wire, and panes are missing from many classroom windows.

Charleston Hill is a middle-class community with a mixture of large, well-built houses and green gardens protected by gates, as well as small houses surrounded by storm fencing. Most houses were built about thirty years ago, sometime after the removals began from the city center, but they have been modernized and upgraded in the interim. In between the large residential blocks are well-maintained parks with brightly colored jungle gyms and swing sets.

Black families were resettled into nearby Mbekweni, a township north of the river, full of small blocky houses painted in pastel colors. Row after row of these neat homes, surrounded by little plots of flowers, give Mbekweni a peaceful atmosphere. It bears little resemblance to the overcrowded, problem-ridden townships closer to Cape Town.[3] While less affluent than Charleston Hill, here there is nowhere close to the poverty of the massive townships where Thandiswa and Ambrose live.

Women in Mbekweni and Paarl East often work at home and the older men can be seen sitting outside enjoying the fresh mountain air. Working-age men are scarce during the day as they fill the ranks of the blue-collar workforce employed by the factories that line the road from Paarl East to Mbekweni. Clothing, textiles, footwear, and now high-tech electronics are all produced in the area and contribute to its broad-based economic structure. People from these working- and middle-class areas of Paarl can walk to the factories from their homes, which makes Paarl's suburbs more stable than the sprawling settlements around Cape Town, in which few are able to find work. Indeed, notice boards line the main boulevards advertising new developments in the Paarl area, suggesting that housing stock is growing.

Just west of Mbekweni lies the Berg River, with views so breathtaking it is hard to imagine that the apartheid state consigned its less-favored racial groups to this area. There is a beautiful, placid lake nearby that catches the light and the shadows of the clouds that pass over it. Large trees line the river, their leaves wafting in the breeze, an image you might expect on the cover of *National Geographic*.

Coloured people who grow up in Paarl are more economically secure and steadily employed than their counterparts who were dumped in townships outside Cape Town. About 23 percent of Paarl's population is unemployed, which compares very favorably to Manenberg, where an estimated 66 percent of the population is out of work.[4] Many of Paarl's Coloured families are headed by semiskilled workers, while those lucky enough to have jobs in Manenberg are more often entry-level workers in unskilled occupations.

Daniel Cornell's father, Andre, was once one of those semiskilled workers. Considered a "fair Coloured" man under apartheid race laws, his family enjoyed slightly more privileges than those who had darker complexions. The Cornells had better houses, lived in better neighborhoods, and had better connections than their darker-skinned relatives. The social capital that came with skin color classification paid off and still does, even today. Andre's lighter

skin and "finer manners," an official criterion of the apartheid color classification system, translated into better jobs and greater respect from those above
him. His bosses were sure he could take on more demanding construction
assignments than his darker colleagues. Andre capitalized on the opportunities by working three jobs at the time and giving it his all, day and night,
weekdays, and weekends.

Today Andre is a respected business owner in the Paarl Coloured community, though most of his clients are White. His firm builds homes in the Paarl
Valley that are each worth R5–6 million ($500,000–$600,000) and manages
construction projects on a large scale. He owns several properties, both in
Paarl and in the elegant Cape Town neighborhood of Strand, and is hoping to
one day diversify to Camps Bay, a stunning seaside town where the average
home runs around R10 million ($1 million). The company has offices in an
industrial park not far from the family home. Surrounded by tall metal fences
with barbed wire on top, the office is fairly bared-boned, with an office for a
secretary, one for Andre, and one for Daniel, now the firm's heir apparent,
having left his job in Cape Town for this berth in the family firm. They have
a large garage and a yard full of equipment where the materials Andre uses
in his business are stored. They are thrifty in their use of these goods; Andre
never throws anything away.

Andre's story is a tale of extraordinary tenacity and strategic planning.
In his life he has gone from blue-collar worker to proud member of the Paarl
"business roundtable," a multiracial organization that absorbed all of the local
race-based mini-roundtables of the apartheid era. He is a charitable donor, a
pillar of the community, and still a full-time manager of his large enterprise.

Andre and his siblings come from a long line of disciplined people.
George, Andre's father, worked as a chauffeur for farm owners but developed
a more skilled job "on the side," as an upholsterer and curtain maker. Andre's mother worked in a factory. In a country whose Afrikaner elites stressed
the virtues of the traditional family, with mothers expected to remain in the
home, the Coloured community always stood in contrast because its women
typically worked. It was necessary since wages were low, even for semiskilled
and skilled workers. This tradition of blue-collar employment was the economic bedrock for the more prosperous Coloured people, and in the Cornell
family it fostered respect for men and women who work with their hands.

Accordingly, when the oldest son—Andre—came of age, it was only natural that he began his work life as an apprentice bricklayer in a well-established
company. On weekends, Andre would add to his income by doing small jobs
on the side. From that beginning came larger and more lucrative construction

contracts. Eventually Andre found a full-time job in construction, while continuing to build brick houses on the weekends. He took on the task of training three of his younger brothers who were also eager to find a path into the industry, while a fourth trained at their father's knee and became an upholsterer and curtain maker. Andre's industrious nature and his capacities for leadership eventually led to his elevation to the role of foreman, showing the kind of upward mobility that a successful Coloured man might hope for in the apartheid period.

His aspirations were for greater independence, though, and eventually those side jobs in construction led him to form his own company. Andre now bids for construction projects large and small and hires subcontractors, engineers, and even architects. He has parlayed profits from his business into a significant empire of properties he owns throughout the valley. Sometimes he acquires houses and rebuilds them for sale; others he rents out, deriving a secondary income stream from them.

Edwina, Andre's wife (and Daniel's mother), has participated in the steady ascent of her family to its present upper-middle-class station. She grew up in Paarl with her parents and two brothers, but since her mother worked in a local canning factory, Edwina spent much of her youth with her grandmother. The extended family lived very close to what is now the main road through the center of Paarl. At the time, it was a mixed-race community but one in which the relations between groups were structured by enforced subordination. The shops where Edwina and her family bought their groceries were owned by White people who would attend to Coloured families only as long as they used a separate entry and exit. They were always the last to be served.

There were lovely public swimming pools in the center of town, but Coloured children could only look through the gaps in the wooden fences around them. On a hot summer day, families in Cape Town love to flock to the magnificent beaches that hug the coast. In Edwina's early years, the best coastal areas were entirely reserved for Whites. Coloured families could frequent beaches like Strandfontein that were rocky and closer to industrial plants. These rules of engagement were not as harsh for them as those that governed the relations between Black and White South Africans, but the hierarchy was clear enough and it is this sense of exclusion that Edwina remembers most from her teenage years in the 1950s.

That was right about the time when all Coloured families were ejected from their homes in central Paarl and packed off to Amstelhof, east of the river. Henceforth, central Paarl was to be Whites-only. The grocery stores in Amstelhof were inferior to those of the city center. They belonged to Indian families who were accustomed to dealing with low-income households. Customers could buy their goods on credit and pay off the debt at the end of the week when the factories paid workers. Shopkeepers became important agents in the stabilization of the Coloured community because they trusted their customers and created a point of contact that enabled them to get to know one another.

Forced removals not only deprived Edwina's family of interracial relations, they also threw total strangers together based solely on their common racial classification. Class differences within racial groups were ratified by the removals, since those who had more money and property ended up in more desirable areas of Paarl East and those without were directed to flats that recall for us the ones in Manenberg.

Paula Joubert High School, a co-ed institution for Coloured students, was the last stop in Edwina's education. She did not finish her matric exams, but instead went to work as a cashier at ShopRite. After marrying Andre, she found another job, in a factory that made bed sheets. These were the kinds of jobs that were typically available to Coloured women, many of whom were blue-collar workers in the Western Cape's manufacturing industries.[5]

Their early years as a couple were dedicated to saving money. Andre worked seven days a week, eager to acquire different skills from the artisans with whom he worked on construction sites. Edwina is clearly very proud of his work ethic and of their mutual commitment to upward mobility through prudence, self-sacrifice, and strategy.

By the 1980s, Edwina and Andre could begin to see the fruits of their success. He was earning enough now as a construction site foreman for her to quit working and become a stay-at-home mother. They had four children in rapid succession: Celeste and Meagan, the oldest girls, followed by Daniel and his younger sister, Kim. Though they started out in fairly modest circumstances, by the time the children were teenagers the family was able to move to an upscale section of Charleston Hill.

Andre built the family home himself, the place where all of the children now return for family gatherings, and it is a living testimony to his skill. A solid brick-faced house, it is surrounded by white walls and graced by a large gate that swings open with an electronic signal. Beautiful flame trees with their vivid orange blossoms tower over the garden just behind the walls, leading to a graceful front door with large white flowerpots on either side. The interior of the house is decorated with fine wooden furniture, giving the living room a stately air without being overly formal. The kitchen, the center of Edwina's world, has a large wooden "farm" table in the middle and an open fireplace of the kind one might find in a snowy country like Austria or Switzerland. Only Kim lives at home these days, but all of the children come around to be together on a weekly basis.

At the back of the house is a large barbecue (*braai*) for grilling meat, a favorite pastime of South Africans of all colors. Here the family gathers for a weekly braai as they have done since Daniel and his sisters were children. These days the company includes their spouses and children. Occasionally they are joined by the Cornell grandparents and assorted aunts, uncles, and cousins. The braai is where the adults chat while the little ones scamper around the back garden.

Behind the barbecue is Andre's dominion, the place he goes to unwind every evening while Edwina readies dinner. His special passion is birds, acquired by having watched his uncle breed racing pigeons. Here seventy Indian ring-necked parrots are flying around inside an aviary he built with his own hands. Powder-blue parrots race through the air, circling others that are fluorescent yellow, emerald green, or royal purple. The preserve is bounded by a garden with spinach and lettuce for the household. Andre designed a water-pump system so the birds can drink when they want to. He gets one of the workers in his construction company to come and clean the place on a regular basis.

The Cornell home, the birds, the property empire: the family has come a long way from its working-class origins, and Daniel, the heir to his father's business, has benefited every step of the way from his parents' hard work and business acumen. Had the apartheid system not come to an end, it is doubtful that he would have been able to experience the kind of upward mobility that is his good fortune now.

Daniel's first home was in New Orleans, a low-income area of Paarl where most of the residents live in flats similar to those that dominate Manenberg but with fresher paint and less debris on the streets. Semi-detached shacks are attached to the flats, just as they are in Ambrose's neighborhood. They house the "backyard dwellers," people who have flooded into an area that might have jobs. The shops on the main road are like those in Lady Grey, selling discount clothing, liquor, adult videos, and low-end groceries. Every so often, a fish-and-chip shop will appear in the middle of a block.

By the late 1980s, when Daniel was about seven, the family moved to their present home in Charleston Hill. Edwina and Andre were in search of better schools for their three children, and before the end of apartheid this was the best a Coloured family could hope to find. As Daniel remembers, the conditions were tolerable even if they weren't equal to those for Whites.

Daniel and his sisters attended Charleston Hill Primary School, which was then an all-Coloured, Afrikaans-language school. Its graduates tended to complete high school and enter the trades, though some went on to the largely Coloured University of Western Cape. In 1994, when Daniel was eleven, Paarl Boys' and an exclusive girls' school, La Rochelle Girls, opened their doors to non-White students for the first time. Celeste and Meagan were offered the chance to transfer from their Charleston Hill schools, but they turned it down because their friends were staying in the Coloured schools.

Daniel and Kim took a different path and enrolled in what were by then "Model C" schools, so that, in Edwina's words, they could "upgrade to the level of the White children." When Andre sent Daniel to Paarl Boys', he was a little uneasy about the transition, thinking Daniel might feel out of place among the White kids. He told him to "work hard, harder than them," to show those rich White boys he was their equal. Daniel remembers some of that pressure but mainly he recalls how different the facilities were, how they telegraphed racial privilege: "The first shocker was, like, 'Wow, a school with Whites. They have swimming pools and a hall for assemblies.' And we would come home to tell our parents about it. No one is sitting in the sun or on dry fields."

The manicured lawns and elegant buildings of a former "model C" school. These public schools are now open to all, but the best of them charge higher fees and, hence, are hard for families of limited means to afford.

Four of Daniel's closest friends, all of them top Coloured students who had excelled in their subjects in primary school, made the same leap. The transition proved fairly easy for Daniel, in part because he was so capable academically. He made high marks, won prizes, and joined the school's swim team. In addition to English and Afrikaans, Daniel added German, and that qualified him for a high school study abroad program in Germany, where he lived with a host family. He came out of that experience as a fifteen-year-old fluent in German and cosmopolitan in his outlook. From a segregated childhood, he emerged a young man with a broad understanding of life in other societies, much like many of his Black peers in the new upper-class communities of Johannesburg.

The racial structure of South Africa no longer provided his only or even his most important set of social coordinates, an evolution that began with his multiracial experience at Paarl Boys' High. This is not to say that Daniel is unaware of the past. On the contrary, particularly when he speaks—with admiration—of his father's remarkable ascent up the economic ladder, he often notes how difficult that was, given the strictures of apartheid.

We gave Daniel a camera and asked him to take photos of things that were important to him in his daily life. One depicts a relic of the old days, benches marked, one for Whites and one for Blacks. When Daniel drives around the area where his company's construction crew lives, he points out how unfair it is that people of color were shoved into substandard housing. He knows that past was palpable for his parents.

> There used to be the Coloured Business Round Table and the Black Business Round Table [similar to Rotary clubs]. After the first elections it automatically became one [with the White Round Table]. At first the non-Whites got the cold shoulder from the Whites and some of . . . the White people left the Round Table; they did not want to belong to it anymore. My parents still continued. My mom said when they had camps or . . . charity events, the White ladies would not talk to her. They would sit in a circle and when she walked past they just looked at her and would just be quiet. My dad was more integrated with the White men. I think it was because it was most probably a male-female thing. Although even today many people mistake my father as being a White person, so they probably thought [he was a] White man with a Coloured wife.

Yet when Daniel considers his own position and his future trajectory, these kinds of racial inequalities have passed into the background. They inform his identity but not his sense of possibility.

Daniel's sister Kim also attended a formerly all-White school and her self-definition began to shift to reflect her new surroundings. La Rochelle Girls was now a "Model C" school, bilingual in English and Afrikaans. The majority of the students were White and the work was more demanding than what she had experienced at Charleston Hill Primary.

Kim says that she never felt the sting of discrimination herself, but she did notice that expectations of the different groups in her school diverged. "In high school, especially when it came to discipline . . . it would only be the Coloured people or the African people who were always in trouble."

> *What type of things did they do?*
> KIM: Smoke. At high school, we had a cafeteria. We had off periods, so basi-
> cally I had seven subjects, but I wouldn't have all seven on the same day.
> We would have two to three periods free, and when you get to grade[s]
> ten to twelve you [had] your own study location, with no teacher. . . .
> You were responsible to do your studies or your homework. But [stu-
> dents would] often . . . walk around or go to the cafeteria and smoke . . .
> And, honestly, it was only the Coloured and the Africans [she laughs].[6]

Kim had friends from all different racial groups, but as she got older she spent more time with White girls.

> Race was never brought up and, funnily enough, at school the majority of
> my friends were White. When I started studying, I would always be with
> the Whites. The other Coloured girls would always say that I want[ed] to
> be "highty tighty," or . . . White. But it was because of the . . . way [the Co-
> loured girls] behaved. Like, for example, with the free periods we had. I
> mean, we had a lot of work. They never used the time to do it.

As she has grown older and moved into the work world, Kim has moved easily into multicultural, middle-class environments. She continued her education at a technical college and studied cosmetics and "whole body" treatments of the kind that qualified her to work in a beauty salon. She has worked on cruise ships, and, like her brother, has traveled internationally, to London, the Caribbean, and Alaska. On board she worked side-by-side with twenty-four other girls in a spa. The guests were from all over the world and were curious about her identity, which she explained as "South African and Coloured," especially to those who thought she looked like she was from Spain or the Philippines.

Daniel's gradual movement into a multicultural life was accelerated by his experience living abroad. His language skills meant that he could interact with the large German community in South Africa. Most of them descend from colonial "pioneers" who farmed great tracts of land in Namibia, and who remain—to a larger degree than many other White ethnics in the country—attached to their language and country of origin. Anna's family is part of this group and even as a fifth-generation immigrant to Africa she speaks German and has attended German schools. Daniel came to his German connection by experience rather than heritage, but it stuck to him and probably had something to do with why he courted Lize, a German girl who works at the country's South African embassy and who is now his wife.

Lize first came to South Africa for an internship position. She had always been interested in traveling, discovering new places and different cultures, and Cape Town seemed like a "great place" to visit. She met Daniel during a night out with her colleagues. He convinced her to "stay a little longer" in Cape Town and they got married fairly soon afterward. Both are hard workers: Lize was working two jobs when we first met her, full-time at the embassy and as a freelance desktop designer at the same company as Daniel. Together they are the essence of a cosmopolitan, interracial couple for whom class identity may well be the more compelling way of locating themselves in the South African panorama.

DANIEL'S WORK WORLD

After leaving Paarl Boys', Daniel faced a decision: he could choose to pursue a university education, for which he was well qualified, or move toward technical training, which would speed his entry into the world of work sooner and move him closer to his father's life in the skilled trades. He elected the latter and enrolled in a technical college in Cape Town where he worked toward an engineering degree. The program played to his strengths in math and his facility, earned at his father's knee, for strict time management and meticulous attention to detail.

It did not take long for Daniel to turn this training into a good job in the city center. Seaford & Associates, the firm for which he had worked for three years when we met him, is an engineering company with offices downtown, near Parliament. The day we arrived, the front desk of Seaford was vacant and the office seemed empty. Daniel explained that the bosses were away; one had just left the building and another was in Saudi Arabia. Clearly, if he stayed with this firm, he could expect international contract work to be part of his life as well.

Here in Cape Town, his office telegraphs professional expertise and attention to aesthetics. The floors are a light-brown wood and they glisten with a high varnish. The smaller offices are framed with large, dark-blue iron beams and enclosed by glass. The walls are a mixture of exposed brick, wood, and steel. A very stylish meeting room is filled with large blue leather chairs surrounding a lovely oval-shaped, polished wooden table. Paintings cover the walls.

The bosses' offices—accessible only because they were gone—are larger and more elegant than the others, but Daniel's workspace befits his station as a junior person working his way up. His desk is in the middle of the office. It is a small space and looks even smaller because Daniel has piled all his paperwork on top of his desk, butting up against a computer screen. In the next office is a Black woman from the University of Cape Town Engineering faculty who has a part-time contract. Daniel's other coworkers, three women—two White, Afrikaner, and one Coloured—and one White man, sit upstairs.

When Daniel wants to eat lunch out, he walks through the vibrant streets of the downtown business district to a little "hole in the wall," the Wellington Eastern Food Bazaar. It feels like a corner of India. Sitar music is playing in the background. Set up as one long corridor, and in keeping with its name, the bazaar offers a variety of dishes from Turkey, India, and China, among others. It is trendy but affordable, which more or less sums up Daniel's approach to life inside and outside the workplace. He cares about style, likes the look of elegance, but is cost-conscious and not over-the-top extravagant.

In all of these ways—from his multicultural educational background to his diverse coworkers and the comfortable apartment he shares with Lize near the Company Gardens—Daniel would seem to have left race behind. There is nothing about his social environment that bears any trace of the segregated life his parents led or that he himself faced as a young child. For Daniel, upward mobility has erased the kinds of strictures that Ambrose faces every day.

Given his position, we might imagine Daniel to be the kind of person who rejects the social policies advanced by the ANC as remedies for racial inequalities. Indeed, between his educational background and his sister's recollections of a similarly elite experience, we might imagine the Cornell children would embrace the doctrine of meritocracy. After all, Kim speaks about the differences between kids who worked hard and studied during free periods and the ones who didn't. Daniel prides himself on his skills as an engineer and chalks his success in life up to his determination.

While this belief in the work ethic is there, it would be wrong to suggest that Daniel opposes affirmative action quotas. He is definitely not aligned with Ambrose or many of the people we met in Manenberg who hate those policies, feeling that the law favors Blacks and leaves them on the sidelines. Instead, Daniel accepts the need for this kind of social engineering and does not try to hide the ways in which they have advantaged him as a Coloured person. Seaford & Associates is a registered BEE company. Mr. Seaford is Coloured and while only a few of the workers are non-White, the company "receives points"—and hence is a preferred vendor—for government jobs because the company is "BEE compliant."

Daniel recognizes that there are structural factors that make a level playing field something of a pipe dream at this point in South Africa. For that reason, remedies like affirmative action are a necessity. His outlook might be characterized as similar to that of the US Supreme Court when it ruled that preferential admissions to universities on grounds of diversity is needed now but should be phased out twenty-five years after their onset.

Daniel is aware that his firm has an advantage in competing for contracts because it is headed by, and has hired, workers of color. He also knows that affirmative action created the conditions under which someone of his racial background might be hired over others. Yet because there are so few people from the Coloured community, let alone the far more disadvantaged Black community, who have these technical qualifications, he had a reasonably easy time finding work anyhow. He would never say his skills didn't matter, but he would be the first to admit that with them, the fact that his race helped the company meet government quotas didn't hurt his chances either. Fundamentally, it is Daniel's human capital that gives him the edge.

This is precisely what Ambrose and Brandon, who both lack qualifications, cannot secure. They have no such edge and when forced to compete with people who are otherwise advantaged, both men are left scrambling to find work at the crowded bottom of the labor market pyramid.

This recognition of what might be called "legitimate advantage" reinforces Daniel's conviction that at the end of the day what matters most is his skill and his work ethic. That is why he is a valuable asset to Seaford. Indeed, it might be argued that he took the harder road by taking his chances in the job market when he was virtually assured a managerial position in the family construction firm. Even the hiring managers at Seaford were surprised he bothered. All along, they expected Daniel to make the move back to Paarl and the security of his father's business, but they respected him for trying to make his own way first.

But the opportunity to work in the family firm came about long before he expected it and years before his parents planned any such transition. In 2011, Lize began to get homesick and worried about her aging parents back home.

She wanted Daniel to follow her to Germany and live there so that she could fulfill her responsibilities to her parents and reclaim her own roots. Daniel was happy enough to follow, though he had no idea what he would do when he got there. Given Germany's strict immigration laws, it would be years before he would qualify for a job like the one he had in Cape Town. Lize could parlay her experience into a position that would support the two of them and Daniel was not averse to spending time in cosmopolitan Western Europe. For all its charms, South Africa can feel like it is cut off from the rest of the world simply by its remote location. Daniel was game.

His parents were not. Their tight-knit family, with its weekly braai, was in danger of dispersing, their future grandchildren growing up in a foreign land. To this traditional couple, the notion that a wife would support her husband did not sit well either. Most of all, the departure of their only son was too much to bear. They set about creating an offer that Daniel and Lize could not refuse: 50 percent ownership of the family firm. For a young man of twenty-seven, it was a game changer.

With the blessing of his boss at Seaford, Daniel resigned his job in the City Bowl and took up a new role as an independent businessman. The learning curve has been steep. Especially, Daniel has had to learn the delicate art of managing across class and racial lines. Though familiar with class gaps in his own family, especially between his father and his uncles, Daniel never before had to negotiate cleavages as he does now. It is an introduction to the managerial perspective on labor. "To manage the guys on-site," he explains, "is a tough job."

> You can tell them things like do this and do that, but if you turn your back they do it completely wrong. Because the problem with construction laborers and even some of the artisans [is that] they don't have a high qualification. Some of them just left grade seven or just left high school and then started working on a building site or started working in construction because that was the only thing they could do. And some of them start as a general laborer and then an assisting artisan and then that is how they acquire the trade. But they don't have any trade papers or qualifications, so you can explain to them something [and] they will not really understand it, but doing the actual work, like just building and laying bricks, they can do well. But reading off a plan and doing some complicated work for different types of walls or bonds, you really need to stand there and check that they do it.

I'm sorry to say this, but it is like they are machines, you know. They are programmed to just lay brick after brick, but when it comes to difficult work they blank. So you have to stand there and say, 'This goes like this,' and so on. In effect it is not really their own fault because once again they were disadvantaged with their education and qualifications.

Here the nuances of post-apartheid life are most visible in a young man who believes in the future of a multiracial democracy but knows that the groups that compose the population are starting from vastly different points. In an earlier era, or under a less enlightened theory, a manager in Daniel's position might conclude that the problems of managing labor have to do with the innate capacities of the workers. That is manifestly not his perspective. Still, whether he ends up doing his part to close some of that distance, through the training and education that his firm could provide the workers, is yet to be determined.

One imagines that he might make that difference, because although Daniel genuinely does not believe that race structures his life, he knows that it had enormous consequences in the past. He can see it in his own family tree. The aunt who passed for White and abandoned her family to make that identity stick in a society that would have rejected her identity claims if the truth had come out. The father who is so light-skinned that his customers thought he was White and gave him business he might not have had otherwise. His mother, who is darker and has had to endure the snubs of well-to-do White women at business community functions, even though she is the wife of a prominent man. These all remind Daniel of the personal impact of the country's social history.

For Daniel, the past is there but it is not the present, and the future depends on what you put into it. That future will not be segregated by race, but it will be divided by class, and those who have put their all into educational attainment, exerted themselves to find opportunities that were not handed to them, and then worked like the devil to get as much out of those chances as possible, these are the people who will come out on top. Daniel would be the first to acknowledge that family resources gave him options in life that someone like Ambrose will never have. But he would also be quick to point out that he deserves credit for driving himself toward higher ground at every turn. And the good life he enjoys—the apartment in the City Bowl, the nice restaurants he and Lize patronize, the travel they pursue—are the rewards that have come to him because of his own qualities.

Daniel's life—and that of his family—represent the apex of what Nelson Mandela and other ANC leaders argued was the real hope for a new South Africa, where investment in high-quality integrated schools, labor market opportunity, and political freedom meet. In this, Daniel would probably agree that he epitomizes what Martin Luther King, Jr., argued should be the highest aspiration of Americans frozen in racial division: a country where the content of character matters more than the color of one's skin. Daniel would accept that this is not an accurate description of South Africa today. But he would also argue, as he did many times to us, that his own life comes pretty close.

CHAPTER SEVEN

The Past Was Wrong, but It Was the Past

SITTING AT A CAFE IN the afternoon sun, not far from her house in the northern suburbs, Brandon's sister Lauren talks about daily life in this Afrikaner neighborhood and about what it was like to grow up in a family with three older brothers.[1] Brandon and Mark are keen for her to continue her education. Neither of them did, nor did their parents, but the brothers now understand the urgency of having a higher degree.[2] They would like to see their sister collect some employment references for herself in a South Africa that no longer resembles the country their parents knew. Lauren explains that for now she is happy working in a jewelry shop to earn some cash and content to live in her mother's house. She is not sure about what she would like to do in the future. Maybe she will try to study fashion design, but she says that she would need to do that at a Cape Town college, which is "very expensive," and finances are tight. She hopes to be able to study part-time and continue work at the shop. She says, "I don't want to do it full time because I have a job and it's really hard to find a job."

Unemployment is rising and income declining among South Africans without higher education credentials, whether White, Black, or Coloured.[3] Apartheid's color bar ensured a high degree of economic security for White people, but no longer. The world economy has caught up with South Africa, introducing the same bias in favor of the well educated that now shapes the labor markets of Western Europe and the United States. This came as something of a shock to Brandon and Lauren's generation of White South Africans. The labor market protections that insulated Whites fell, competition increased, and the successful ones were those with credentials honed through higher education.[4] Because this trend coincided with, and some would say was exacerbated by, remedial quotas that redress the historic exclusion of the majority population of Blacks, the free fall for many White South Africans has been profound, and the tendency to look first toward remedial policies rather than skill differences as the underlying reason has become a political

sore point. The experience of inter- and intra-generational downward mobility has seeped into every corner of the Bowles family.

Lauren is optimistic about the future of South Africa as a country. Her
boyfriend, Johan, however, is not. He believes there will be few opportunities
for Whites, especially White males, and that infuriates him. Having graduated with a two-year diploma in 3D design, he has been looking for a job for
months, unable to find an entry-level position. He blames the ANC and its
"reverse apartheid" policies of Black Economic Empowerment and affirmative action. These policies are meant to provide positions only for Black people, independent of whether or not they "can do their job," he argues. People
who are not qualified will be accepted, while he will be rejected. Why? Because his skin is White, he tells us. And that is why he has no future in the
country of his birth.

Lauren disagrees. One can "always make a plan" to either continue studying or find work, she admonishes Johan. She speaks with hope about the relationships between people from various racial backgrounds, and, in sharp
contrast to what her mother and many around her have always tried to tell her,
thinks of people of color as being more or less like her: "You think Coloured
people rob you and they're gangsters and stuff, but if you work with them
they're actually so nice, just like normal people." Yet Lauren is scared. She
avoids watching the news, saying, "It's very depressing, really, because they
[emphasize] all the stories about death and burglaries and everything." She
asks us what it is like to be doing fieldwork "with Black people" and hesitates
before she gathers the courage to ask, "Do they really all hate us?"

The 2009 elections brought emotions to a fever pitch among Brandon's
neighbors in the northern suburbs. Anxious about being left out of the
ANC's policy formulations, afraid for their personal safety given the saber-
rattling presidential candidacy of the ANC's Jacob Zuma, and the increasing personal insecurity caused by crime, White voters were on edge. Zuma
hardly helped matters by appearing at election rallies in the company of radi-
cals, singing the anti-apartheid "struggle song," "Awuleth' umshini wami." It
calls the faithful to "bring [me my] machine gun" and celebrates murderous
attacks on the Boer oppressors at the time of apartheid. The firebrand ANC
youth league leader, Julius Malema, added fuel to the fire by claiming that he
"would kill for Zuma."

For residents of the Northerns, this sounded all too likely. It was not simply a revenge fantasy aired to rally political support. To them, it gave all indications of being something closer to a plan of action, or at least the rough
blueprint for one, and it fueled fear of attacks by the Black majority. Visions

of violent land-confiscation of the kind that happened routinely in Zimbabwe, and the near certainty of diminished job opportunities in the country of their birth, seemed only too real.

Brandon and his friends recounted stories to us of farm attacks: murders of White farmers that had happened, they thought, "for no reason" other than revenge or hatred. In social media and blogs, Afrikaner South Africans spoke openly of genocide against their race, displaying gruesome images of White people murdered in cold blood. "Yah, well, it's been brewing for quite a while," Brandon's friend Pieter notes, shaking his head.

> PIETER: I don't know what the origins are, but rumors spread and they turn to general stigma, especially among White populace. Um, everyone here probably knows of this whole rumor going on, that if Nelson Mandela dies, the ANC or whoever would arm up and try to exterminate us . . .
>
> *But do you think that this fear that 'they will kill us' is spreading amongst White people?*
> BRANDON: I don't think people think that radically, do you?
> PIETER: Not that extremely, but it is on everyone's mind, at least to some extent. I'm pretty sure everyone's heard this rumor.

Even though Brandon and many of his friends are not convinced that there is any such plan afoot, with all the rumors and belligerent talk on the air, a lingering fear that "they maybe really do want us all dead" remains in the back of his mind:

> When you hear a guy like Malema saying, "We'll kill for Zuma," you think, "Oh, fuck, maybe they will kill us, man." . . . You hear these rumors about . . . they're going to extinguish the whole flipping White race . . . and you think—can't it just explode all of a sudden? It could. What if there's a mentality that we don't know about . . . maybe a lot of people are thinking that. . . . We don't know.

"IT WAS NOT TO BE SHARED"

Brandon does not come from wealth. His family is what would probably be described as working class in any other country but South Africa. No one in the Bowles family has had a college education. Brandon completed his secondary schooling, but, following his father's suggestion that he should "get a trade and a skill," he did not go past high school. He is trained and experienced in installing home security systems. He has his own small company but it is a fledgling enterprise. At times, it has proven hard to find clients—a situation exacerbated by the global financial downturn that has left less money in the hands of the overseas investors who are often his customers.

Brandon often struggles for money and lives hand-to-mouth, without savings. He admits to spending beyond his means, enjoying "the high life," partying, driving into the mountains for weekends, and spending money as soon as he earns it. He has often voiced ambitions to "get his marketing going" but nothing comes of it.

Every so often, Brandon has toyed with the idea of attending university, of studying part-time while working—but he has settled instead for the entrepreneurial route, which seems to hold more promise for a White man in what he views as a Black man's world. It was different when Brandon's parents were young. His father, Ian, had a good job in the corporate world, without having needed a college diploma. That was an important benefit of being White in apartheid South Africa. The protectionist labor policies that barred people of color from high-status occupations made it a seller's market if the seller was White and limited the need to invest in higher education in order to lead the life of a professional. Ian earned enough that his wife could stay home to care for their four children.

Everything changed in the 1990s with the victory of the African National Congress. At the age of fifty, Ian was dismissed from work as a result of the new Employment Equity legislation that requires companies to transform their employment profiles to reflect the demographic reality of the country. New entrants to the white-collar world began to edge out the older workforce. Ian remained unemployed for a while, and the family considered moving overseas, away from this new government that clearly did not have their interests in mind. Ian tried to capitalize on his ancestral visa from the United Kingdom and moved to England for a time to try to find a better job. He returned to South Africa within a year, though, disillusioned by the realities of the British labor market, and he decided to start his own pool-service company to make ends meet. After Brandon's parents separated, money was hard to come by. Brandon's mother ended up living on what he considers "his money," the inheritance left by his grandfather that was to have gone straight to Brandon.

Brandon suffered his own crisis of confidence about the future of the White minority in the new democratic South Africa. After his matric exams at the end of high school, he too decided it was time to see if he could find a better path in another part of the world. "There was just so much talking," he recalls. "So much fear. And people were angry. I was really negative too. I struggled to find work and that type of thing."

He left to join a traveling rock band in the United States and spent two years on the road with them as a set-up man, traveling through Canada and the "lower forty-eight." He spent a little time in the United Kingdom as well, and he considered moving to Holland. But in time, just like his father, Brandon came to realize that South Africa was really his home. He missed the mild weather and his own culture. Afrikaner values—close-knit families, conservative morals, inward-turning social relations—could not be duplicated elsewhere. And on the bright side, he explained, his fears about the political and social turmoil that might follow once the ANC consolidated its control turned out not to be entirely warranted. "I thought South Africa was doomed," he said. "It was only when I came back that I realized [that we are] obviously only reading all the bad—and I reckon you just have to be positive and try and make good, especially if it's somewhere you really want to live. So there's no point in being negative about it all the time. . . . I just didn't like England at all. I didn't like the amount of people—it was too busy. Here we have this outdoor lifestyle and space. And it is home, you know."

Of course, his home is a far more complex place than it was in his childhood. Brandon is often angry about just how his country treats him and his kind. The ANC's policies of redress, from affirmative action to Black Economic Empowerment, do not seem consonant with the idea that race should not matter. Indeed, to Brandon and many of his age-mates, these policies betray the public claims of the leadership—from Nelson Mandela onward—that the objective of the post-apartheid period would be to build a colorblind society. What is so colorblind about quotas, Brandon wants to know?

He gets the idea that, given centuries of oppression, it is time to "let others take the front seat." Yet he argues that the crime for which the ANC seeks redress—the crime of apartheid—was not his doing. No one in his generation had a say in White supremacy, but they are now the ones who see their options truncated. The past may have been wrong, but Brandon wants to know whether the present state of corruption and these new forms of racial discrimination are truly the right corrective.

He now lives in the southern suburbs of Cape Town, an area home to mainly English-speaking Whites. Rondebosch is a cosmopolitan, multicultural environment with a vibrant student community since the University of Cape Town is close by. Some neighborhoods here are upmarket, with leafy lanes that exude an air of stillness. Doctors and lawyers make their homes in

Rondebosch. This is where the leading schools of the province are located. Much like the Northerns he is familiar with, these southern enclaves are distant from the bustle of city life, but the urban setting is closer. Turning out of the smaller lanes onto the highways that lead to the city, the "crossroad economy" is alive. Street vendors come up to cars idling at a light, selling hand-made beaded artwork, paintings, hats, garbage bags, clothes hangers, or miniature fans. Whatever is in fashion will be offered for sale there by the side of the road, where drivers have to slow down for "robots," South African slang for "traffic lights."

Off the main road in Rondebosch, life is calm and the hassles of the crossroads are easily forgotten. The area where Brandon lived was slightly less wealthy than most of Rondebosch, which helps to explain why Coloured and Indian families have moved in alongside young Whites. Brandon rented the house he lived in, and he sublet to a number of students. Although situated in the suburbs, the house itself had fallen into a gentle shabbiness. A wooden gate swung on broken hinges, the driveway was unswept, littered with leaves, and bits of disintegrating junk mail had blown into flowerbeds. Despite its worn appearance, the house boasted a decent-sized swimming pool in the front garden, although it was often green, murky, and swamp-like despite Brandon's efforts to maintain it. A war was being waged with the landlord about general maintenance. There were always several towels hung up on the railing around the pool, various belongings scattered around the patio (surfboards, bicycles, odd bits of wood, empty beer bottles), and a rotting wooden cable wheel stood as a table on the patio surrounded by mismatching plastic chairs. The centerpiece of the patio was a large, well-constructed stainless steel braai inherited from Brandon's favorite grandfather, who made it by hand and passed it down lovingly through the generations.

After the landlord ended Brandon's lease and threatened to cause trouble over damage to the house, Brandon moved in with his father for a couple of months, back in the Northerns. They have never had an easy relationship but it is part of Afrikaner culture to pull together when someone in the family needs help. Brandon does get along well with his brother Mark, who he says shares his values and ideals. They also have same dry sense of humor and enjoy going on hikes—and hitting the bars.

It is in the company of his brothers that Brandon has revealed aspects of himself that had been invisible to us for months. Like many people in the Northerns, Mark is not too keen on Black South Africans. Nor is their youngest sibling, Danny, for that matter: he has been arrested for getting into fights and after making racist comments to groups of Black youths. Mark and Danny are quick to judge Black politicians corrupt, Black social movements as threatening to White interests (and to the stability of the country in general), Black people as untrustworthy, and efforts to address decades of discrimination as nothing more than reverse discrimination and therefore evidence of duplicity or hypocrisy. Apocalyptic visions of the country as a failed state, one step away from Mugabe's Zimbabwe, are often heard in their company.

In our presence, Brandon himself never seemed to reject or judge anyone on the basis of race. He spoke about having Black friends and was especially fond of those who got his sense of humor. He felt uncomfortable with "the k-word" ("kaffir") that some of his old neighbors still used. Yet Brandon never confronted anyone who expressed racist ideas: "I think it's wrong, but I don't have to force my world upon them." The awkwardness of the transition period following the end of apartheid, the daily challenge for Whites of revealing and then concealing racial animus, made Brandon something of a chameleon. It was tempting, at times, to think that he was deliberately concealing his true feelings. In the end, we decided this conclusion wasn't quite right. One side of Brandon remains the creature of his upbringing, the other is trying to find a place in a country that has changed dramatically in his lifetime. Both sides of Brandon are real.

We had seen similar ambivalence in Anna, the architect, who would patiently and firmly explain to us, time and again, that she did not agree at all with the racist views she would hear around the dinner table of her well-off family on their farm in Namibia. But she also said that she felt she could not challenge her family. It would be disrespectful to the elders, so instead Anna and her sisters would just mumble under their breath, "Well, it's not really like that," and squirm in their seats. Unlike Brandon, though, Anna was careful not to be put in a position where she could be interpreted as agreeing with her elders.

Anna was always much closer to living in a "rainbow nation" than Brandon. She was less distressed about her place in the country and more secure in her own multicultural identity. She felt German, Namibian, South African, and White, all at the same time. Mingling with the Afrikaner and English communities, she had also shared a high school classroom with Black and Coloured students, with whom she easily had become friends. Anna did not adopt a strong identity that she had to defend, hence she did not feel the sting of stigma that comes from belonging to the Afrikaner community that has been held responsible for all that is wrong with the past.

Why were the two so different? Anna's place in the upper middle class, several rungs above Brandon on the socioeconomic ladder, gave her a cosmopolitan persona that was virtually the opposite of Brandon's self-presentation as a working-class stiff. Anna's class background cultivated in her an ease with life, much like Daniel's, that gave her some distance from the complexities of South African existence. She had spent a year in Barcelona, not because she was troubled about the future of her own country or the place of White South Africans in it, but because she wanted to experience what life overseas was like, to immerse herself in the historic architecture of Spain's most flamboyant city, keen to make friends in different places. Easy-going, open-minded, and curious, Anna had a multicultural bunch of friends at the University of Cape Town and that allowed her to get closer to non-White communities in the country than many of her White peers.

Was it her family's money that eased her way into the life of an independent, confident young professional? Yes and no. She certainly knew that if she got into trouble she could fall back on her mother's or father's financial support. Though they are divorced, they are both supportive of their children. But there was more to Anna's confidence than that. Her store of cultural capital, bequeathed to her by a well-to-do family with countless connections to offer her, made a difference. There was never any question that Anna and her sisters would attend university. It has been a given that one day, when she has a family, her children too will attend college. Building on that solid foundation, she guided herself through her mid-twenties, navigating successfully through her architecture degree, part-time jobs, and world travel.

For most of the time we have known her, Anna's life in Kalk Bay was almost idyllic. Cozy in her little room in a seaside flat, Anna was entirely self-sufficient. She paid her rent and living expenses from the modest salary she was earning at the architectural firm in town, a job she had gotten, she said herself, "through connections." The savings she was able to build up helped her afford her post-graduation travel. Anna was frugal, keeping her expenses to rent and food, but she is also not particularly materialistic and had little desire for luxuries, apart from traveling and discovering places and cultures new to her. Part of this attitude toward money reflects the way she was raised. She was taught to expect that material things would not simply land in her lap. "We had enough [when we were children]," she explained, "but never abundance. When we wanted a bike, we had to wait till there was a special occasion." Her upbringing taught her how to save for such special occasions, and so, knowing that she would want to return to college, she had started drawing up a budget and making plans for the expenses. She would not be able to save enough in the months to come before school started, and she "hated asking [her] parents for money," but she knew that one of them would probably come through to help her with tuition. The rest she would manage on her own.

The upscale side of the seaside town of Muizenberg, near Kalk Bay, where Anna moved during her years as a student at the University of Cape Town, which is a train ride away.

When she completed her final year in architecture, Anna decided it was time to go and see a little more of the world. It wasn't that she was running away from South Africa. She had a sense of freedom and agency that allowed her to figure out how she could go about traveling the world on a tight budget. Anna studied carpentry and spent six months in Zanzibar learning Swahili. She finally went to Switzerland, where, through connections, she got a job at an architectural firm in Zurich, a place she described in a letter home as "rather expensive: imagine paying three times everything," and she continued to travel throughout Europe.

When we got together for coffee in 2012 during one of her short visits back home, we listened as she wondered out loud how long she would want to stay "overseas." Life is different there, she said: "People have so much." Here, in South Africa, her work could have more meaning, she was convinced of that. But she also wondered out loud whether she would want to raise children here, in Africa, or there in Europe. Would she not be able to give them more opportunities there? Would things improve for the better in South Africa or would it remain more insecure than what she had seen in her affluent environment in Switzerland? This insecurity about life and fear over public safety has not always been such a big part of life for young Whites in South Africa. Growing up during apartheid, Whites had the privilege of freedom and personal security because the separation of the races and strict curfews guaranteed that no "people of color" would hang around the upmarket "Whites only" areas in towns and suburbs. They were protected by total segregation. "I'm White," remembered one of Brandon's acquaintances.

> Life was great living under apartheid. . . . I was privileged . . . Apartheid was exceptionally good to me. . . . [and this was] generally true for White South Africans. I had the education, I had the schooling, I had sporting facilities, [and] later, in university, I was more involved and [had] more of a conscience. Otherwise being a White South African was a great thing.

Of course, Whites did interact with Black and Coloured people in a very limited and unequal way that at the time seemed simultaneously (and paradoxically) "normal" and unnatural. Brandon and his friends used to play with

The majestic Table Mountain is the backdrop to the more exclusive part of the city bowl, where well-to-do families live, surrounded by high walls.

the children of Black laborers, but they were never allowed to eat together or to visit each other's homes. One Afrikaner young man remembers wondering why his Black friend would never join him for dinner: "I had a Black friend when I was small, seven [or] six years old. It was our maid's boy. . . . We used to play like crazy, I could never understand why he couldn't sit at our dinner table, because his mother would drag him away." It had all seemed strange, but, when questions were asked, parents would dismiss them vaguely. In the end, Brandon, Anna, and many around them had come to understand that these friends were "different," that they would never be "on the same level." "If we were walking up the hill," Brandon recalled, "they would have to push the bicycle up for us. And if we were in the go-kart, then they'd be pushing us in the go-kart. That was something that was . . . it was just the way it was. It was normal."

The great South African playwright Athol Fugard captured this awkward sentiment in one of his best-known plays, *Master Harold and the Boys*, the tale

of a young White man during apartheid who thinks of his Black servant's son as his best friend until he awakens to the power he can wield because of his superior social position.

Even in relatively liberal White families, whether Afrikaans or English, separate and unequal treatment was most often "just the way it was." "It was them and us," says Keith, a young English-speaking White man in Anna's university circle of friends. "My folks taught us to respect everyone. We were not allowed to call the guy who worked in our garden a 'garden boy.' He was always a man and he was the gardener. And we were never allowed to call the domestic who worked in our house the 'housemaid' or the 'house girl.' She was a woman and she was our domestic helper. . . . And my folks were kind and looked after their domestics, you know, as well or better than most people would. But it was them and us, it was not to be shared."

Automatic understanding of the "way things were" had been the situation for generations. Karen, Anna's mother, recalls how she too "accepted it the way it was." "You wouldn't argue it or fight it," she says. "And I went to an Afrikaans school as well. So I was pretty much brought up in an Afrikaans, what would they say, *vreeslik nationale* [terribly patriotic] environment, you know, very much for the Whites." In turn, Karen never spoke with her children about politics and why race relations were the way they were. Anna does not raise the past with her older relatives, knowing it would be impossible to question any of it with her mother or especially her grandparents. For many of that generation, things then were "exactly right." Johan, Anna's grandfather, spoke about how his relationships with Black workers had always been "good" but never closer than a strictly boss-to-worker hierarchy, as he believes it was intended to be. He maintains that even today it is a good thing that most Black people remain living on the peripheries of the cities. Should, for example, more Black people (he calls them "workers") move into his own area of Sea Point, it would quickly deteriorate, he is sure. It is best to keep the races separate. He adds, "That may sound racist, but it is true."

A CULTURE OF FEAR

The protections enveloping Whites unraveled in the 1980s as the anti-apartheid movement mushroomed into an international sanctions movement. Internal politics became more fraught and violent. ANC targets were always intentionally military or police-related, but the mere fact that a Black army was swelling in the midst of the right-wing state was enough to send waves of apprehension through the White communities. Mariza, a young Afrikaans woman, was ten in 1989. She dimly remembers what the transition period felt like to those on the "wrong side of history."[5] It was, she says,

> quite scary, because we all kind of realized that this was a small bubble that we were living in. . . . There was this fear of terrorists. . . . In the farming communities at the time, or even before transition, there were a lot of . . . attacks. My grandfather was murdered [on a farm]. That kind of made people very fearful, because it just seemed that there would be this complete lawlessness. And these weren't political attacks. That is what also really shocked people; these were just armed robberies. . . . These [White] people had something, and they'd usually been [foremen] on the farm, and you know that kind of thing. . . . After that happened, a lot of farm security came on board. Like previously our house was left open all the time, and suddenly you lock the house at night, and alarms were put in.

Then in the 1990s, the long-awaited turn to freedom for Black and Coloured South Africans instantly became an impossible and perilous situation for many Whites. Whites on the political left, many of whom had gone into exile and supported the sanctions movement, joined their African allies in celebrating the impending downfall of the racist regime, and many veterans of the struggle returned home to participate in building the new "rainbow nation." Other liberal White thinkers too, those who had stayed in the country more quietly disagreeing with the state of apartheid, savored the possibility that the apartheid rule was coming to an end. For them, the idea of a "nonracist, nonsexist real South Africa" finally seemed possible; times were "very, very exciting," the air filled with celebration.

But for thousands of White South Africans, the end of apartheid was the beginning of the end of their way of life, or so they believed. Some Black people, including Amanda and her family, spoke openly of their hopes to be able to move into "the houses of White people." Needless to say, families like the Bowleses and their neighbors in the Northerns were not keen on that idea. In places like Newlands, many families began packing their bags.

Brandon and Anna are too young to remember much about the period that followed Nelson Mandela's election in 1994, but they do recall that the adults around them were apprehensive, that they were saying that their social world was "going to change so much." The two just didn't understand why. Suddenly people around them were talking about wanting to leave the country or were stocking up their cupboards with tinned and dried food, preparing for the worst. Karen told us, "Especially the Afrikaans people, a lot of them were talking about the big danger. . . . People didn't know what was going to happen. There was so much insecurity."

For Brandon's mother, Gerda, and her friends, the memory of that time twenty years ago induces a shiver and mourning for a lost world. "Everybody was scared," Gerda says, "because we thought . . . they were going to take our houses, because they had already promised [that] for years." Her friend Anita concurs: "I was so scared, I promise you. That day when I went to vote, I cried. I was so scared. I thought it would change just like that and they [would] throw us all out."

Some of Brandon's friends were removed by their parents from the government schools they attended and shifted into private schools, an outmigration familiar to Americans who remember the white panic in the South after the *Brown v. Board of Education* decision by the US Supreme Court, declaring that "separate" could never be "equal" and hence paving the way for school desegregation. White flight into private institutions accelerated rapidly thereafter. Even those who were slightly less panicked were nonetheless concerned about the potential loss of their property, their sources of income, and their ability to provide for their children. "It was very uncertain," explained Karen, Anna's mother.

> It could have gone another way. A lot of credit must go to those politicians. . . . It could have changed completely the other way round. Sort of a Zimbabwe scenario. You [didn't] know what could have happened. And people were anxious. . . . A lot left in 1994, or just before, just after, because of the uncertainty. . . . A lot of them went to Australia, New Zealand, and a lot from the German community went back to Germany. Whether that's now better for them I don't know. But they just said crime already had started to increase at that time, and they didn't know what education would be like for the children. And . . . because of affirmative action they were scared of losing their jobs.

Violent retribution for decades of suppression was a specter haunting the Whites of South Africa, and while this never transpired as a political movement, violence of another kind did indeed grow quickly. Crime—robbery, burglary, street assaults—became the staple of the evening news and the consequences touched the lives of both Brandon and Anna. Karen was attacked in her house in 1993, after coming back from dropping her children at kindergarten. Homeowners started erecting walls and fences around their properties in desperate attempts to keep themselves and their families safe. Many sought weapons training in order to be able to protect themselves from the "*Swart gevaar*"—the perceived "Black danger" posed by the majority group. One of Brandon's friends told us: "My mum remembers all the White [farm] women being trained on how to use a pistol and that kind of stuff . . . by the police, the army."

Brandon and his friends "used to camp in the back garden, and then crime and stuff started really suddenly." Now they had to get used to living behind locked doors. Anna too remembers the moment that her neighbors started raising fences around their houses, topped with jagged glass or barbed wire, in Pretoria, where she lived as a child. Where Anna could once run straight from her back door, through the garden, and onto the street, she now had to navigate a fortress. She felt isolated and claustrophobic.

> If you walk through the streets of Pretoria, you see these high fences. Everyone has a dog, everybody has an alarm system, every house has barbed wire around it and electric fencing. . . . When I was a child, the house had a big front garden and big back garden. The front garden was just grassed and looks onto the street. . . . Black cleaning ladies used to sit there and chat with their friends—and kids used to play there. . . . It must have been 1994 when crime generally started increasing, a lot of houses got broken into, and suddenly everybody started putting up fences. . . . People . . . now have walls with barbed wire, and always have dogs. . . . We used to climb over and through the fence, and then people made their fences too small for children to fit through.

Anna detested the burglar bars and the barbed wire. She swore that she would never live like that once she was grown up and could make decisions for herself.

> I could not live in a gated community because I feel it inhibits my freedom . . . and I feel like a bird in a golden cage. People can't visit me and I can't visit people—I'd like my house to be open, for people who'd like to come in . . . and I feel it creates a non-space between all these fenced-off areas. So I never liked it, even when I was younger.

Given this high level of White fear, it is almost ironic that the most devastating impact of crime, especially violent crime, falls on poor people, mainly

Wealthy suburban households are barricaded behind wrought-iron bars, electrified barbed wire, and security cameras. South Africa has one of the highest levels of inequality in the world and notorious crime problems that disproportionately impact the poorest areas but generate anxiety in rich neighborhoods as well.

those Black and Coloured residents of the townships. South Africa is consistently identified as one of the most dangerous countries in the world, with a murder rate that is more than four times higher than the international average of approximately 7 per 100,000—the country's murder rate is at 31.9 per 100,000, and the attempted murder rate is about the same: 31 per 100,000.[6] Most murders in South Africa happen within family or friendship circles, but they are concentrated mainly in areas with high poverty levels. On the other hand, aggravated robbery, carjacking, and house burglaries that often turn violent keep the higher-income communities on edge. Between 2002 and 2010, South African crime figures indicated a 100 percent increase in house break-ins.[7]

The iron control of the apartheid regime had meant that people of color could not move about freely and were under constant police surveillance. Wynand, a White farmer of the Eastern Cape whom we visited, remembers very well the apartheid-era curfews that meant that White areas would remain "White only" after a certain time, which meant he felt perfectly safe. "In Upington [a rural town in the Northern Cape]," he remembered, "at nine o'clock a siren went off: no Coloureds in that town. If Blacks were out after that time, they were put in jail. That was the best time for me as a White to live there."

When freedom of movement was restored, not only liberty but crime returned. This helps account for the despair expressed by many White South Africans. Yet Black people were far more vulnerable to crime. Thandiswa's sister Abbie, for example, fled Khayelitsha for the Eastern Cape to protect her family from attacks. She blamed Nelson Mandela for increasing disorder and the crime that crept into her world as a result. When we asked Abbie whether it wasn't of paramount importance to strike a blow for freedom, she answered, "Freedom for what? Freedom to starve? Freedom to worry about assaults if my children go outside?" She felt safer under the apartheid state because she was not a political activist and worried more about street safety, which declined markedly as apartheid fell, as she sees it.

Abbie originally had thought things would be better after the end of apartheid, and she was disappointed when it seemed to her that they were not. The members of the White middle and upper class had *expected* the situation to deteriorate, and they were worried that they would become the target of revenge for the repression of Blacks under the old regime. Their fear is reflected in the security measures around their houses. The sense of vulnerability remains.

Amelia, an Afrikaans-speaking young woman committed to the new democracy, wonders how much more fear and violence she can take:

> I mean, to be quite honest, often I've wondered ... what's the point [when] you say, "I can't live here anymore"? ... Within my family, we've all experienced quite a lot of violence. Like I've been mugged at knifepoint, my mum was hijacked at gunpoint, my grandfather was murdered. I almost feel like, "How much closer does it have to get ... until I'm like raped, and then will I leave?" Or will I not? ... I think that where the defining line [is] for me is when I no longer feel safe within my own home. And I've felt like that at times. Like I was house-sitting once and someone broke into the house ... People really do have this fear of violence. .... I love South Africa, but it's such a sad happy country.

STAYING OR LEAVING?

Many Whites have left the country. Exact data are hard to come by, but according to analyses contributed by the South African Institute of Race Relations, approximately 16 percent of the White population left during 1995–2005, an exodus of 500,000–800,000 people in a decade.[8] Since then, the figures have increased, with a surge after 2007–8, it seems, possibly related to the ousting of Thabo Mbeki, Mandela's successor as president, and Jacob Zuma's run for the presidency. In 2008, figures indicated a continued "high rate of emigration of those who reach working age in the White population group." Large numbers of those from ages fifteen to thirty-nine are leaving the country, and this is often cited as representing a "brain drain" from the country.[9] Emigration is facilitated by the fact that many South Africans—especially those who are highly skilled—are dual nationals with a passport from elsewhere. Many South Africans of English descent, for example, can apply for a so-called "ancestry visa" to allow them easy entry into the United Kingdom.

Many more, it seems, may be set to go. The *Business Day* newspaper, based in Johannesburg, reported that "about 20% of South Africans planned to emigrate or were seriously considering it, according to a survey published in May 2008 by a global market research company, Synovate. The option to emigrate was most popular among young and middle-aged South Africans, the group with the most valuable skills."[10] A more recent study conducted with close to 1,300 students at the University of Johannesburg indicated that 66 percent had contemplated leaving South Africa and settling elsewhere. The majority of those were either White or Coloured—but Black students too had considered leaving the country.[11]

Employment insecurity plays a significant role in outmigration. Suburban residents blame ANC policies, particularly Black Economic Empowerment and affirmative action, for their predicament in the labor market. Many see these policies as favoring people of color only on the basis of skin tone, not on competency. To this they add frustration at what is widely perceived (at least by major newspapers and opposition politicians), as overwhelming government corruption. These forces undermine entirely any sense of trust in government, and a deep cynicism has set in: government is incompetent, having taken institutions that functioned well and destroyed them through favoritism.

The Cape Town newspaper *Business Day* maintains a website with figures on emigration and where readers can post their stories. Readers also can post anonymous reactions, and many of these reinforce the view that the political machine in South Africa has killed any chance of functioning social services and left citizens with no reason to believe that things will ever improve. As one put it:

> I made a promise when I got married 17 years ago that no matter what I will protect my family even if it means that I have to relocate to a foreign land. I did not vote for apartheid [to continue] in 1990. Currently finalizing my MBA studies in SA and busy sourcing great opportunities [overseas] to secure a future where you can sleep at night, not spend a fortune on security systems and pay additional guards to patrol streets at night. Why is all this necessary? Already 13 years into a new democracy and it seems nothing has changed in the African culture.
>
> I left SA for good in May 2006, taking my wife and two children with me. . . . My people are now being tortured, murdered and raped just for being White, yet the government refuses to acknowledge SA has a severe crime problem and the police are unbelievably ineffectual.

Similar sentiments were in the news in 2009, with the well-publicized case of a young White South African filing for refugee status in Canada, based on a "well-founded fear of persecution on the grounds of his race." He claimed to fear "discrimination, harassment and possibly death" if he were to return to South Africa.[12]

Many White expats continue to hurl unbridled and racist criticism from a distance. But White South Africans are not united in their opinions. Some have become more optimistic about the fate of their country and have started to argue that all this talk of departure is a mistake. Sally-Jane,

a young woman responding to the debate over "the need to leave" on a local youth blog, asserted, "I love this place and I am not leaving. I will fight
and I will help and I will work to make this a better SA for all. I have a responsibility to do that. I have a duty to my country and to the millions who
suffered when I benefited."

In fact, many Whites who departed have since decided to return.[13] Others
wish they could come back now that they have had a close look at the alternatives. Johan, Anna's grandfather, noted that many who left at the time of the
transition are now looking for a way back. The quality of life in South Africa,
he says, and the spaciousness, is hard to do without. "Nowhere in the world
do you get a landscape like this." But he also thinks that those who left never
really feel at home elsewhere in the world, "especially the Afrikaners—they
were the first Whites to really settle, [and] this is their home." Bianca, a White
South African who is much younger than Johan, has been thinking about
leaving, but she too knows that life "overseas" isn't all that wonderful.

> I know that a lot of South Africans who leave the country have a hard life,
> like, you know, . . . not just your standard of living, but a hard life because
> you never fit in, and you miss your country. And I think it sounds very
> romantic and up in the air, but people do—people pine for their country
> until they die. And I met some people in Canada who were like that. They
> were so sad. Like, I just wanted to say to them, "Go home, go home! Like,
> you guys are so sad, you eat *bobotjie*, and you talk about home the whole
> time. Just go home!" Ja . . . So I don't want to be one of those.[14]

After a period of time "on the outside," homesickness coupled with the
knowledge that the country has actually managed the transition fairly peace-
fully leads—at times—to return. Many Whites recognize that South Africa
has managed something unusual: a fairly orderly transition from something
close to an autocratic society to a living democracy. As Rob, a friend of Brandon's, explained, it seems that the predictions of the ANC are coming true,
and while there are still "lots of problems, it's a thing that can be made right—
and we can all live in harmony together."

Of course, this optimism can easily run aground when the nightly news
of crime strikes fear into the hearts of Whites, who then imagine themselves
the next victims. Like his sister, Brandon avoids the television news and the
tabloid press, keeping his distance from the endless list of violent attacks or
exposés about corruption. Ignoring the bad news makes it easier to stay positive. But it's not a sure-fire strategy and it often fails. When Brandon looks

around for institutions that might provide solutions to problems like crime, he cannot find them. The ANC government does not seem concerned with the issues that bother White people, in his view. The more power they have, the less confidence Brandon has that anything will improve.

This sober recognition inspired him to take political action. In the run-up to the 2009 elections, Brandon staged a Facebook campaign to get all his friends who had emigrated to exercise their vote to make sure that the ANC would not gain full majority rule—a situation that, as was constantly repeated by opposition parties, would give them the power to amend the constitution unilaterally and to shift power away from the local government structures to the national government. The debate on Brandon's Facebook wall went viral, with racist slurs threaded among moderate voices trying to temper the rage. South Africa, said many of those friends living abroad, is "going down the drain," because the ANC is corrupt, because the needs of White people are no longer taken into account, and—again—because of crime and violence.[15] These worries were sometimes fused to the old apartheid ideology, which counsels that interracial mixing is a recipe for disaster:

> L: I don't even recognize the current regime of black domination and ma-
> jority politics. Who is standing up for ME and MY people? Who is
> standing up for MY culture?? NO ONE. I am against mixing, inbreed-
> ing, trampling of the Whites. Fuck the "New SA."
>
> H: But us Whites are still grabbing at straws. The current ORDER is ANTI-
> white in its ENTIRETY. Ai, the poor misled white people—they all wor-
> ship that woman [Helen Zille, leader of the Democratic Alliance (DA)]
> now. They believe . . . that the DA will make a paradise of SA. We whites
> WANTED to give them control, we WANTED to sit with the boys
> arms-around-the-waist *HAND OM DIE LYF* [supportive and friendly],
> we WANTED their "peace" . . . and now yeah, WE'VE GOT IT!! Only
> God will be able to help us.

Others countered by pointing at the willingness of so many to make this multiethnic country work, the strong economy, and areas of progress. Some straight out rejected the racist angle:

> G: You high-holies might just get a big surprise hereafter. I don't think God
> likes discrimination. . . . You use God as a motivation for hate, racism
> and brainwashing. . . . It's disgusting. . . . I'm glad your time is over. You
> make me ashamed to be an Afrikaner.

T: I'm just amazed at the utterly racist comments that have been made by some here. It is hate from both sides, where is the middle way then? . . . My actual opinion is . . . if everyone feels so strongly that there is no party for them, then . . . seeing as we are living in a "democratic" country, establish your own party!

Racist or not, Brandon's friends agreed that the ANC was "not their party." The more extreme voices claimed that not even the DA, the former National Party, represents their needs anymore, as the party now has Coloured and Black members. They are not alone with their sentiments. Years after the election, in May 2011, one freelance Afrikaner reporter summarized the mood this way: "The feeling among the Afrikaner community is that of isolation, withdrawal and ignorance about South African life. Many of us refuse to entertain politics because we are formally unrepresented in the national debate and thus we are at the mercy of 'die swart gevaar.'"[16]

The disconnect from the present political reality is not limited to the Afrikaner community. Even Anna, with her open and liberal ideas and dreams of a true "rainbow nation," would tell us she had never actually engaged with post-apartheid politics. When she eventually did talk about politics, she did so very cautiously. "I don't know, for me, even when I voted last time, I didn't think about it too much; it didn't affect me too much. . . . I feel I've been sheltered from politics. My family isn't very political at all." She attributes the apolitical stance of her family mostly to the fact that they are German Namibian, and so they would therefore automatically feel disconnected from South African politics, but race figures as well: "My gran would *never* vote for a Black party, *ever*. She just wouldn't, because they're Black and not her."

Since the power positions have changed, the older generations of Anna's parents and grandparents can no longer regard the current government as "their government." "It must've been a bit different when the apartheid government was ruling," she says. "I don't know, but I think my parents probably felt . . . that their views were represented more then than now. . . . I think my parents and many other people from their generation feel that the government doesn't represent their views . . . because it's a different culture, a different race, I guess, but not them. It's not their government really. They would never call it 'our government.' [For them it is] 'the government,' 'the South African government.'"

Among Brandon and his friends, the ANC's social restitution programs are a major thorn in the side. Pieter shook with emotion as he tried to express how much he loves his country, how much he wants to stay, but how alienated he has become:

> [The ANC] makes it extremely hard for a White South African to vote for them . . . nothing they've said, nothing they're pitching at us, nothing they're telling us is convincing us at all. Especially during this time when we are in this phase, if you call it that, where employment, or getting employed is a very, very hard thing to do. . . .
>
> When I ask people, you know, "What do you find is the biggest issue when trying to find a job?' . . . the first thing that always comes to mind, especially with White people, is Black Economic Empowerment. The typical story always goes that you've got a person who's got a couple of degrees somewhere, somehow . . . actually I think the story was some person tried to enroll into university, he got the grade requirements more than sufficiently, [but] he was told straight up: "You would be accepted, but in order to accommodate previously disadvantaged people you are not allowed in."
>
> This makes it extremely hard for a White South African to just cope with everything here. It's come to the point where we cannot tolerate it any more. It's come to the point where you're getting quite a lot of radical ideas and thoughts.

Young White South Africans argue that they were not part of the machinery of apartheid, and they do not agreed with its philosophy, yet they are asked to bear the consequences of redress for its failures. A newspaper blog captures this sentiment well, in the reply of a young man who had decided to leave the country: "My reasons [for leaving] were simple . . . no opportunities for white men. I was too young to be part of the process of apartheid yet I was discriminated against for being White. My chances of promotion were severely minimized because every company I worked for was terrified of having a white man promoted above any other race."

This kind of discourse is openly reinforced by leaders of the Democratic Alliance Party, whose campaign literature argues that ANC policies are a form of reverse discrimination and will ultimately be the undoing of the country, not just because they are unfair but because they will place unqualified people in positions of importance, undermine the nation's efficiency, and "re-racialize" a country now committed to the colorblind strategy articulated by Mandela back in 1994.[17] Brandon and his friends reject the apartheid regime because it was, in Pieter's estimation, "just wrong." Yet they also think that the playing field today is closer to being level than most Black people would credit.

Black youth counter that this perspective ignores the ways in which the past isn't really past. The damage of apartheid has, they argue, created after-effects that have saddled them with unwelcome burdens. The social fabric of their communities and families was destroyed by forced removals, inferior and inadequate education crippled their parents in the labor market and ensured that they would lack the cultural, social, and economic capital to foster mobility in succeeding generations. As one young Black student at the University of Cape Town put it in an editorial, "It's not about whether or not there exists a group of genuine White people who embrace Black people as equals."

> It is about the past injustices suffered collectively by black people under the hands of white dominance, from colonialism through to apartheid, right through to a racialised economic ownership under the democratic black led government. . . . The inequalities we often see, whether [in] income, ownership of industries, spatial inequalities . . . infrastructure for education, private health etc. in suburban areas, often favours white people . . . over the black majority. . . .
>
> Let us be frank, the white people in this country continue to live a life of privilege, not because the ANC government is engineering this, but simply because the structure of the economy dictates it be this way. . . . If white people were genuine [about social equality] they would be at the forefront of preaching land redistribution. . . . No white person in this country has [failed to] directly or indirectly . . . benefit from the brutal history of colonialism and apartheid.

Brandon and his friends do not take issue with this account of the past, but they resent having to take the blame for it now. From Brandon's perspective, "the past was wrong but it was the past, and let's now move on." He utterly rejects the claim that he has been the beneficiary of apartheid—his parents, perhaps, but surely not his generation. And if their age group has not benefited, then "why should I apologize?" one of his friends asks. Adam, another friend, feels his life has been hijacked by history: "Our generation rather resents being saddled with all this horseshit. . . . I'm pissed off that I've passively inherited all of these hang-ups and these sort of half-formed racial instincts. . . . Yet having to pay the price or having to take the back seat because your dad had the front seat before doesn't feel fair."

The full impact of the past on the present and future of the rising generation is not easily grasped. Social media sites, blogs, and face-to-face encounters often throw simplistic solutions in the air, leaving people like Brandon
without many tools to sort out what is wrong or right, what is feasible or a pipe
dream. Accordingly, he is often not sure what he really believes and is prone
to shifting positions from one sentence to the next. At times he has insisted
that it *is* time for Blacks to "take a front seat," seeing that Whites did benefit so
much from the past. But it has been difficult for him to come to terms with the
lingering inequality that makes it hard to claim that seat if one needs skills or
contacts to secure it. So in the next moment Brandon's voice rose in irritation
over the lack of fairness involved in remedial policies.

> I think a lot of young White guys, we haven't benefited from the new
> government. And then, of course, we grow up sort of not benefiting from
> the old government, so we only see it as bad instead of good. And there's
> more crime, and there's probably more poverty and more shit going on.
> And life's become harder for us. Even if it's become better for the general
> population, which I'm not even so sure about. But the new government
> hasn't done us any favors at all. I mean, there's adverts on television go-
> ing, "Old Mutual are selling shares, but only to Black people." And it gets
> you angry [because] it's supposed to be fair now, and it's really unfair. So
> I don't know."

While Brandon doesn't put much action behind these opinions other
than sighs and an occasional bout of activism during election season, he has
friends who are edging toward a kind of radicalism that could be dangerous.
Pieter asks, "How much can you tolerate? You come to this point of desperation where you really become fed up, completely fed up, and then you seek
alternatives: leave the country or resort to crime, you know."
    Brandon and his young White male peers are not unusual. National sur-
veys of social attitudes make it clear that Whites widely oppose policies of racial redress.[18] Eighty-seven percent of White respondents reject the idea that
"there should be preferential hiring and promotion of black South Africans
in employment," 84 percent oppose the notion that "government should give
preferential contracts and tax breaks to Black business," and 82 percent reject
the statement that "government should pay money to the victims of apartheid
as reparation for the history of discrimination."[19] This opposition is especially
strong in the Afrikaner community.[20] The opposite is not limited by age, however. Young White adults, despite growing up in the new, democratic South

Africa, oppose these policies as much the older White generations do.[21] The prospects for racial reconciliation are not improved by the punishing consequences of the worldwide recession that has taken a profound toll on the labor market prospects of the younger generation in South Africa and in much of Europe and the United States. When opportunity abounds and jobs are there for the taking, it is easier to accept remedial policies because there is enough to go around. When unemployment rises to 25 percent, as it has in South Africa, too many people of all colors scramble for a piece of the pie. Sadly, despite the complaints voiced by Brandon and so many of his friends, it remains the case that unemployment is far worse for Black people in South Africa. But relative deprivation has its own consequences, and that is an important part of the dynamic in the Afrikaner community: they are worse off than they were in the past, even if they remain more privileged than those they have grown to resent.

Some, like Anna, genuinely recognize the structural disadvantages of the past and the constraints on Black mobility that operate today. Even so, BEE and affirmative action are simply too much for them to have to deal with. Anna is clearly aware of the unequal education offered in her own upmarket suburb where she grew up, and the schools in the townships:

> The Black schools there, in the Black areas, they'll learn about microscopes and this and that, and how to do a litmus test and stuff, but no child there has ever *seen* a microscope in their lives. . . . At Westerford [the school she had attended] they gave us such good resources and you can basically, just by attending all the classes . . . you can easily get 80 percent marks, you can really just get that. Whereas in Khayelitsha . . . [there are no such resources in the schools].

Anna realizes also how severe the consequences of apartheid urban planning have been. She knows that her suburban life has been so much easier than that of those who were deliberately placed at the peripheries of the cities.

> I can't believe how well planned it was, if that was your aim. Like if your aim was to disadvantage people, then they have definitely succeeded. I think we also learned . . . that . . . they [apartheid urban planners] planned the routes especially so that people would have a really long way to travel. So instead of going straight from A to B, they have to go from here, to there, to there, to there. . . . I think they've looked at it a lot, the planners at UCT [University of Cape Town] and they're trying to rectify it, but it's obviously a slow process.

Yet despite this social awareness, Anna too has felt discriminated against, and she had felt deeply frustrated when asked to tick a box designating her race on her application form for university entrance. She felt she was putting herself "into a box" and that "this is racism, you know, it's nothing else." She was not accepted to the program she chose, because people of color were ahead of her in line for entry into medical school. Even though redress of past inequalities is necessary, she bridles at the idea that this is the way to right a wrong. Just like Brandon, Anna swings back and forth between a rejection of the process and an acceptance that concerted effort is needed to redress a past in which inequality was purposely created.

Not all White youths we spoke to reject policies like BEE, but liberal voices are not heard among them that often, and they are definitely heard even less often among Afrikaans youths. Mike, an English-speaking young man at the University of Cape Town, told us that he thinks BEE "spooks people more than anything else. I mean everyone says, 'Oh, reverse racism, why should we stick around here?' . . . but I think that there's a lot of negative press attached to BEE, when I actually personally feel it's a very positive thing. I support it 100 percent. . . . I don't think that change is going to happen without it."

Sigrid, Anna's sister, was among those who took a strong stance when she said that she generally found that White males "are still incredibly advantaged and they like to complain a lot." She said, "I think that the greatest apathy is among White males . . . [who] should get off their butts . . . it's really up to them—there's so many opportunities to become entrepreneurial and to do business stuff in South Africa—and I think it's a pity that they do not take more charge of it. And it's always like, 'Oh, I'm a poor White male who can't get a job.'"

A young woman in Brandon's group of friends agreed, noting, "White people have to be more resourceful than they had to be in the past . . . stop bitching and moaning about it." Anna's mother, Karen, who herself experienced the consequences of BEE when she said she had to "sit back just to give other people the chance," agrees too. Rather than feeling resentful, she feels young White South Africans should shift their focus and take ownership of the situation: "What's to suffer? You've just got to put your shoulder to the wheel and work just as hard as everybody else. . . . There's no place under the sun for you now that is reserved for you. You will just have to work as hard as everybody else."

Michal, an English young man of Jewish background, also expressed a resoundingly positive attitude toward BEE, racial quotas, and general restorative justice in the country. Seated at a café in one of the inner-city suburbs that overlook the Cape Town skyline and harbor, he spoke with passion about how growth will not be possible without providing extra opportunities for those who experienced discrimination. Asked what he thought about, for example, racial quotas at UCT, he answered:

> I think it's fantastic. . . . It's very important to have racial policies at the university. Man, forget the Whites, get as many Black students as possible . . . this is why apartheid ended, you know. Let's educate the rest of this country. Get more Black businesses in this country . . . it can only be good. . . . And BEE, the same, man. . . . I haven't been in the position yet where I don't get a job because someone else, a Black guy is given the job. But I think that I will be okay if that does happen.
>
> . . . In terms of ideology, I believe it's the right thing to happen. . . . But not to give someone an opportunity just because of their skin color, but people who are getting the jobs are highly qualified . . . it's a myth that they're taking Blacks without any qualifications, and putting them into top jobs because of BEE—it's a myth. It doesn't exist, and if it does exist it's a bloody stupid way to run a company. There's brilliant Black people in this country, with brilliant qualifications and minds. If they get a job ahead of me, with the same qualifications, I'll deal with it, man, we're trying to build up the country here.

Michal believes that Whites complain too much about BEE and affirmative action and that they are too used to having the advantage. "I went out last night to this bar, and there was this guy . . . telling everyone how's he's a professional lawyer and his work's at stake because of BEE. . . . I was saying how I won't be able to get a job in a law firm because I've got dreadlocks, and he said, 'No, you won't get a job in a law firm because you're White.' It's just . . . so lame, it's so old and it's so lame." Michal saw current policies in the broader framework of remaining structural constraints and inequalities:

> UCT didn't create the (racial) categories . . . they still exist. Apartheid fucked up this country good and proper. . . . You can't suddenly say, "Apartheid's finished, let's ignore it." Because if you do, apartheid's not ever going to finish, you're still going to have Black people living out in Khayelitsha and not in the universities, you're still going to have Whites living in towns and in the private schools. . . .
>
> You need to actively take steps to fix it, and UCT, the way they need to do that [is] by saying, "Cool, if you were considered as Black we're going

to deal with you in this way, and if you were White we'll deal with you in that way." Hopefully it won't be there forever, you know.

Many Whites, however, were skeptical of more than policies for social redress. The perception of high levels of corruption in every rank of the ANC, coupled with its quest for "total power," has led to high levels of mistrust and vocal worries about the end of democracy.[22]

> BRANDON: Why do they [the ANC] want two-thirds [a two-thirds majority in the elections]? Because obviously they want to shake things up, hey? Because otherwise they'd be happy with winning by, I dunno, 60 percent or something, but they want more.
>
> PIETER: It strikes me as a party that wants absolute power. And that's never a good thing. . . . So the problem is trust. I don't trust the ANC at all. I see no reason to trust them at all.

PROUDLY AFRIKAANS?

Brandon and his Afrikaner age-mates have given a lot of thought to where they fit in South African society. They are searching for a way to maintain an Afrikaner identity that stands at a distance from the radical racial Afrikaner philosophy of the past, which was "just wrong," while maintaining those parts of the culture and its values that have nothing to do with racial hierarchies.

The "tightness" of Afrikaner communities with their prescriptive rules also meant they were caring and supportive toward insiders. People looked out for one another and still do, especially in the rural farming areas where families often live several kilometers away from their closest neighbor and remain dependent on one another to send warnings about flooded roads or seek help because a car has broken down. Houses are warm and welcoming, with food and hospitality on offer for the odd visitor. Gender roles and responsibilities are clear and strict, as an acquaintance in the Eastern Cape explained: "Ninety-five percent of Afrikaner women will still do the cooking, and the man stands outside with his buddies. . . . Today, the younger generations, the women are starting to become an equal partner. But on the farms, no. Even until today, the man doesn't cook—he doesn't even think he may be allowed in the kitchen."

Life doesn't change quickly or easily in Afrikaner communities. One of the farmers we met out on a vast tract of dairy land in the Eastern Cape observed, "I don't think there was ever any farmer or *boertjie* that liked any change." When the time of the transition came, and relationships between farmers and workers were supposed to change to the benefit of the workers, "nothing changed really." Wynand left his farm years before we met him, when a severe drought struck the province and the farm was failing. Yet he carried a sense of stasis on his shoulders. Nothing changes; nothing should.

> [In the north], in Gauteng, there it is especially clear, there it is Afrikaans, nothing else. No Colour[ed or Black people], you are White and whatever you do is right. You are Afrikaans, you rule. That's how it is. . . . They were against this change [the transition]. You vote no in that election [the referendum organized by the National Party at the very end of apartheid, to ask whether Whites could agree with a change of power structures]. No Blacks. No, [you are] against. They still live like that. . . . The government changed, but nothing changed. You still live like that. . . . They [Blacks] have to still say "*baas*" [master].

Against this cultural backdrop, the world *did* shift under their feet. We heard bitter complaints about the labor rights that had been extended to the farm workers, how it was simply impossible to work "like that" on a farm. Wynand claimed to have always treated his workers fairly. He gave them "one sheep to eat every two weeks" and did not charge his "labor" any rent to stay on his land. But he railed against the union rules that now dominate farmwork:

> Now they want to do teatime, lunchtime, and all that. . . . [At] one o clock they have to [go back to their places] for an hour and do nothing, and five o clock they [go for the day]. And I mean it does not work like that . . . on a farm. . . . And there is a scale [minimum wage] that they have to be paid. . . . So it is a bit more difficult for the farmers [now] . . . and they know about it, the workers. So there is no way [you can avoid it] . . . they expect it, this is the way the government wants it to be now, so it must be like that.

With the opening up of the international markets since the end of apartheid, large multinationals have moved into the South African farming and especially food distribution industries. Price setting for the commodities they offer is now determined by large supermarket chains and distribution companies like Parmalat or Nestle that decide how much milk, for example, they will buy from which farmer, under which conditions, and at which price. The practice pits neighbor against neighbor and makes it particularly hard for smaller landholders who lack economies of scale. All the while, the amount of land that is under cultivation is decreasing. In the apartheid years, farmers were heavily subsidized, but those supports decreased sharply as the ANC shifted public spending priorities to the needs of the majority. Today farmers rail about the loss of these critical investments and are bailing out, selling to agribusiness firms willing to offer a good price. The farmers hold back some land and start game parks or lodges that appeal to tourists. This is their only hope, the farmers complain. They cannot make it in the agricultural business that was their ancestral way of life. They believe that land claim cases will pull the land out from under them.

Up until now, the approach to land redistribution in post-apartheid South Africa has been based on the willing buyer–willing seller principle. Although the constitution provides a clause for expropriation, it has never been applied. The majority of land remains in White hands, yet farmers often complain about land restitution claims. Wynand explained to us that a friend and fellow farmer had been sued by a Khoi family that claimed to have been the original owners of his farm. The government conducted research, found that the land belonged to the Khoi 300 years ago, and took the land, paying market value to the farmer, who had to sell. His story seems practically impossible, as the constitution only provides the opportunity for people to log land restitution claims for dispossessions that happened after 1913.[23] Yet Afrikaner farmers do wonder about the future of South African agriculture. In their minds, the government is creating a disastrous situation. One older farmer, Kobus, almost shouted at us in despair:

> It cannot be sustainable the way it's going now, because the people who are running the country do not know what they're doing . . . they do not understand how important agriculture is for the country. . . . South Africa made its own fertilizers . . . today most of it's imported. . . . Electricity . . . why has electricity got out of control? Because it hasn't been managed. . . . Now they face a huge problem. Now we have blackouts, blackouts cost money. . . . I've had to buy a generator!

Another farmer explained how there used to be a state veterinary service during apartheid that offered free care of his livestock. It exists no more, or, as he said, it had "gone to the dogs" and now "you are supposed to just look after yourself."

One of the most liberal Afrikaner women we spoke with in the Eastern Cape explained this sentiment as a consequence of an insular life that refused to recognize that the country had changed. It was possible to be that way, she explained, because formal desegregation had not been accompanied by any real measure of racial interaction. "Most Afrikaners do not have contact with [people of color who would be] non-gardeners, non-farmworkers," she explained. "Their only frame of reference is the chappie on the farm, the laborer, or the chappie who works in the garden. They do not know the new generation—they don't know the [Black] girls coming out of the Collegiate, the very grand girls' school next door—that there are Black ladies walking out there. You close your eyes and your ears and you will not know . . . they do not know that."

Older Afrikaners, especially from the Gauteng and Free State provinces, are described by their younger White counterparts as very insular and "backward" in their ways of interacting with other races. "All they talk about is the kaffirs and *swart*," said Cara, a young Afrikaans woman whose family's history in the country traces back to the early eighteenth century. Young Afrikaners, she says, are "desperately trying to be different, different from what [our people] were, that whole *Voortrekker* background. . . . Part of the reason [younger Afrikaners] are here [in more liberal Cape Town] is because we don't want to associate with that."[24]

CARVING OUT A "NEW" SOUTH AFRICAN IDENTITY?

Young Whites are indeed trying hard to renegotiate their realities, choosing those parts of their culture they appreciate and can be proud of and dropping others they perceive as regrettable. With the transition to a new democratic system and the rejection of the apartheid past came a strong sense of shame for some in the Afrikaner community. Blamed for all that had been and remains unequal and wrong in the country, many have tried to create distance between themselves and the Afrikaner world. One Afrikaner young man told us he did not find "anything to be proud of in being Afrikaans. . . . I find the history of repression and discrimination, you know, it sickens me." "There's . . . a lot of people not wanting to be Afrikaans because there's such bloody negative connotations to it. It's uncool as well," said a young Afrikaner woman.

Brandon rejects this perspective completely. He cultivates pride in Afrikaner culture and heritage and stands firm against those who would try to wipe it out, whether by shame or ignorance. The drive to make Stellenbosch University—the only remaining explicitly Afrikaans-language university in the country—into an English-language university, and the fact that old Afrikaner street and place names are being replaced by new African names, inclines Afrikaners like him to feel defensive. "I'm just scared that sooner or later they're going to start trying to completely wipe out Afrikaans as a language," a young woman in his social set complained. "Everything's becoming more Zulu and Xhosa and English, and you see less and less Afrikaans everywhere. Like, even, they took it off the notes, off the money. . . . That's why I'm so scared for the language, because it's getting less and less, and that's what's worrying me. I mean, because then, kind of, that's like your identity gone, because now you have to speak English."

Brandon's friend Alex describes how, after a period of feeling alienated and ashamed, many young Afrikaners are starting to own up to their identity in post-apartheid South Africa:

> These days . . . people are actually proud to be Afrikaans. For the first time in ages, there's a total turnaround. . . . I think because of apartheid, or the end of apartheid, Afrikaners didn't know where they belonged, and slowly but surely they realized that they're just as much part of South Africa and they are allowed to be proud of their culture and their heritage . . . Afrikaners now, they've realized that they'll never ever be in power again; there will never be the day when you get an Afrikaner Nationalist Party. But there are other ways of asserting your identity. Through culture: through sport, through music, through language. And it's happening.

Reconstructing race relations is a pressing task for young Afrikaners. They are looking for a way of differentiating themselves from the racial animosity that was the hallmark of "their people" in the past. A young woman recalls the way in which her family used to depict other races when she was growing up, "thinking of anyone who's not White as not really being people. . . . When they used to speak about other colors or races, it was like 'they,' you know, it's not people, it's just like objects. Not like people with feelings and lives of their own." Things are done differently now, she says. The schools opened up to children of other races and so interaction became easier, more natural. Slowly the change brought about by the children's interactions could lead to minor shifts in awareness among the older generations:

> [It was] weird for [my parents]—me wanting to stay over at a Black girl's house. And things that they still actually do, like if the maid comes, then she's got to drink from that cup and [eat from] that plate and it's . . . under the sink and she knows that that's her stuff. You know, those sort of things, they're still very much alive, I think, in most families. . . . I remember also

at school in Uppington, I always grew up with the idea in my head that Nelson Mandela was, like, this criminal and . . . this really bad person. And there were these songs, . . . these things that kids make up; I can't remember how it went, but it was, like, "He's a criminal and he must be killed," like, "shoot him" . . . And then later on in life you learn about this guy, and he's such an amazing person, and just the stuff that he's done . . . But we weren't taught that at all.

With its melting pot of cultures and a university that attracts students from various backgrounds, Cape Town is an experimental playground for young White people who want to create this new way of doing things. Anna is one of them. Her architecture friends are a very mixed bunch of people. Spending all those long nights working together, she says, it really doesn't matter where you come from. All working toward one common goal creates bonds—skin color no longer matters.

Yet she is quick to point out that most of her friends, even though of a different race, are of a similar class. None of them are from the poorest areas of the townships and all of them share certain interests and likes. They are either all students in the school of architecture or she met them at high school and connected with them in the context of an upper-middle-class background. They "think the same way," like the same things. At that point, cultural differences enrich the relationship rather than undermine it. Says Anna,

If you've got the same education as someone else, it's very easy to relate to that person, no matter what, and their skin color doesn't matter, or the culture doesn't matter. I can easily get along with people who have some interest in art, or, you know, that kind of thing, because I like it, no matter what their culture, because there's some common point.

So are you saying cultural differences are still there or do they disappear?
No, then they become more valuable, because you can learn from the other person.

Despite the open-mindedness and wish to create a truly integrated multicultural society, Anna too admits to sometimes "changing tune" depending on which group of friends she is hanging out with. The trap of judgment or prejudice is never far away. Referring to the lower-middle-class Coloured area of Mitchell's Plain, often mentioned in the same breath with drugs and gangs, she reflects on how she chooses her words and shades her opinions based on the people surrounding her: "If you're in a White group of people it's easy to make comments—I try not to do it, [but] maybe I do, I dunno—about an area that's not so good. You know, you'd say, 'Agh, who wants to live in Mitchell's Plain?' But . . . if you are with Coloured friends you wouldn't say that, because some of them might very well live there. And actually I don't know that area so I actually can't say."

Anna and Brandon find themselves in the emotionally draining position of hoping for the better for their future and fearing the worst for their country. Protected by a privileged position based on the exploitation and discrimination of all those deemed "non-White," their families had managed to build up easy lives in affluent areas, with large houses, top-notch schools, and managerial jobs. Especially in Anna's case, land, wealth, knowledge, and connections accumulated that ensured her an enviable starting point at the time of the transition into this new "equal" South Africa. She was light years ahead of the vast majority of non-Whites.

When policies of redress blocked her first vocational desire to become a doctor, she was only slightly shaken. She quickly settled into her second choice, capitalizing on the education she received at one of the best universities in the country and the network of ties to equally educated and well-off friends and connections. Her life continued with few ripples "after freedom."

Brandon's path has been more complicated. As a White man, he has enjoyed privileges denied to Ambrose and Thandiswa, but class has intervened to separate him from the more comfortable life that Anna enjoys. He did not have the same kind of educational credentials to fall back on as Anna, and the older generations in his family lack the money and land that Anna can rely on. When his father lost his position because of BEE legislation, another managerial position was not easy to find without the right kind of educational degree.

Brandon's was also a more complicated identity, firmly grounded in Afrikaner values and beliefs. Caught up in the overpowering fear and insecurity that hung over the Afrikaner community at the time of the transition, both Brandon and his father thought they had no future in South Africa, and both of them left to try to make their way in other countries. Both returned disillusioned by the difficulties in the overseas labor markets and realizing that perhaps South Africa was not that bad a place to be. Turning to entrepreneurship, they each started businesses from scratch.

Brandon may be financially insecure, but Ambrose and Thandiswa would change places with him in a heartbeat. When times got tough for Brandon, there was always some extra cash to be found somewhere, and if the going got even tougher, he could wheedle some money out of his brothers or his dad.

Yet, unlike Anna who has a basic faith in people of all cultures, Brandon worries, and his Afrikaner community encourages such doubts and troublesome questions. Will the vast Black majority still living in poverty in the townships one day turn against people like him? How can he protect himself against violent crime? What hope can there be for reversing his downhill slide if the corruption of the ruling party continues unabated?

Oscillating between fear and hope, Brandon wonders how to position himself in this new, so-called equal and nonracial South Africa. He believes that the country truly could be successful in the future, rejects the racist past, and, at least much of time, questions the intransigence of the far right. But unlike Anna, who has adapted to the consequences of the ANC's policies of labor market quotas, Brandon bridles at the barriers they present to his community and questions how the party moved away from its original commitment to "colorblind" social policy. The reality that White graduates in the country still land more better-paid and stable jobs than their non-White peers, does not register in his mind, perhaps because these "winners" have the education that he lacks.[25] Rising inequality that privileges those who have pursued higher degrees is clipping the wings of Brandon's peers in ways that simply didn't happen in the old days. This limits his horizons and exposes him to economic insecurity. But for Brandon, the starkest change is racial, and he is on the losing end of a transition that has intervened to create upward mobility for those who are not White, and consequent downward mobility for him and his father. In the backs of their minds, the question remains about whether they might one day have to leave their country to find a path toward security and safety.

CHAPTER EIGHT

Movements and Migrations

SINCE THE END OF APARTHEID, millions of migrants—mainly refugees from the war-torn and politically unstable parts of Africa to the north—have poured over the borders into South Africa, the wealthiest country on the continent.[1] Some seek the beacon of human rights and the security of the rule of law. In spite of the troubles that certainly persist, this is what South Africa has come to represent in the wake of Mandela's triumph: a peaceful democracy where political parties contest for power at the ballot box rather than at the butt of a gun, a place where due process reigns and the dirty wars of the past—that saw thousands disappeared into prisons, never to be seen again, or shot on the streets—have been replaced by heated but peaceful political debate.

Some come—as Suzanne and her children did—looking not for political freedom but simply for the right to live. They are the victims of ethnic persecution in countries such as the Democratic Republic of the Congo (DRC), Somalia, Rwanda, and Nigeria, where interethnic, African-on-African enmity has been spurred by elites competing for natural resources like oil, diamonds, and minerals such as bauxite that are needed to power first world economies. Armies on the payroll of corrupt leaders who stand to benefit from these riches have everything to lose from democratic power transitions, and nothing distracts attention more from the millions missing from national bank accounts than genocide. The Rwandan Civil War of the 1990s, the murderous violence in Mugabe's Zimbabwe, and more have led to ordinary people on the run, just ahead of the gun, the machete, the torch.

Economic aspirations power the movement of people across the continent as well. Post-apartheid South Africa bears a striking resemblance to the United States in its magnetic power to attract migrants looking for a better life. The juxtaposition of Mexico and much of Central America, with millions of impoverished peasants looking for upward mobility, and the United States, with its vastly higher standard of living, has produced the same outcome: illegal immigrants willing to work hard at wages at the bottom of the American pyramid. Millions of dollars in remittances flow across the border, as hardworking migrants send their paychecks home to pay for the stuff of life in villages thousands of miles to the south.

In South Africa, uneven development spurs internal migration too. People move to areas with higher employment opportunities but also better infrastructure and services and stronger community organizations. At times these movements seem unidirectional, but thousands make a round trip from cities to rural areas and then back, with movement sometimes depending on illness, unemployment, and high urban crime.[2]

The Western Cape Province receives thousands of migrants from the much poorer Eastern Cape Province, which is mainly rural and plagued by corruption in local government. While the Eastern Cape is home to a robust agricultural economy, the best and most productive land is still largely in the hands of White farmers who employ Black labor in much the same way that American agribusiness relies on migrant workers from Mexico. Relations between landowners and their laborers are tense, so much so that private armed patrols are common, ostensibly to prevent the farm murders that periodically hit the headlines. Leaders of the Democratic Alliance Party believe that the best land is in the hands of traditional chiefs who allocate land to locals who use it for subsistence farming and hence do not provide jobs for landless farmworkers. Regardless of landownership, employment opportunities are low.

The economy in many of the northern provinces, such as the Free State, Mpumalanga, and the North West Province, is dominated by a mining industry that provides dangerous jobs at slightly better wages for those who live long enough to enjoy them. Drilling for platinum in the bowels of the earth can break the body. No wonder that many look for other places to live.

Off in the distance, the wealthy, tourist-rich Western Cape Province glitters like a jewel. Cape Town, its capital, has a bustling center with a well-heeled elite willing to pay for drivers, nannies, landscapers, car guards, restaurant help, and all of the other service jobs that come with a more developed economy. Another life, a better life, seems possible to those to the north, and that message streams across social networks, now often via the cell phones that are nearly universal. Tales of riches, of life beyond the township, exaggerate what is likely to happen to any particular family or aspiring migrant.

Amanda and Thandiswa are part of this migration. Born in the Eastern Cape Province, they moved west in search of better opportunities. Some, like Amanda, have found them, and her good fortune sends signals back to her home in Port Elizabeth, inclining those who would like to follow a similar path to pack their bags. Others, like Thandiswa, have not. For her, the migration has proven to be something of an empty promise, though she would be the first to admit that life might have been worse if her family had stayed in the Eastern Cape.

In the years between the World Wars, millions of Black people in the American South turned their backs on King Cotton and streamed out of the region, bound for Chicago, Youngstown, Washington DC, and New York. Whole blocks in those northern cities bore the imprint of that Great Migration, memorialized in Nicholas Lemann's stunning book *The Promised Land* and Isabel Wilkerson's tour de force, *The Warmth of Other Suns*. For most, this was a one-way trip away from the worst aspects of Jim Crow and toward the possibility of industrial jobs. They settled into segregated urban enclaves in the northern cities that gave birth to the ghettoes we know today. Sociologists recounted the social organization of these enclosed communities, with their own barbers, politicians, church leaders, teachers, gangs, drug lords, and street hoods.

Not that these newcomers were particularly welcome. The arrival of African Americans by the millions into the White enclaves of the urban North was sometimes greeted by bombings, shootings, and fire. And that was during a growth period in which there were jobs to be had. When World War II ignited the domestic economy, the men and women of the South were readily absorbed into an industrial economy that was thirsty for blue-collar workers. Competition was keen, of course, but burgeoning factories—even those that were occupationally segregated—needed labor. When the war ended and unemployment lines began to grow, racial antagonism and Black unemployment grew side-by-side.

Migration in South Africa has followed a similar path, with familiar consequences. The country's strong economy was built on its wealth of natural resources, and by the middle of the twentieth century South Africa boasted an extensive transportation system, electrical power grid, and large manufacturing industry. After World War II, manufacturing increased, following trends of urbanization and consolidation in the farming sector. But by the mid-1980s, South Africa had witnessed a downturn. During apartheid, the country became a pariah state. Sanctions from the United Nations bit down and the divestment movement in Western Europe and the United States caused a withdrawal of foreign capital, an increase in the cost of imports, and serious inflation. The economy stagnated, one of the reasons why the National Party government felt the pressure to end apartheid.[3]

When apartheid ended, the barriers to international commerce came down. South African dairy products, beef, and wine began to appear on shelves across the world. The Chinese government came prospecting for minerals and, as elsewhere in Africa, began investing in infrastructure and extractive industries.[4] American corporations ramped up their investments. From one point of view, this was a tremendous boon to a country that had grown economically isolated. From another, it was an accelerant for inequality.

Take agriculture, for example. Farmworkers in South Africa have been hurt by mechanization and the increase in large farms while small farmers are driven out of business. During our sojourn to the Eastern Cape, we heard many White farmers lament (to put it mildly) the rising cost of fertilizer, driven by the skyrocketing cost of oil. Without it, they cannot compete. With it, their costs of production are rising and their profit margins melting. Labor feels that bite eventually. With democracy came the unionization of farmworkers and demands for minimum wages and respect for human rights, and this led many White farmers to cut their workforce, expecting that it would become "more difficult to manage farmworkers" and to cover the increased cost of paying them.[5] Farm strikes in the Western Cape in 2012 were successful in extracting promises for higher pay but led to another round of retrenchments as the owners claimed they could no longer afford the bill.[6] Where this equation no longer works at all we see farms entirely abandoned and a rural proletariat that is permanently unemployed.

Economists have proclaimed the present the "era of inequality" and hearken back to the 1920s for metaphors to characterize the extremely unequal distribution of wealth. The same trend plaguing the United States, the United Kingdom, and other advanced postindustrial societies has landed like a body blow on South Africa. Where industrial labor could once command reasonable wages it is now buffeted by robotics and a flood of cheap labor coming across the border.

On arrival in the Western Cape, migrants (foreign and domestic) find labor markets that are saturated, unable to absorb everyone who wants a job. Millions of locals are barely managing.[7] The added competition fuels anger and resentment, feeding ethnic and national stereotypes. "Those people" are the ones who want what "we" have, when there is not enough for "us." "They" should go back from the place "they" come from and stop taking, stop upending the local social structure. Most of all, "they" should disappear, because their very presence undercuts wages, reducing what was a shaky hold on a viable life to a desperate scramble. Unemployment rises, and young men with nothing to do hang around the townships looking for any opportunity, whether or not it's legal. It is not hard to see why the trade in drugs and guns flows into that void.

In the last five years, South Africa has seen increasing riots, strikes, road blockades, and arson in the townships. Foreign African shopkeepers, often Somali, run small *spaza* shops (tuck shops) interspersed throughout the Black townships like Khayelitsha. These are patronized by residents, short on cash, who need small amounts of everyday goods. Given their long-standing history with trade culture, Somali immigrants know how and where to buy in bulk, and together with relatives, friends, or colleagues who own shops as well, a single shop owner in the townships can find ways to lower prices below what his indigenous rivals can afford. Somali and other foreign traders find ways to access money through their networks, and they offer products that local shopkeepers cannot get their hands on. As the locals struggle to compete, they are not above wielding the force of prejudice. Foreign traders and shopkeepers have had to face the rage and distrust of local communities.[8] They all have stories to tell of how they have been verbally abused, intimidated, attacked, and their shops looted or burned out.

The situation exploded in 2008. A chain of attacks against foreign nationals erupted first in the township of Alexandra near Johannesburg. Angry locals had decided "the foreigners must all go," and groups of armed Black South Africans started attacking, looting, setting fires, and killing immigrants and refugees. Two people were killed and forty wounded, and then the violence spread across the country, eventually reaching Durban and Cape Town. In the end, over sixty people were killed, hundreds were wounded, and several thousand foreign nationals were displaced, fearing for their lives. Survivors said it was "surreal" to see people they knew well and sometimes even shared houses with all of a sudden turn against them, vowing they would "kill all the foreigners."[9]

Refugee camps were set up to host most of the victims, while churches, mosques, and various community organizations opened their doors to provide shelter and food.[10] The African National Congress appeared to be embarrassed but impotent to stop the violence. Countries along the South African border that had harbored ANC activists during the struggle against apartheid, giving leaders shelter in a common fight against racism and near-slavery, now found their emigrant citizens targeted for bloodshed inside this "beacon of human rights."

The atmosphere has calmed, but tension remains. In the run-up to the 2010 World Cup, rumors spread through Cape Town that "[foreigners] won't be safe when the Cup is over," causing great anxiety among immigrants in various parts of the city. Since 2011, anti-immigrant attacks have recurred, though not on the scale that overtook the country three years earlier. It was a grim reminder that immigrants are not always welcome and may not be safe.[11]

Millions of refugees living in South Africa watch their children grow up in an alien land, among people who do not really want them there, children who are losing their native languages (Kiswahili, French, and Lingala, to name just three). The life these migrants fled was worse, however, than what they have here. The violence and hatred Suzanne witnesses in South Africa trigger frightening memories of the horrors she left behind in the DRC. Suzanne no longer wants to remember her trek to Cape Town or the events that forced her and her three children to embark on their journey to South Africa. From Congo to Zambia, then to Tanzania and Mozambique, they were on the run for two years, traveling in furtive spurts from one outpost to another. In the back of trucks, on foot through the bush, wading across rivers that define borders, with her three-month-old infant tied to her back, Suzanne dragged her family to safety. She twists her hands in her lap when asked to recall how she managed such a feat, and she stares off into the distance, with tears welling in her eyes, when she explains that she didn't know where her husband, Eduard, was for months on end or whether they would ever see one another again.

They have seen enough of this kind of brutality to last a lifetime. Eduard's father was murdered in their home in the DRC, his cousins torched to death in their car, and he escaped only because of a borrowed army uniform that enabled him to run long enough to be out of immediate danger. These are the memories the family Kalle carries from their last years in Congo, now ten years in the past. Like the Jewish people of Eastern Europe who survived the Nazi-era Holocaust, only to discover that pogroms were starting up in Poland once again, refugees like Eduard and Suzanne experience reflexive terror when mobs attack people in the Cape Town slums because of their ethnic identity. Could their DRC experience happen again?

No one would willingly go back, even if their new neighbors do not want them. They stay and face the disdain and disrespect in Cape Town, the muttering under the breath, and the assaults aimed at them while waiting in line for the home office to dispense legal papers. "*Kwere-kwere*"—"foreigner"—has become a standard local term of insult. People like Suzanne turn away and try to shield their children from such a harsh reception. Their kids, in turn, shush the parents when they come to school speaking Swahili. "We don't want anyone to know where we came from," Suzanne's daughters tell her.

ARTHUR MUTOMBO

Burundi's first Hutu president, Melchior Ndadaye, elected in 1993, was felled by Tutsi assassins later that year, igniting a wave of murders that saw somewhere between 50,000 and 100,000 people—mainly innocent civilians—die in the year that followed. Tutsi civilians were massacred by Hutu peasant militias, and Hutus died at the hands of Tutsi army recruits. It was a civil war that marked one of the bloodiest periods of African history.

One of those who lived through it was Arthur Mutombo. Born in Burundi in 1977, he was in his early thirties when we met him. Hutu by birth, Arthur was among the thousands of young men who were hunted down by the Burundi army starting in 1995. "Soldiers, who are supposed to protect the people, nearly 95 percent of them were Tutsi," he recalled. "They would come into Hutu communities and kill mostly young men, like my age. . . . They accused us of being rebels. If they came into the neighborhood, there would be one guy who was fighting them with guns, then [it would be] all of us fighting with guns. They don't care. They will make sure all of us die." At the age of eighteen, Arthur fled for his life. He spent two years in the neighboring DRC and then tried to go back home. But the situation there had gotten worse. "My parents said, 'It's better that you go,' because I was quite a revolutionary boy. I go where people are fighting with guns, and me, I'll take a knife or stones and go help those who are fighting. . . . My parents could see that they would lose me. So the easiest way was for me to leave [home], to bounce and go away."

The lucky ones among Arthur's friends found their way to Europe. Thousands of Burundians fled the wars of the 1990s and made new homes in Belgium, the former colonial power in Burundi, where French is spoken and the history of the two countries is intertwined. But that option was only open to the few who had the connections to make it past the well-patrolled entry ports to Europe. Arthur says,

> There were Burundi people who were in Belgium before the war. They went there to study. Some immigrated there. But the majority are the ones who went there because of the war. And those ones . . . had people [family, friends] who were in the government. . . . They helped them to get the visas. Yah, so for people like us, who did not have nobody in high places, it was not easy. So we just had to bounce.

And bounce he did. Arthur spent several years in refugee camps in the DRC, Tanzania, Malawi, and Mozambique, in a pattern familiar to people like Suzanne. Taken together, those years on the road were full of hunger and loneliness alternating with fear of discovery and the fury of rejection. None of the countries Arthur passed through were happy to see the flood of refugees fleeing the wars in Rwanda, Burundi, and later, the DRC—all were poor, lacking in the most elemental resources needed for their own people, much less for the refugees. As soon as they could muster the bureaucratic or military wherewithal to move the refugees out, they sent them packing. Arthur found himself in the back of container trucks, on foot through mud and dust, looking down the barrel of a soldier's rifle. He learned to search for people who spoke his mother tongue, Kirundi, or, failing that, the pan-African tongue, Swahili. Only when he could locate people who shared his background did he feel even a modicum of safety.

South Africa became Arthur's dream destination. He finally made it there after about two years on the run. Like thousands of others before him, he landed first in Johannesburg, where he set out to find work. In Burundi he had been trained as a barber and a hair salon operator, a portable trade that put him in good stead when he first hit the streets of Jo'burg. His first employer thought well of his skills but within a few months grew worried that Arthur would set up an independent business and become his competition. To avoid such a fate, he bought Arthur a bus ticket for Cape Town, where Arthur went to work for one of his brothers who also had a hair salon.

The new job was in the City Bowl that cradles the craft market where Suzanne and her employees sell clothes and beads. Arthur moved into a shack in Khayelitsha and quickly became an object of interest among women in that section of the township.

> One week. I lasted only one week in Khayelitsha. I was quite young and, you know, when you're still twenty, your blood is hot. So, I was staying in this house, and there are young girls and I'm young too. So they kind of like who I am. I left in the day to cut hair and come home in the evening. . . . The girls see that I go to work, not like the boys around them [who are unemployed].

Because Arthur did not speak a word of English, and no one in his new neighborhood spoke Kirundi, he couldn't communicate easily and missed the nuances of conversation. What he did catch were the obvious looks of interest from the young women and the mutterings, posturing, and glaring eyes of the young men. Within a week the conflict was open: "Those boys, they like girls, girls who don't like them. Those girls liked to be around me. Me, I didn't care.

I wasn't even [interested] in them. But the boys who were around, in their minds they were thinking, 'This boy is a foreigner; these girls, we want them and they are busy wanting to be with this [foreign] boy.' When I came out [of the house], they would speak to me in the Xhosa language, which I didn't understand. I would just say, 'Ahh, I'm rushing to take my bus to go to work.'"

Arthur had inadvertently trod on a touchy aspect of relations between foreigners and locals. Unemployment among South Africans remains excruciatingly high. The International Labour Organization estimates that 20 percent of unemployed young men are not even looking for work anymore.[12] This situation leaves many young men feeling disempowered, unable to live up to what many of them believe a "real man" should be: independent, successful, tough, and a provider for family.[13] To see other men, strangers to their communities, come in and fill positions they cannot access inevitably leads to frustration and anger. It is a recipe for trouble. The mother of the house where Arthur was staying could see an explosion coming and urged him to clear out. "She told me, 'Listen, my son, you are a very cool boy. You know, you respect me even more than my own children [do]. You do things more than my children do for me. But I don't think this is the right place for you to stay. Is better that you go out and look for another place somewhere in town, not around here.' I spoke to my employer and he told me, 'If that woman told you [to leave], then it's better that you do.'"

Arthur found his way to quarters in Observatory, a vibrant, arty residential area, just east of the Cape Town city center, which hosts a multicultural crowd, including many university students. Arthur located several countrymen from Burundi whom he had known casually in his teenage years there. He had been aware that they had migrated to South Africa as well, but he had not known how to find them until he hooked up with a network of refugees with contacts all over the country and indeed the world.

Arthur has now been in South Africa for nearly twelve years. He cuts hair in a shop conveniently located near the taxi and train station junction in Claremont, one of the more upmarket southern suburbs of Cape Town. Part barbershop, part makeshift tailor shop, and part public telephone service, the business seems to have a steady trade. The woman who owns the business sells garments she makes. A man runs a cell phone repair shop in the corner. In the back, a pool table has been set up and a few Burundians gather there every day to play and gamble.

Arthur's apartment is in a block of flats within walking distance of Cavendish Square, a fancy, large shopping mall in the heart of Claremont. A two-bedroom walkup with a view of Table Mountain, it is a far cry from the shack lands of Khayelitsha. It would seem that he has managed to do reasonably well for himself, that South Africa has turned out, after all, to be a place where a man with a portable trade can make a life. Surely he plans to stay?

"A future here as a foreigner?" he muses. "I don't see a future here. For the past twelve years I've been living here. I don't have even one South African person [about whom] I could say, 'This is my friend.' I could not say, 'I am going to visit my friend who is South African.' I know people who say that [these people] are friendly, but for me . . . I don't agree."

The onset of the xenophobic attacks in 2008 deepened Arthur's view that he will never belong in this country, not in the way that its native people do. His customers, most of whom are native-born, have apologized to him for the behavior of the few, ashamed of the way that they were treating fellow Africans. They found it hard to account for the violence and felt responsible for the fear that someone they value—who has cut their hair for years now—feels while living among them.

Arthur has tried to rationalize the violence, to invent his own explanations for why it became so serious. He concluded that apartheid was responsible. Extreme racism has damaged the souls of the South African people, he believes. Not the White people, he hastens to add, for they were already racists. It is the Black people of the country who are consumed by hatred for foreigners, and the only sense he can make of their behavior stems from the twisted logic of apartheid.

> We're all Black. They are Africans just like us. I don't have a problem with [South African] Blacks. If I could help, I would, because they are my people. Some things they say and do are part of the system, the past system, the apartheid system. They messed up their minds, made them believe what they are not supposed to believe. I kind of forgive those who did all these wrong things, yah. I can't sit there and judge and say, 'They kill foreigners.' Yes, we [have] got those who think, 'I don't have a job because of foreigners.' Some even believe they don't have [a] nice woman because of foreigners [he laughs]. You get me?
>
> Most White people are racists. That I won't pretend. I won't lie. You can see racism in their faces. You get me? You see Coloured people thinking that they are superior to Black people. They're clever, more than us Black people. Obviously you get Black people . . . who hate, who have that racist mind. But for me, that's because of what the other races have done to them in the past.

The experience of living under apartheid, Arthur argues, has created soul-destroying conditions, leaving irrational hatred and contempt that spills over into violence. "They say stupid things. They see me and say, 'You, in Nigeria, you eat dogs.'... I'm not Nigerian.... I've never been to Nigeria. But you ridicule me because I look like I'm Nigerian? So, I just [try to] forgive them. The apartheid system has just messed up their minds."

The epicenters of the anger are the overcrowded, poor, often informally developed areas of townships like Khayelitsha, the least expensive places to live and hence the first stop for African immigrants who have only what they could carry. When Arthur wants to epitomize just how bad the tension can get, he tells a particularly grim story. One of his friends from Burundi boarded a train, only to be confronted by township boys spoiling for a fight. "He was married and his wife was pregnant. They threw him out of the train while it was moving. He didn't survive. People, they say, 'Listen here, man, the townships are not for you. It is not your place.' I knew where to go and where not to go. So you won't see me walk around in townships on my own."

Arthur recognizes the conflicts in South Africa and within the Western Cape specifically, where identity politics divide Coloured and Black South Africans: "The Western Cape will be better one day, the day the Coloured people accept that they are Black. These Xhosa people, this is their home; they'll never go nowhere. In this town, the Coloured people do not accept that Xhosa people belong here. They think that Xhosa people come from wherever, from Transkei. But this is their country. The race issue here ... between Black and Coloured people ... there's that hate, that hatred between those two."

He understands that poverty feeds anti-immigrant violence. It's a pity, though, he explains, because what poverty ought to catalyze is the recognition that all Black people—no matter the shade of their skin—deserve their fair share of the nation's wealth, which remains largely in the hands of Whites. It is the legacy of apartheid that prevents Coloured people from understanding who their real allies should be. And that division, between peoples of color, prevents them from uniting against the one group that is, at least in terms of resource division, the proper target. As Arthur says, "Most of the White people, they're rich. They have money. If you look out my window, see those houses [points toward Fernwood, a wealthy neighborhood at the base of Table Mountain]. There's no Black person there ... it's only White people who stay there. Those houses are supposed to belong to Black people.... Eighty percent of their money they did not get legally, you get me? There are so many Black people who died in the mines to get that money there."

What will it take for that day to arrive when the nation's Black majority finally lays its hands on the riches that should always have been theirs? From Arthur's perspective, the resolution is visible in the distant future, if not for his generation, then for those who come behind him: "Our time will come, don't worry. These Black kids growing up now . . . they are going to better schools, better universities. So I'm sure [they will have a better life]. Even if they won't be my family, at least they'll be there. You know? They'll be there, and I'll be happy to see that."

REFUGEES ON THE MARGINS

Camp De Doorns was one of the refugee enclaves set up to provide shelter to displaced foreigners who were no longer safe in the townships. Set near Worcester, in the middle of the grape-growing region of the Western Cape, it was a rough collection of tents in the open air. More than two years after the violent attacks began, the residents of De Doorns remained, stuck in a bureaucratic limbo and pinioned by fear of future violence. The inhabitants were mainly from Zimbabwe, the failed state just over the northern border of South Africa, where Robert Mugabe and his army have driven the country into an economic freefall of uncontrolled inflation, widespread police violence, forced evictions, and growing malnutrition. They were Shona-speaking people who had migrated to Stoffland, Majoks, and Ebuleni, informal settlements not far from the De Doorns refugee camp. They had come to look for work in the grape arbors and vegetable farms during the harvest season.

A local teacher explained that when these Shona laborers went to the farms in the morning, White farmers would divide them into groups. In one line stood "the foreigners," and in the other line were "people with South African ID documents." The farmers divide and conquer, driving wages down by relying on competition between these groups.

The economic downturn that gathered force worldwide in 2008 spread to South Africa, pushing employment down and ratcheting tension up. At the bottom we find desperate migrant workers who must earn their bread on a daily basis or have nothing to eat. They are pitted against equally worried local workers who watch jobs disappear and what they see as favoritism toward foreign workers grow. Tinashe, a Zimbabwean stuck in De Doorns, explained that tempers boiled over as job possibilities melted away. "They come up with stories like, 'You people are getting underpaid. You are taking up all the jobs and we sit with no jobs.' And they say we are taking all of their things like cars, TVs, and hi-fis, all kinds of accusations, and then at the end of the day, they attacked us. . . . There is just that cold blood between us. There is hatred."

Tinashe has been coming to South Africa to work in the fields since the mid-1990s, though he has stayed in Pretoria for most of that time. He saw the same xenophobic reactions there. "Whenever they want something," he complained, "they take the law into their own hands and do whatever they want. . . . "It has always been like this. Even last year it was like this. But they never pushed the people out before. They just [would go on] talking and talking and threatening and threatening. Like saying, 'You must go back. We're going to kill you. We're going to ban you.'"

The threats escalated into the widespread violence of 2008, and the scale of the brutality was unprecedented. It was then, Tinashe explained that "they burned people. They burned seven people last year." Under that kind of pressure, these migrant workers, who had put up with the punishment because their families back home were desperate for their earnings, fled the townships for refugee camps.

At the entrance to De Doorns, a security gate was manned by a young man who insisted on a signature and a license plate number to permit entry. Otherwise, there did not appear to be anyone in charge. The Red Cross tent that was supposed to be an administrative center had been abandoned, with an empty table on its side in the interior. People had hung their laundry along the wire fencing that surrounds the UN tents. Conditions were squalid, with latrines overflowing and the resulting stench almost unbearable. Children were playing in dirt contaminated with human waste. One child had recently died of diarrhea. A single water tap was crowded with women looking for potable water. Food had to be trucked in since nothing grows here. "We are not used to [living] like this," Tinashe noted with indignation. "We are not refugees, even though we live mostly like [them]. Every service has been taken out now. No more electricity. There was a fire brigade here, but they are gone. There was the Red Cross; they are gone. There is no clinic here. So we are no more than refugees now."

De Doorns accommodated about 1,400 people on a pitch the size of a football field. They remained in this depressing place because they were afraid to go back to the townships from which they were evacuated and did not have anywhere else to go. Some would leave the camp during the day to return to work, but they came back at night since it was not safe for them to sleep elsewhere. Many would have liked to return to the townships if only they could have been assured of their safety. They felt stuck. "We are waiting to hear from the government," Tinashe explained, exasperation rising in his voice.

> We can't decide on anything. We can't go back to the locations if they don't say we can go back. [The government] doesn't talk to the community, so we can't leave. Because we are afraid for our lives. We can't just go like that. We need assurance that we will be protected. Because these people, they don't have respect for life. . . . So we are waiting for the government to give us direction. Which way must we take? Where do we go from here?

Our fieldwork was two years into the migrant workers' stay in De Doorns and there was no sign of that direction yet. In some of the areas where the first attacks in Cape Town had happened, local people themselves had been the first to apologize and set up plans for foreigners to return. But for many who remained in the camps, there was no certainty. Local universities, NGOs, and community leaders all tried to smooth a way for the reintegration of refugees, but the inhabitants of De Doorns remained scared and insecure about their fate in the townships.

Nyazondo, a community leader and informal mayor of De Doorns, had been trying to get some answers on behalf of his people. He had met with the ANC's minister of justice and a local official in Winchester, but they were more interested in talking about labor relations on the farms than in reintegration, he said. Nyazondo had inquired of them what security measures would be put in place after the farming season ended. No answer was given. Some camp dwellers were beginning to consider what had been unthinkable: return to Zimbabwe or Congo. What would await them there was enough to make most shudder and shake their heads. "For me, if I go back to my country," one young Congolese man told us, "the only job that is available is to take a gun . . . that is the only job, to join the army. We are not safe in our countries and we are not safe here. People will try to get to another place, whether Namibia or Zimbabwe. Often it is worse back there. But it is better to die at home than here."

BLUE WATERS

Three kilometers from the beach, in Strandfontein, about twenty-five kilometers outside of Cape Town, Blue Waters could have been a resort under different circumstances. Instead it was a refugee camp.[14] Situated on a dune landscape dotted with low shrubbery typical of the windswept Western Cape shore were white tents barely able to withstand the sea winds, home to hundreds of foreign African nationals. Blue Waters was one of three camps set up for people who had fled the townships of Phillipi or Khayelitsha. Human rights organizations arranged for buses to collect foreigners and bring them to safety here soon after the xenophobic violence began in 2008. Most left their homes suddenly, without any time to gather their belongings, and arrived with nothing but the clothes on their backs. Some people in Blue Waters made do by fishing and selling whatever they did not eat. Dried fish could be sold on the roadside, with customers rolling down their car windows to buy what they wanted. Alternatively, they combed through the suburbs in search of gardening jobs. This was not the life they had known before, as one man explained: "We were living like you people before. We were studying or starting a business."

Studying became a luxury. Everyone had to work to survive. "That's what happens to people who have nothing. They got no school, nothing. They just have to survive. They have to go and live in the locations [townships] where people don't want them." Another man added that if people see that you are successful in the townships, rather than try to find out how that good fortune came about and perhaps try a similar path, "they prefer to kill you." Nonetheless, Blue Waters residents had worked to eat. If they were lucky enough to find a paid job, they had to watch their tongues, no matter what abuse they might have suffered. "We must have no complaints," they told each other.

TRADERS

Suzanne has managed to escape such a fate, in part because she has skills that have served her well, though not the ones she developed in nursing. She did not even try to put her formal training to use in South Africa, but her education and her worldly wisdom has bequeathed to her the capacity to gather information, speak with authority, and command the respect of others. Suzanne has built her business up from nothing, becoming quite the entrepreneur along the way. It was not the occupation she chose for herself years ago in Congo, but over time Suzanne has adapted to the notion that she has a talent for business and the qualities of a leader.

Greenmarket Square, where she makes her living, began as a slave market in Cape Town. During apartheid it was a place for farmers to bring their vegetables to town, a place for White people to sell their wares, Suzanne explains. When apartheid fell, Africans from other countries began to bring curios to be traded, and the selling of fresh produce moved to supermarkets. By the mid-1990s, the square had become a major tourist destination for the region and Suzanne one of the informal leaders of the market women who work there. They depend on her to explain what can be a confusing business climate, particularly as to regulations governing who can sell, what can be sold, and in what kind of stall they can display their wares.

Actually, "confusing" does not adequately convey what the market traders experience at the hands of local government. Foreign sellers are not always welcome in the public square, and the municipal regulations they encounter often seem designed to push them out, perhaps in favor of local merchants. Sometime in 2008, after countless public pronouncements about its willingness to work closely with the market sellers, the city council passed an edict to the effect that only one "spot" could be allocated per family. For Suzanne, this was a direct threat since her husband, Eduard, also operates a stall, and the dual income is essential to the family's well-being. Moreover, rumors began to circulate that the council was planning to shut the market down entirely to re-pave the cobblestones in preparation for the 2010 World Cup and the expected influx of tourists. Such a move would endanger the livelihood of hundreds of families.

Greenmarket Square, in the center of the business district, does a brisk tourist trade in African crafts. Suzanne has a stall here and in several other open-air markets. Many of the market women are immigrants like her, but it is a thriving business for South Africans as well.

Many were afraid to object, but Suzanne insisted they meet as a group to address the situation. At this gathering, Suzanne opined that they needed a lawyer and should pool their resources to enlist one who would sue the city fathers on behalf of the traders. The matter was dealt with in the Cape Town magistrate's court and the verdict was in favor of the market traders. The city council was given a finite time period to complete the restoration. Greenmarket Square was to be divided in half, with only part closed for construction at a time. At Suzanne's suggestion, market people worked on a rotational basis (she was there three times a week), and over a seven-month period the project was completed. The limited space still imposed a hardship during this time— Eduard lost his stall, as did others—but when it was done, business returned to normal and the council learned to think twice before taking these people on in a political battle.

City leaders know now that the foreign sellers will fight, and Suzanne emerged as a force to be reckoned with. On reflection, she says that she learned how important it is to know one's rights, to be willing to speak up when there is an injustice. While many in her exile community feel the brunt of exclusion and have come to see themselves as inferior, Suzanne is adamant that if you pursue what is just, the country can become your home.

She has taken this point of view to heart and put it to work outside Greenmarket Square. An acquaintance came to Suzanne in tears because she had been informed that her bank was about to close her account because she did not have an up-to-date residence permit (which must be renewed periodically). Home Affairs, the office responsible for renewals, was dragging its feet—not an uncommon occurrence—and the consequences were falling on this poor woman's shoulders. Suzanne told her that injustice must be countered forcefully, marched her to the bank, and told the manager in no uncertain terms that her friend, who could not speak English, deserved better treatment. She explained in authoritative tones that what the bank was doing was not allowed and that if they had "an issue," they should take it up with Home Affairs. "You should act as a bank and not masquerade as the immigration police," she argued. The branch manager was completely unsympathetic and a shade contemptuous, and so Suzanne said she would take the matter further—to the bank's provincial manager. She contacted a German friend known to be helpful to refugees, who then came with Suzanne and the woman whose account was to be closed to a meeting with the "higher-ups." The sight of this delegation seems to have unnerved the provincial manager, who backed down and ruled in favor of Suzanne's friend, whose account was kept open despite the out-of-date ID.

From these experiences, Suzanne has developed a philosophy that guides her and gives her a sense of purpose. She understands that people in her position cannot rely on the powerful. They must do for themselves and for others at the bottom of the hierarchy. "Rich people never help poor people," she explains.

> The poor, they help each other. They know how poorness is [what it means to be poor]. You can see, even in the train, who they ask for money. Before the beggar goes to the first-class cabin, he goes to the third-class and they get a lot more money there. Those people in the third-class are poor like them, but they help. [They] are sensitive to someone who suffers. Because they know how to suffer, they know how to sleep hungry. The rich people, they never know how it is to sleep hungry. If you [tell me], "I sleep hungry," I will feel it. I know those things.

A lesser person might come to believe that it is only the foreigner who feels the sting of poverty. Suzanne is sensitive to the rejection that refugees and migrants experience at the hands of South Africans, particularly those who have little and fear competition. But she is also a keen observer of the inequalities that beset the country and understands that there are millions of native-born people who have nothing, who are victims just as she has been.

> Everyone have their own problems here in South Africa. Even the South Africans . . . I saw a girl who was working for me before. She came to see me with eyes that were [swollen], like someone beat her. I ask, "What's wrong?" She says, "The people they attack me, they steal phone and beat me." I say, "Wooo. I think it's only foreigners that they are beating." She says, "No! Even us! They are doing the same thing."

It would be easier, in many respects, if the foreign population could unite in a common quest for a place at the table. Sadly, as Suzanne has come to recognize, they are internally divided and wary of one another, just as the South Africans are leery of them. Undercutting prices, angling for advantage, and muttering slurs are common among refugees and migrants because they are all after a slice of the same pie.

Suzanne's capacity to see beyond the immediate concerns of her family, her people, is essential. She knows that they are not alone in their worry, that everyone around them is beset by the same pressures. And while that does not lead easily to solutions, it leads away—she hopes—from the kind of murderous violence that has infected the townships.

To raise that kind of moral voice above the din of xenophobia will take more than one trader in the market square. It will require the leadership of people with more clout. One of them might be Antoine Muadi, formerly a human rights lawyer in the DRC. In the course of his work there, Antoine uncovered evidence of election fraud, which placed him at odds with the ruling regime, a dangerous position in a country fraught with ethnic violence. Along with much of the rest of the legal profession, Antoine left in a hurry, destined for South Africa.

He had been to South Africa when much younger and a member of a Congolese national sports team. That visit led Antoine to realize how many Congolese immigrants were in the country. When the time came to flee, he realized he would have friends to turn to, including some distant Congolese cousins, if he could find his way to South Africa. With the help of his refugee network, he made it to Cape Town and set about trying to find work in the legal profession. It was a rude shock and a sudden confrontation with downward mobility, a common experience for the most skilled migrants. "Since I am a lawyer, I started out at the Cape Law Society. I said I was a lawyer. They said considering that I didn't get my [law degree] here and am not South African, I cannot work as an attorney. From there, I went to the High Court, to an advocacy office. It was the same answer: you are not South African, you can't work here."

In some respects, Antoine was not surprised. By the time he finished making the rounds of the courts, he had met people like Fabrice Musamba, a car guard living in Maitland with his wife and daughter. A law student and apprentice lawyer in the Katanga region of the DRC, Fabrice too had run for his life. Packed in the back of a container on the back of a truck, concealed from view, he had made his way on back roads from Katanga to nearby Zambia and from there to Zimbabwe. There armed vigilantes shut down the refugee camp where he sheltered. At last, as exhausted as he was relieved to be alive, Fabrice landed in Cape Town, where he has lived for the past six years. The job he has found as a car guard does not even provide him with a salary. He looks after the cars of hikers who are hiking up the mountain during weekends. He survives on tips of one or two rand per car, but as he is there all day for a lot of the time he can gather a couple of hundred rand (about $20) on a good day. There are thousands of well-educated foreigners who have fallen into the abyss of downward mobility like this. Most will have to wait for their children, educated in South Africa and beneficiaries of their parents' human capital, to ascend the occupational ladder and rescue the family's middle-class heritage.

Having come into contact with many people like Fabrice, Antoine recognized that he would need to lower his sights if he was going to survive. His first paid job was on a construction site, but it lasted for only a day—he earned R100. Lacking a residence permit, he was unable to find anything more regular. Since the legal profession was out of reach, Antoine's next task was to figure out how to explain himself to potential employers. "I drafted my CV and went looking for a job, anywhere. I put my qualifications down on it. I was not ashamed to note that I am a lawyer. I say, 'Yes, I'm a lawyer, but not in South Africa, in Congo. But I am looking for any job. And they say, the job we can offer is in the kitchen. And I say, 'Okay, good.' They paid me R390 [about $39 a week]." This is how lawyer Antoine was put in charge of peeling potatoes in the back of a Cape Town takeout restaurant. Ten hours a day, less than $40 a week.

It is hard to keep a smart man down, and within a few weeks Antoine figured out more efficient ways to prepare potatoes, winning himself a promotion to the French fry station—and gaining the enmity of his fellow kitchen workers. He worked long days in the kitchen and put in many hours thereafter on his English-language skills. Moving from restaurant to restaurant, Antoine graduated from the back of the kitchen to the front of the counter and to the role of headwaiter. He was still making very modest money, but at least he felt a degree of satisfaction in his ability to move up.

All the while, he kept in contact with the legal clinic at a local university where he first had inquired about work in his profession. They specialize in human rights law and eventually they had an opening for someone with a legal background who was fluent in French and English. Antoine landed the job and has never looked back. Today he is the proud recipient of a master's degree in law, but he is perpetually aware that he is one of the lucky ones. He says, "I know a lot of people, even those with MA degrees in law, like me, who are working as parking marshals or security guards. There are so many here."

To a degree, virtually all refugees and migrants start out with certain advantages, though they may not be able to capitalize on them for many years, if at all. Emerging out of war zones or countries ravaged by poverty, they are the ambitious, the networked, and often the best educated of their compatriots. Those with fewer advantages are often stuck, unable to flee. They may wish as fervently as Suzanne or Antoine to get out and take their families with them, but lacking the material means to bribe a border guard, pay off a truck driver, or latch on to relatives who have gone before them, they are unable to move. It is hardly accidental, then, that we find lawyers, nurses, mechanics, and teachers among South Africa's refugee population.

The most fortunate of them are able to rely on their human capital and return to the professions they left behind. But for every Antoine, there are probably twenty Suzannes who will never work in the professional fields for which they are qualified but whose smarts and energy will see them through to other careers. Their children are likely to assimilate into South African society and, fueled by the aspirations of their parents and the benefits their parents can provide (especially relative to those less fortunate), some will qualify for university and become upwardly mobile. Sadly, there may be even more refugee children like those growing up in De Doorns, who will not see the kind of success that Suzanne's family has already experienced. Their futures are dim.

For parents like Suzanne and Eduard, there is pride in the accomplishments of their children, but there is also more than a hint of regret. They are products of a culture that was far more conservative than the westernized one in which their children (five of them now) are growing up. "You couldn't smoke at school or kiss a boy," Suzanne remembers.

> You couldn't drink at school. They had a lot of discipline that I don't find in South Africa. Here I can see [kids] wearing the [school] uniform, kissing in the streets. . . . I can see the teacher smoke in front of the kids. Even the kids smoking! Children bringing the knives to school, children swearing at the teachers. . . . We had discipline at our school. You couldn't swear, you couldn't even shout or answer to your teacher when he is shouting at you. You have to obey him like he is your father.

Her immigrant friends agree that discipline is lacking in their adopted country. Sylvie, an immigrant from Cameroon, sent her children back to her home country to be raised by relatives rather than see them adopt the modern ways of South Africa.

> Life is not good here for my children because the words . . . that are coming out of my child's mouth! I don't like it. Things like "fuck." They don't want Mommy and Daddy to have authority over them. Sheesh. I prefer for my child to come back here when he is at an age that he can understand good and bad. When he was small—three years old—he was talking about "moffy" [a slang term for gay]. He says, "This boy is a moffy." I say to him, "What do you understand about being a moffy?" In my country [no child] would know about [such things]. We only read about it in books. In my country I have never seen a woman smoke cigarettes. So there are lots of things which are corrupt in South Africa.

These conservative norms about how children should be raised, how discipline should be maintained, are in keeping with immigrants the world over, who are often more traditional in their expectations than the host societies where they find themselves. Letting go of those values is hard for them. It is tantamount to acknowledging that they will never go back, that the future lies in a new land where they will never quite belong.

Of course, compared to the fate of the thousands of people who got stuck in refugee camps like De Doorns, this is perhaps not such a serious concern. For them, the costs of remaining in South Africa are far more consequential. They have languished in squalid conditions for years. After the closure of the camps in 2010, some were moved to so-called Temporary Residence Areas (TRAs) set up by the city of Cape Town when clearing stretches of informal settlements to prepare them for new housing developments.

We found some of the families after their relocation to the "TRA Symphony Way." Residents had renamed the area Blikkiesdorp—literally "Tin Can City"—as it consisted of rows and rows of steel containers that look like railroad cars, planted on a desolate stretch of land on the far edge of town. Blikkiesdorp houses a mix of Black people and Coloured "backyard dwellers" waiting for a new home, along with refugees who are foreign nationals. From the center of Tin Can City one can see silver jets lifting off from the

Blikkiesdorp, or "Tin Can City," as it is known, is a temporary residence area for refugees and displaced South Africans who were cleared out of "backyard dwellings" and the N2 highway construction zone. It is a bleak, barren, dust-blown settlement, where families live in zinc cabins and children play in the sand. The people we met here had been living in Blikkiesdorp for over two years.

Cape Town airport in the distance, but no one in this place is going anywhere. They are living in the midst of gritty sand and boredom. There are no stores, trees, playgrounds, or ponds in Blikkiesdorp. Residents feel as rejected and despised as any racially subordinated group was during apartheid. Some of the children living in these camps will die young. Others will see their education interrupted at the point of no return. Many will become depressed by their surroundings and angry—justifiably so—about their treatment.

THE GREAT MIGRATION, FROM THE INSIDE

The mass movement of people like Mam'Cethe, Tata Boya and their children—Thandiswa, Zakithi, and all the rest—from the poorer provinces such as the Eastern Cape and Limpopo to the wealthier areas such as the Western Cape and Gauteng rearranges the population landscape of South Africa. Urbanization is on the rise: thousands have decamped for cities—especially Johannesburg and Cape Town, and to lesser degrees Pretoria and Port Elizabeth—leaving some regions depopulated and making others overcrowded.[15] They are moving in the same direction as the refugees and migrants from other countries and are often greeted with the same lukewarm welcome at best. In the poorest receiving communities, like Khayelitsha or Nyanga, some of those who came before them would prefer that the newcomers go back to wherever they came from.

Tata Boya, Thandiswa's father, was part of that mass movement from the Eastern Cape to the Western Cape. Ngcobo, the rural community that is the original family seat, lies deep in the apartheid-era "bantustan" of the Transkei, which was declared an independent homeland by the regime and left to stagnate.[16] It was nothing more than a labor reserve, disgorging thousands of migratory workers, mainly men like Tata, who left their families behind to move to the more industrial areas around cities such as Cape Town, in search of wages they could send home.

Tata left Ngcobo nearly fifty years ago in search of a job. Mam'Cethe explains that he went first to Johannesburg but did not want to work in the mines, and so he came to Cape Town in the 1970s. The family first settled on a farm where Tata still works today. They then moved to Crossroads, at that time an informal settlement plagued by high levels of violence. After the Western Cape government decided to start building houses for Black people again, the family was eventually given a house in the 1980s, in the township of Khayelitsha, which was then new.

Tata Boya continued to work on a Kuils Rivier farm, while Mam'Cethe and the children stayed in Khayelitsha. Thandiswa went to school nearby in

Lwandle. On the weekends, they would join Tata in Kuils River and would ready firewood for sale to the braai stalls in the townships.

With life settling down in their new world, why did Thandiswa's family continue to maintain ties to the Eastern Cape? The cattle they left behind in Ngcobo, the only real cushion or bank account they had, were not safe.[17] Some were dying mysteriously, a problem they attributed vaguely to witchcraft. Some had clearly been stolen. They needed to be moved, and the Kat River Valley near Seymour seemed to be the right place for them. "An old man [who also had land near Seymour], told us about the [pastureland]," Mam'Cethe explained. "He said we should go to Seymour because it would be possible to guard the livestock there."

It was possible but only at the sacrifice of seven years of Thandiswa's life. From her mother's perspective, living in such a beautiful valley is not such a hardship. She doesn't really understand Thandiswa's complaints, her sense of abandonment. But they come from different worlds. As many women of her generation, Mam'Cethe remembers the independence of rural life and would not mind returning to it even now.[18] "I'm tired of having to buy everything here [in Khayelitsha]," she says, "whereas on the [eastern] side we farm our own food. . . . I can plant my own in the garden. But my children, they will never be able to live there. Not when they are unemployed. They must work here and be able to live. There will be no place for them to work at, whereas we could live there on our pension money. We can live there with our pension."

In Ngcobo, Mam'Cethe grew vegetables, and they had milk and meat from the cattle and raised chickens and goats. The family did not want for food. The strictures of apartheid did not reach into the homelands. There were no pass laws, no Afrikaner police to contend with. Ngcobo was peaceful, poor, and self-reliant. Thandiswa's sister Zakithi remembers that life. It was not a time of want and deprivation. The Eastern Cape of today bears little resemblance to Mam'Cethe's idyllic memories, however.

For some internal migrants to Cape Town, relocation from places like Seymour is permanent; they will never return to the communities they came from. Others may participate—as individuals or as a group—in a round trip, or may even find yet another place in the country to stay for a while. Children may move ahead of their parents; parents may precede their children. They can be separated for many years, as Thandiswa's son has been during the years he has lived in Seymour with Zakithi. Most of the Xhosa families now in the Western Cape maintain roots of some kind in the regions from which they have come. Indeed, the very definition of family may stretch across thousands of miles and multiple households, with wages, goods in kind, houses, cows, and land exchanged, sometimes loaned, and children circulated for years at a time across extended kinship groups.

Clan structures facilitate this kind of movement and represent a form of interconnection that has withered in the Western world. A clan is generally a collection of kin, often quite distant from one another, who recognize a common ancestor, who may by now be hundreds of years in the past if they were ever living people at all. Thandiswa's clan is Qwathi and its members probably number now in the thousands. The responsibilities that clan members have to one another can be quite elaborate. Those who bear the same clan name are expected to step forward and help people who may be total strangers.

When we first started to get to know people in Khayelitsha, we worked with a young research assistant, Xola, who helped with interview translations from Xhosa to English. Xola is from Willowvale, a small town in the Eastern Cape Province. He came to Cape Town to attend the university and arrived without knowing a soul, with almost no money, and with very little idea of how to find housing or navigate the bureaucracy of his college. No one in his family had ever attended university before and he had never been outside the eastern region of the country. He got off the bus in central Cape Town and wandered around the City Bowl for a few hours feeling lost and hungry. Somehow—mostly via text messages—word got around to his clan members that one of their own had arrived and needed help. In no time, Xola had a place to stay, a modest amount of money in his pocket, and people he could rely on. None of them had ever heard of him before. His clan identity was all they needed to know: he is one of them.

This is, no doubt, the original safety net in rural regions where a shortage of food or a weather disaster leads people to need assistance from those far away. But it has great significance in a migratory society where young men like Xola find themselves a long way from home and in need of help. The exogenous nature of marriage patterns, the imperative to "marry out" beyond one's patrilineal (and matrilineal) kin, spreads the clan structure far and wide and helps to insure that those who know enough about these traditions can access a support structure built for the agrarian past that is no less useful in the industrial world.

In much this way, Amanda Yelesi's migration has left her with anchors in two worlds. She makes her living and conducts her active social life in the upscale parts of Cape Town. But her daughter, Lindiwe, lives with her grandmother, Zondwa, in a Black township outside Port Elizabeth. Amanda is on the phone every week checking up on Lindi's progress in school. She has come back to Port Elizabeth to visit occasionally, including the all-important time when Zondwa was trying to get Lindi into one of the better schools there, the one Amanda herself had attended. Amanda came scurrying back to Port Elizabeth to talk with the headmaster and remind him of her loyalty to the school, leaning on him to take her daughter. In this respect, Amanda is not an uninvolved parent even though she hasn't lived with her daughter full-time since she was an infant and probably won't unless Lindiwe joins her in Cape Town years down the road.

As a migrant from the Eastern Cape Province, Amanda often feels that she is not fully accepted by the people she works with or goes out with at night. The fact that she is from the Eastern Cape, that she has responsibilities to contribute to her family's expenses, including the need to build Vusi, her (male) cousin a house after his initiation, separates her from the middle-class community of Cape Town. Indeed, Amanda feels that Capetonians hold her at arm's length.

> They look down upon us because they are from the Western Cape and we are from the Eastern Cape. They think we are a bit behind. I don't have any female friends who are actually from the Western Cape, their values too different. If I hang out with them, then they'll see that I now live in this one bedroom and I share a flat with four other people, while they are living at home and spending their money on their Guccis and other stuff. But we have responsibilities, we send money home. I want my family at home to be fine, my mother and my grandmother and my kid. And so if you are not like them, they look down upon you and they judge you.

Amanda doesn't live in the townships and the people whose judgment she fears don't either. The status conflicts she experiences stay with her in the City Bowl. When internal migrants move into the interior of the townships, in places like Nyanga, the tension between newcomers and old-timers, all South African, can become as pronounced as the conflicts that divide foreigners and the native-born. Some township residents complain that these more recent Eastern Cape migrants are "just coming into the Western Cape" all the time, setting up squatter camps, and then expecting to receive a house straight away. Township residents may have been waiting years for government houses and some get furious at the very idea that anyone who has just "wandered in" would try to jump that queue.

Americans are no strangers to these kinds of tensions. Southerners often feel themselves judged as slow by northerners. Californians are regarded as too "laid back" by fast-talking city dwellers in the East. Europeans have their own regional stereotypes and they can be as derogatory. Some Flemish-speaking Belgians detest the Walloons, French speakers. Many Italians from the north do not consider Sicilians part of their nation. Regional differences in economic structure and cultural heritage can easily become fodder for stereotypes and ugly forms of discrimination that are more than simply annoying.

In South Africa, the fault lines that separate foreigners from the native-born have dug deep trenches in the social landscape. If the internal migration streams keep up, it is not unthinkable that tensions will grow sharper between those who have been in the cities for longer than the newcomers from poorer rural provinces. If that social distance simply divided regions of the country, or enclaves in the cities, it would be cause for concern. Powerful forces of international capital flows, natural resource extraction, political instability, uneven development, and even national social policy are translating into the movement of people across thousands of miles. They are leaving families and languages they understand, venturing into the unknown where they have to create new lives and learn the languages of others. And they are moving to the same cities, townships, and neighborhoods. Cheek by jowl, they must contend with competition for all that they need: jobs, housing, food, schooling for their children, citizenship papers, and even lovers.

In South Africa, a country that required a revolution to overturn invidious apartheid, differences are rearing their ugly heads once again. This has already led to bloodshed, evictions, and the erection of refugee camps and squatter settlements for the dispossessed. To see a place like Blikkiesdorp, to feel the grit and sand blow through your hair and confront the endless, bleak rows of steel containers that its residents have lived in now for more than two years, is to glimpse a South Africa unrecognizable to the people who fought the struggle for freedom and dignity for all. It is a nagging thorn in the side of the wealthiest country in Africa, the place that hopeful migrants look to for a future better than the war-torn or starvation-plagued ones they have left behind.

For many, the migratory experience translates into a lost generation or two: lawyers working as car guards, nurses selling craft goods in Greenmarket Square. They do what they can to get by and, like immigrants around the world, hope that their children will bring the family's fortunes back into alignment with their sense of dignity. For millions, that kind of upward mobility is a pipe dream. That is a challenge to South African democracy.

CHAPTER NINE

Political Heat

ON APRIL 8, 2009, TWO weeks away from the national elections in South Africa, the eighth election season since the end of apartheid, Amanda Sophotele is talking politics over drinks, after work. "Politics . . . it's just one big joke!" she exclaims.

> The country, South Africa . . . we were all fighters, we were standing, we were unified, fighting for a common purpose. Which was achieved! A small dot at the bottom of the map, South Africa . . . proved to the whole world that it would stand together and fight for a common goal. And after the apartheid era, we didn't fall apart, we were still functioning. Functioning! But now? We're a joke! We are a joke. We are just like the closest thing to Zimbabwe. Right now. Our politics are . . . all about power, greed, corruption. But [politicians] are all hiding behind banners that [say that we will] "make a better life for all South Africans," that's their favorite slogan. But no-o-o [rising sarcasm]: "we wanna be the ruling party so that we can push all you other people down and make you do whatever we want you to do." No-o-o! I'm not falling for it, I'm not buying it. I don't buy ANC, I don't buy DA, I don't buy IFP. . . I don't buy anything. I don't buy it!

This was the year after the ANC's National Executive Committee ousted President Thabo Mbeki, making him the first South African head of state to be recalled by his own party. The ejection came after long-standing accusations that Mbeki had been involved in a conspiracy to undermine the ANC party leader, Jacob Zuma. Zuma had been linked to fraud and corruption in a multibillion-rand arms deal. Bribes were allegedly paid to members of the ANC, including Zuma, to grease the wheels for contracts to supply new army materials and vehicles. Zuma and his allies protested their innocence and maintained that the investigation was a political witch hunt instigated by Mbeki and his followers. The High Court eventually ruled that the corruption charges and subsequent court case against Zuma were illegal. Too many interventions from high political figures had rendered an independent investigation impossible according to the court. The case against Zuma was dropped and a short time later the ANC pushed Mbeki out of his presidential post.[1]

Disgruntled cabinet members stepped down in solidarity with Mbeki, and a number of provincial premiers resigned as well. Prominent members of the ANC left the party, vowing to inaugurate a rival Congress of the People (COPE).[2] Bitter conflict over the purpose and aim of the new party, its "betrayal" of the ANC, and the suspected role of Mbeki in the formation of COPE were fought in the press, all in the run-up to the 2009 elections. The new party's platform had not been fully developed, but one feature that was publicized caught public attention: COPE suggested the end of Black Economic Empowerment employment quotas that had worked against Whites below the age of thirty. In this, COPE acknowledged the perspective of people like Brandon, who argued that they should not be punished for events of the past. In many ways the new party presented itself as wanting to be a more color-blind version of the ANC.

Alongside COPE, and especially visible in the Western Cape, the Democratic Alliance campaigned vigorously against the ANC, attempting to gain the votes not only of White South Africans, but especially Coloured and Black citizens.[3] Once the Democratic Party (DP)—which was itself descended from the Progressive Party, a relatively small, White-led party opposed to apartheid—the DA was reborn in 2000, when the DP merged with the former hard-right National Party. Some of the former NP members would later leave the DA, with Marthinus van Schalkwyk, former leader of the New National Party, making the almost unthinkable move of joining the ANC. Led by Helen Zille, former anti-apartheid activist and journalist who had exposed the news of freedom fighter Steve Biko's death in the 1970s, the DA would grow into strongest opposition party in the country.[4]

Its rise in the Western Cape had been and remains cause for serious unrest within the ranks of the ANC and its Youth League, whose members have attacked the DA as a Whites-only party, antagonistic to the rights of the majority. An endless series of verbal—sometimes racist—attacks back and forward between Zille and ANC Youth League leader Julius Malema were broadcast throughout the 2009 pre-election period.[5] DA supporters spread a "stop Zuma" slogan and focused on the lack of progress on infrastructure, corruption surrounding the Zuma administration, and fears over the consequences of one-party rule should the ANC become politically dominant. Zille pointed out that should the ANC win a two-thirds majority, it would be in position to pull more power to the national government's level rather than to municipalities. Her warnings spread by DA supporters inspired Brandon to launch his Facebook appeal to win more expatriate South African votes for the DA.

Voters seemed to have true choices between parties, yet thousands joined Amanda in sitting out the show. Amanda did not register to vote, because, as she explained, there was not one party she believed in. Instead, she told us, all she saw was "power and greed" among politicians.

Her mother and grandmother, and many others of the "struggle generation," could not fathom how their children could throw away a right for which they had fought for so long, the freedom they thought they would not see in their lifetimes. Amanda's mother, Zondwa, says that surely the ANC *has* made a difference in the lives of many:

> [The year 1994] was like a dream. Like I say, I never thought it would happen. You know, the day it happened we cried. A lot of us, we cried because for us, as the older generation, we never thought it would happen in our lifetime. We thought it would happen in children's lifetime. But it happened with us . . .
>
> I mean, as from [1994] up to this time. I feel like [government has] done a lot. The houses, things like pension. There was a certain age for us Blacks that you could not get your pension. But now people get it, even sick people get it. [Back] then, there was no such. That is why I'm saying now. . . . I feel government [has] done a great deal. . . . Things have become better, man.
>
> [Under apartheid], I couldn't go and work in Cape Town because I didn't have a pass to work in Cape Town. The minute I get to Cape Town, [whenever someone] there would find out that I'm from Port Elizabeth, I would be . . . detained for some days, then deported back to Port Elizabeth. You see, but now I can go and work anywhere in South Africa, wherever I feel like. That's why I say there's a lot . . . in South Africa that has changed. . . .
>
> You know that old government was just around to give people hardship, hurt them, and oppress them. . . . [Yes], people are in need of houses but if you could just have a look at how many houses have been built. There has been lot.
>
> I don't want to dwell on the negative—I see the positives, the positive side of things. And things are still going to happen. We just need to be a little bit more patient.

Zondwa's daughter Amanda has run out of that patience. She speaks angrily and bitterly about the backlog in service delivery and what she perceives as the ANC's (and everyone else's) unwillingness to really do something about it, the air of corruption and rudderlessness. She wonders what kinds of ideals politicians believe in. "We don't have a common goal anymore. . . . What are we standing for? What's everyone standing for? What am I standing for? What do I believe in? What does Zuma believe in? What does Mbeki believe in? . . . I don't know! . . . They say 'we're gonna improve this, this, and that,' but they've had all this time! And it's just not working. It isn't."

She would not deny that the government has made some efforts. "They are trying, they are. I'm not saying that everything has been completely bad, but it's just that there's more bad than good." Too many of the high hopes, she feels, have gone entirely unanswered.

In 1994, the ANC won the elections with promises to create a new, all-inclusive, colorblind South African society. It has pursued elements of that program ever since, and there is much to show for it. Stretches of shack lands that previously had no running water or electricity have been cleared, and over one million "proper" houses have been built, with sanitation and power.[6] Informal areas in many townships have been upgraded with toilets and water taps. While huge gaps separate good schools—ones supported by private fees and public resources—from the underperforming ones that have little or no fees to rely on, all South African children are guaranteed access to education, at least officially. New clinics have been built. Universal old age pensions, child allowances, and disability grants stream tax monies to poor households that previously received nothing and faced hunger and homelessness. Labor market restrictions have been lifted and employment equity and Black Economic Empowerment goals installed, aimed at mitigating the inequalities in the labor force created under apartheid. Companies are now expected to make sure their employee demographics reflect the demographic realities of the country. Quota and scoring systems benefit especially those non-Whites who have able to access higher education.

As a result of these efforts, a new Black middle class has slowly emerged, mainly young people, like Amanda herself, who have some form of tertiary education.[7] They hold more or less stable jobs with monthly salaries of R5,000 or more and have access to private medical care, time to spend on recreation, and, for those who can afford it, access to high quality schools for their children.[8] Yet for Amanda this is simply "not good enough." She points to the stain on the nation's honor that millions of South Africa's Black people remain trapped in poverty, stuck on the outskirts of the cities.[9] Their lives are circumscribed by sandblasted, remote townships created under apartheid. They cannot access proper schooling, and they are faced with hour-long commutes into the city to low-paid jobs if they have employment at all.

These realities nip at the heels of the new middle class because many have family members who continue to suffer these indignities, relatives they feel obligated to help. An active remittance economy links people like Amanda to family members in other parts of the country, even though many of those sending remittances, including Amanda, are not completely secure themselves. She sends part of her pay back to Port Elizabeth to help her grandmother and support her daughter who is in the care of her mother. As mentioned, Amanda and her sister also shell out money to support the needs of their younger cousin, Vusi. But the help Amanda provides drains funds she needs for herself. It is not surprising, then, that she is plagued by the fear that she could slide back down into the lower class. The slow progress of the country in uplifting those at the bottom of the class structure hence becomes a personal issue rather than an abstract political question.

The obvious wealth of White citizens, who continue to enjoy privileges unknown to the vast majority, rankles. The fancy City Bowl apartments and luxurious suburban homes contrast sharply with the dwellings in Nyanga and Khayelitsha. If these class divisions fell along race lines alone, it would be hard enough. Today, though, a nouveaux riche Black political elite enjoys outsized wealth. From Amanda's perspective, these are powerful people who could make a difference, if only they actually cared.

> My biggest frustration [is] going into townships. I mean, look at people who don't have proper sanitation. I mean, the living conditions there are just ridiculous, while these politicians are living a posh life. And . . . as I have said before, the only time they come down to the grassroots levels is when they need votes, when it's close to election time. After that they never go back. It's the same thing over and over again.

Amanda's friends are frustrated with the political establishment, especially because it *is* Black. The dismal conditions of the majority are supposed to matter to these politicians. Instead, Amanda argues, they are busy enriching themselves. The arms deal and the cloud of corruption surrounding Zuma was bad enough. Local politicians too were accused using taxpayers' money for private luxuries: unnecessary and expensive travel and hotel stays,

million-rand parties, contracts awarded to ANC members—including then–
Youth League leader Julius Malema—and the list goes on.[10]

> SHEILA: They [the ANC] are so busy defending Jacob Zuma that they for-
> get about the people on the ground, and that is the fundamental prob-
> lem. Fifteen years later, you still get people living in shacks, . . . people
> you know. . . . It is a sad state of affairs.
> TRACY: I would agree that it has only been fifteen years. We most defi-
> nitely need more than fifteen years to eradicate levels of dire . . . pov-
> erty we have, but we could have done in fifteen years much more than
> we have. The middle class has grown by heaps but . . . the poverty
> levels have not been eradicated to the same degree. . . . The point is
> the split that said "build the middle class, build the ruling class." That's
> how they do it with BEE [Black Economic Empowerment]: exclude
> the rest.

Fueling the outrage of the Black middle class been the unmistaken emergence of elites who are described as having "used the government's BEE programmes to gain wealth and influence."[11] Many of the "nouveaux" now belong
to the top echelons of the ANC or COPE. Amanda's friends and colleagues
criticize these people for being concerned with their own wealth while paying
no attention to the fate of the majority, who are living in shacks by the side of
the highway. An endless stream of newspaper reports on the millions of rand
being blown on parties feeds the disillusionment, and personal experiences
confirm the media accounts.

> LUTHO: I am not into any party politics [but] I was invited to . . . come and
> join [a workshop for young professionals], because of working with so
> many government people. They invited me and said, "you know what,
> come, we have this support group." The support group, it's a wing of
> young professionals linked to ANC, it is organized by the office of the
> premier. You know, at the agenda [meeting], they were talking all about
> a long list of jobs that were under government.
> SHEILA: Jobs?
> LUTHO: Jobs, like director position jobs and . . . and like tenders are go-
> ing to come and how we should align ourselves and position ourselves
> so that when . . . when I get to be a card-carrying member of the ANC,
> at the end of the day, they said, I will be a big member of the ANC and

then I will be seen as a loyal person and I will get one of the things that I want. . . .

So you see . . . even the approach that they are using; it is no longer [part of] the politics to say, "We have socioeconomic challenges in our country, let's sit down and find ways of how to address some of those jointly." Because for me, when I got the invite, I thought, "We are going to look at what will be our contribution as young professionals into the challenges that the country is facing. . . ." And that should be the platform that [these gatherings should be] used for. But basically when we got there, they were saying that there is going to be this post that will be coming from the office of the premier, but we need to be so sure that we are card-carrying members of the ANC, because if you're not, then you can't apply for the position.

Amanda pointed to the money being wasted on large parties by politicians out only to win their vote and then focus only on their own preservation.

When I went home during the December holidays, they were campaigning. COPE in Port Elizabeth [PE]; you stepped out of a bus in PE, it's like, "Hi, how are you. Are you COPE-ing?" And young people would join COPE because COPE has got the coolest parties ever. When you get there, you get money. You get meat, booze, drinks, everything. . . . We partied the whole weekend, from Friday to Monday, all under the COPE banner. . . . This is all the money that they are wasting.

Doubt and accusations of betrayal were voiced among the rising generation everywhere we went. We heard it among Thandiswa's neighbors, Anna's friends, Brandon's family, on Ambrose's Manenberg streets, and in Daniel's upper-middle-class environment in Paarl. The extent of this skepticism was more than confirmed by a 2012 national survey conducted by the Institute for Justice and Reconciliation (IJR). Forty percent of Black Africans younger than thirty-five expressed little or no confidence in political parties, as did two-thirds of young people of other races. Almost half of all South African youths were convinced that "leaders are not interested in people like me," and 46 percent claimed to have witnessed instances of corruption in their own communities.[12]

Dismay was especially high among those who, at one point in their lives, had been part of the ANC. Khanya, one of Anna's friends, recounts how her parents had been part of "the army," had gone into exile, left their children. The family's political background was firmly rooted in the struggle, with her grandfather imprisoned on Robben Island, where Nelson Mandela was incarcerated for decades after his conviction on charges of sabotage and conspiracy against the apartheid government. Today, she says, the disappointment over the state of the country and excesses of the powerful who have betrayed their history is especially heartbreaking for those who sacrificed so much. "My mother tells me that after all these years, and being away from home, being away from her kids, . . . to come back [to find] a few people who are running this country [into the ground] . . . [is so disappointing]."

> Mum tells me, "These people, I worked with them, we were in the army together, and all of a sudden they come back home and they've changed. And they're following a different vision . . . ministers who are in the government, ministers who don't do what they're supposed to be doing." I mean, like the minister of education, for instance: your job really is to make sure that the education system runs efficiently. You know, money's allocated to the right places, that kind of thing. . . . Sure you've got some very good schools in the country, but there's a lot of kids who do not have classrooms, who do not have textbooks. And we've got money. After I voted for them, and knowing they were also in the struggle, [hearing them] saying we need to change this country, we need to transform this country, and then they come back and where's the change? So I guess [my parents are] disappointed. Really, really disappointed.

Those who have been living in poverty their entire lives, who remember the high hopes and today live the shattered dreams, feel a greater anger. In a discussion group with Thandiswa's neighbors, one woman, Thosama, explained how she could not see why she should bother to vote in these elections. There was no one she trusted anymore, no one like Mandela who had led South Africa to freedom. Today, all Thosama can see is a president who is so sullied by the criminal charges surrounding him that it is hard to trust him or believe he truly has the best interests of the country in mind. "I won't vote," Thosama said almost defiantly.

> I don't know who to vote for, you see. The parties are breaking up, you don't know who to follow, there is a lot of scandal, there is a lot of fraud, so . . . I don't know who to trust. . . . Previously we could trust [the ANC] because it was Nelson Mandela all the way. I mean, he is still the guy who fought for us, who went to jail for twenty-seven years. I mean, he has done many things, we are free today, [and] he is the icon that I look

up to. . . . Now how can I vote for a criminal?. . . How can you say you want less crime [when] you are also a culprit, you are involved in crime?

Thandiswa's younger neighbors are particularly outraged by the ways that ANC politicians turned their backs on the unemployed and undereducated. One of them, Andile, said she was not going to vote.

No, it does not do anything for me as a young person. It was going to be my second time voting [laughs]. I am telling you, the only focus is when they are going for elections, and they come to your home [and] they promise this and that, and after that it never happens. I am telling you, I finished schooling in 2004. I have been struggling to get work till today. I am not going to vote. . . . My [résumés] are everywhere, but I am sitting at home, not working. They are not focusing on youth, they only focus if you are a member of a certain party. They work for people who are . . . members of the party. If you are like me, you don't support any party.

This is not idle talk. In 2009, many South Africans, especially younger ones, did avoid the ballot box. While the country boasts a high voter turnout, it has actually seen a sharp decline: 85.5 percent of all eligible South Africans voted in the historic 1994 elections, but only 64 percent did so in 1999, and just under 57 percent voted in 2009. In the 2011 elections for local positions, nearly 75 percent of South Africans between twenty and twenty-nine chose not to vote, but were instead "more likely to have taken part in violent street protests."[13]

In the poorest areas of the country, politics seem to be shifting from the polls to the streets. Sometimes described as a "rebellion of the poor," demonstrations have brought an estimated two million people a year out to protest, especially in the shack lands. The gatherings have grown increasingly violent.[14]

In reaction to the protests, Zwelinzima Vavi, general secretary of the Congress of South African Trade Unions, has publicly distanced himself from the wasteful behavior of some of the new Black elite and warned that the unrest among the poorest could well be a "ticking time bomb."[15] Trevor Manuel, previously the minister of finance, has said that corruption would be the biggest threat to any plan for development the country could come up with.[16] Archbishop Desmond Tutu has lashed out at corruption and BEE deals that continue to exclude the masses and serve only to enrich those who are better off. Tutu has warned repeatedly of the dangers of ignoring the lower classes. As far back as 2004, the BBC quoted the archbishop as worrying that the system of BEE deals could be "building up much resentment which we may rue later. 'Grueling, demeaning, dehumanizing poverty' experienced by millions of South Africans was the biggest threat to the country's security."[17]

These kinds of critiques led many to believe that what was needed most was for the ANC to face a credible opposition that could constrain the power of the dominant party. As one young man explained: "I voted for [the DA] because I believe in challenging the ANC's power as much as possible. They should not be in power any more. They are not doing a proper job. So I voted for the party who were most likely to win. . . . Everyone in the Western Cape voted DA. That's one good thing I'm happy about, . . . that the DA won the Western Cape. Now people can see how a properly run province can compare . . . to the ANC running a province."

The condemnation of the ANC clearly reflects the self-interest of White South Africans who lost control of the country in 1994. But it is more than that, Whites told us. The ANC is unable to do anything right, even for its own people. "They [Black people] are worse off today," we were told. Teachers colleges had been closed—"so where are teachers supposed to be trained now?"—and technical schools have been shuttered: "there are no more qualified nurses." From the White perspective, education has gone downhill: "They had to throw all the White teachers out, and now look at the state of our education. Their own children are not being taught anymore." Finally, the abysmal condition of the townships did not inspire faith in the ruling party's competence. One White woman in the northern suburbs offered the example of a Khayelitsha day-care center supported by her church community, without which the children would have gone hungry.

> MARIEKE: They [Black people] are themselves worse off than what they were.
>
> *They are worse off now?*
> ANTOINETTE: Yes, they are sitting in the squatter camps. What kind of a life is that for the little children? They get sick. It's terrible. Our church has a crèche in Khayelitsha, a lot of churches collected money for the crèche, and they built the school. The little children come there to be taken care of.
> MARIEKE: What does that tell you? The Whites have to go again to take care of them and improve their life standards.
> ANTOINETTE: The little children look healthy, beautiful. They come in in the mornings, get their porridge. They get juice. If they are sick they get

their medicine or whatever they need, they get de-worming pills. Then they get cooked food, and they all have a little mattress and they go sleep. Then they get another sandwich when they go home at five, so the parents don't really have to give them more food. They are taken care of, they get fruit. It is all donated, they don't buy it themselves. There are two schoolteachers that keep it going, plus another one that cleans and takes care of the place and so forth. The University of Stellenbosch takes care of the students.

Manenberg is worlds away from the Northerns, but Ambrose and his mother think along similar lines, though with an even stronger tinge of racial conflict. The Black men ruling the country do not care about Coloured or White people in the country, they feel. Ambrose's diary is filled with anger toward the ANC for the way it favors Black South Africans:

> On everyone's lips lies the fear of the ruling party who emphasise Black Empowerment, Black will rule alone, that is what they say. Whites will leave the country, Browns, Indians and other nations will live like slaves under their rule. They believe that they were the only ones who went through hardships during the apartheid era and they forget about the other non-Whites who were in a similar position. . . .
>
> Black people are laughing at what is happening to Brown people, because they are progressing while we stay on the ash-heap that is why at least another 5 years lies in their hand to rule and to let us go further down the drain.

Ambrose is convinced that the only thing Black politicians are after is "our mothers' and fathers' hard-earned money," and he has called on people to vote for the DA. But even more, he called on the community to help "sort itself out." If no help were to come from government, if government was "only out to push us further into this hole," then the only solution was to stand up and struggle against "corruption and fraud, fighting, and crime."

Ambrose's desires to see Manenberg become more beautiful and life for children and youth more meaningful, less violent, and less hopeless. The ANC has no place in this dreamscape. Hence, almost in unison with Brandon, Ambrose beseeched his people to "vote DA" and support its "vision for the future."

Ambrose recognizes that the ANC "brought freedom" to those who were previously oppressed, but gratitude for that history, he thinks, should not limit rightful expectations that government is responsible for improving conditions for everyone. Surely mere participation in the anti-apartheid struggle does not justify government mediocrity or worse. Apartheid, he argued, is a thing of the past and cannot be an excuse for damaging policies that are equally racist:

> *And now it seems as if we all were a part of and supported Apartheid and now we must all suffer for what others have done. . . . People with Grade R certificates sit in Parliament, because [they were] part of the "struggle."[18] What about the people, from the next generation, who were not in the struggle but are more competent about leadership and have experience to do the job? Apartheid is for olden time's people to try and open old wounds to win votes.*

Liberal Whites who were once part of the anti-apartheid movement were not far from Ambrose in their opinions. Shack lands should have been eliminated. Crime should be under control. How could it ever have gotten to this point? From their perspective, corruption is not an accidental by-product of poverty. It is the *reason* why progress has been so slow. Things could have been different were it not for catastrophic moral failures in the ANC leadership.

While once a strong supporter of the ANC, Gilad now says he cannot vote for the ruling party anymore. "The new government is as nondescript for me as Gordon Brown in England or Sarkozy in France. It's just a government," he commented with disgust. "Just a bunch of politicians who are pursuing their own interests."

The gulf between the political elite and the people is shown by a recent public opinion poll, the Reconciliation Barometer.[19] Government is a distant bureaucracy. Hence, if anything is to come of their lives, they will have to do it themselves; that is the view of nearly 50 percent of South African young adults.

Their elders counsel patience. Ambrose's father, Patrick, voted for the DA in the 2009 elections but wondered whether that was truly the right thing to do and whether it was truly justified to be so hard on the ruling party. "I heard [it said] that the ANC had done nothing for the people, but the ANC *did* do a lot for the people, they removed many wrong things. People need to remember these things. . . . The ANC removed the death sentence . . . friends who grew up with me went to the gallows. The ANC removed this for the people, they need to think about that . . . they made us free. . . . They should give the ANC a chance to still build the houses, but now the people have turned on the ANC."

Young people have lost not only their confidence in the ANC but the sense of duty their elders feel to support the party that led the country to freedom. Khanya, a Black woman in her mid-twenties, explained, "You know, I can walk away. I don't have to be an ANC member." This was hardly the norm in her family:

> We are probably the first generation of people in my family, for instance, who can vote outside the ANC. Like, I have a choice. You know, my grandmother, it's not even in her far-off dreams not to vote for the ANC. And for my parents, . . . the ANC is like family—they're not a political party, they're not a religious group, they're family. . . . But I think for the first time we live in a generation where we can. We can decide: maybe not the ANC.

Her thoughts were echoed months later, when members of the Freedom Generation registered in national opinion polls that they are "not as swayed by history as their elders" and that the majority of them have "no party allegiance."[20]

CURIOUS VICTORIES

Despite the widespread sentiments of disillusionment and distrust, the ANC won the 2009 general elections, as it had all previous elections since 1994, with an overwhelming majority. It narrowly missed a two-thirds majority but still triumphantly claimed 65.9 percent of the vote, leaving the opposition parties behind with 7.4 percent for COPE, 4.6 percent for Inkatha, and 16.7 percent for the DA, now the largest unified opposition in the country. The rise in the DA's support has been explained, however, mainly by the "decline in support for other opposition parties" rather than by a decrease in votes for the ANC.[21]

Given the frustration we heard throughout the Western Cape in the run-up to the elections, how did the ANC victory come about? "Liberation solidarity"—of the sort evinced by Ambrose's father, is certainly part of the answer. Voter turnout decreased, but, among those who did vote, the majority of Black citizens clearly saw no alternative. Khanya explained: "My grandfather from my father's side was in Robben Island, was jailed and stuff during the apartheid times, and also [he] died in jail, and my dad as well. So, yeah, politics is more than just a topic of discussion, I guess it's where they come from. They tell you they're ANC through and through. . . . Some people are, like, 'Yeah, I'm part of a political party,' but for [my relatives] it's bigger and it's deeper." A young Black man, Mandla, notes that the ANC was "like a school" for his elders, not just an organization, and his grandfather, who was part of the ANC, can't understand voting for any other party.

We heard many express similar sentiments, especially among the liberal elders, but also among young people. There is a remaining support for the ideals and the values that the ANC and its Freedom Charter once stood for, and there is nowhere else to invest that political sentiment. Lulama, a young man from Anna's circle of friends, explained that he didn't agree with what the government was doing but intended to vote, saying that "at the root of it all there is . . . a principled vision . . . of what this country is all about and what the democracy is supposed to be." He wanted to contribute to that vision and align himself with the ideals of the people who gave their lives for the country.

Andiswe, an older woman in Thandiswa's neighborhood, expressed the sentiments of many who voted for the ANC and always will: "We got freedom. Now we are free to go, [we] are free to walk around, and we don't get asked where is our pass. . . . Twenty-four years [ago and more], they struggled a lot, went to prison, [got] shot at and chased by dogs, all of that [for our freedom], so why should I vote for another party that was not visible at that time? You see, that's the only reason for voting." Her neighbor agreed: "The ANC was fighting for the struggle. . . . They struggled for us, [and] now we are grown up and see other parties. Now we say, 'ANC is full of shit,' excuse my language. It's not right, man, it's not right [laughs]. I grew up in the ANC. I am gonna vote them until I die. I am not gonna lie to you."

Even though the doubt surrounding Zuma was high, the ANC was still seen by many as the only valid, functioning party that would create a better future for all. A young man in Thandiswa's group had described Zuma as "not clever enough to be our president," but he explained the ANC itself was the only organized force for change. Thandiswa herself agreed. She has a responsibility, as she sees it, to insure that her children will live under ANC rule.

> My children [are still very small and] can't speak for themselves, so by voting the ANC, I am speaking for them. I am the one who is going to foster for their needs to be met because I . . . put my X in the ballot paper for the ANC, so the next government will be the ANC. I am going to force them to deliver because I voted for them.

Perhaps Zuma was not an ideal presidential candidate. Perhaps the ANC had been slacking and corruption high. Nonetheless, Thandiswa insisted, the democratic state is working. Civil society *does* work. It may take government too long to deal with people's needs, but people do have the means to exert pressure on the politicians they voted for.

Of course, the Western Cape is distinctive, with Coloured people—who generally gravitate to the Democratic Alliance—a numerical majority. Not surprisingly, then, in 2009 the ANC lost control of the province and landed in second with 31.5 percent of the vote, compared to the DA's 51.46 percent. That victory set off anxious jitters among Black people in the Western Cape, especially in townships like Khayelitsha.[22] We heard people wonder whether they were safe in the province. Would the DA bring back the "Whites only" signs that the old National Party had favored? Was "another form of apartheid" soon to arrive?

Where do these fears come from? The run-up to the 2010 World Cup is part of the back story. Helen Zille was mayor of Cape Town during that time, and in preparation for the arrival of millions of soccer fans she engineered local legislation that removed Black and Coloured traders like Suzanne, whose presence she decided would not project the right image during the festivities. After some were evicted from the (mainly Coloured) Mitchell's Plain market, the informal trader organization there sought broad support against the city's approach, pointing out that informal trade is the only way many poor South Africans are able to sustain themselves and their families:

> Traders without permits are left without the ability to continue their businesses after many have been trading in the Town Center for over 20 years. The community is behind the Traders and we will continue to fight for the rights we know we deserve. The poorest of the poor continue to be marginalised in a country that claims to be democratic. Traders ask for support and solidarity.[23]

Zille's stance on internal migration was another sore point. She argued that migration from the Eastern Cape and the northern provinces was overwhelming the townships around Cape Town. Her comments raised the fear that she would declare internal migrants unwelcome and perhaps even deport them, a common practice during the apartheid era. Thandiswa's neighbor Qondiswa was openly afraid of this outcome. "Helen Zille said people from Eastern Cape must stop coming here," she complained. "People from the Eastern Cape they come here because it is their country. . . . People need money, so people come from there and they come here, they come here to work, they don't just come here to sit."

The DA's public pronouncements continue to be scrutinized for anti-Black animus. In 2012, Zille referred to Eastern Cape young people who came to the Western Cape in search of a better education as "refugees."[24] The remark sparked widespread outrage, with an ANC spokesperson describing Zille's statement as racist and "typical of the erstwhile apartheid government's mentality that resorted to influx control measures to restrict black people from the so-called white areas."[25]

Many Black people describe Zille as an authoritarian with little appetite for entering negotiations or openness to taking the concerns of non-White South Africans into account. "That is what [frightens] me about her," Amanda explained. "Her sense of 'it's my town, I am law, and you will do as I say' is scary to me."

Some White liberals seem convinced that Amanda has it right. The DA is not an authentic supporter of the rights of the poor, and if they ever were to control national politics, it will not be good for Black and Coloured people, Colin asserted.

> The DA was founded . . . on White sectarian politics. I'd feel the same way I feel about a Catholic Separatist Party in Northern Ireland, or a Unionist Protestant Party. . . . I'd feel the same way about any sectarian party. The worst is any sectarian party [that] doesn't give place in themselves for the diversity of their constituency. Women and Blacks but particularly Blacks, because [the DA is] a White party. And they're anti–affirmative action, which is to me the core issue in South Africa: affirmative action.

How can you place the emphasis on merit, Colin wonders, when the starting positions of South Africa's racial groups are so different on account of the deep tracks of apartheid? How can the DA overlook the fact that Whites have what they have because Blacks were oppressed for so long? The "merit game," as he calls it, simply doesn't work in a society that has systematically deprived the majority of its population for so long. He says you can't suddenly say to Black people, "'Okay, we're all equal.' It's ridiculous. It's appalling. And I am appalled [by] anyone who is against affirmative action."

WELFARE POLITICS VERSUS MERITOCRACY?

The ANC and the main opposition party share very similar views on the legitimacy of the country's social safety net. Both recognize the extent of inequality in the past and acknowledge the responsibility to support the poorest people in the country through a system of welfare grants. Both have warned against the creation of a nation dependent on excessive state support and the unsustainability of a system of "payouts" that relies on the tax base of only about 12 percent of the population.[26] Yet in the eyes of the Black majority of the country, the DA is the more reluctant supporter of the welfare state: the DA's commitment to the needs of the majority is weaker and more begrudging.

The ANC's manifesto places its main emphasis on the creation of a "united, non-racial, non-sexist and democratic society," and it aims to do so by "the liberation of Africans in particular and Black people in general" as well as by "uplifting the quality of life of all South Africans, especially the poor."[27] Given this emphasis, its support for state pensions and child support grants comes as little surprise. Without this infusion, the proportion of the population living below the poverty line would be even higher.[28] Approximately sixteen million people—nearly 30 percent of the entire population—now benefit from the social grant system, and there are measurable indications that this redistribution has had positive effects on material hardship, health, physical stature, school attendance patterns among children, and on the capacity of job seekers to look for (if not find) employment.[29]

The social security system does nothing to create pathways for upward mobility. But it does prevent widespread deprivation and hunger for those who are eligible for state support, particularly mothers with children and the elderly. Its existence has transformed grandmothers in particular into valued relatives because they now command a modest but reliable income stream that can help support the needs of families who lack sufficient earnings from wages.

In theory, the DA also supports this system of social security "as long as [welfare grants and state assistance] are kept within what it considers reasonable limits." But instead of making the needs of poor people central to their policies, the DA manifesto emphasizes the need to create "an open opportunity society," individual responsibility, and the need to "empower as many citizens as possible to help themselves over the long run."[30]

They have warned against a social grant system that becomes nothing more than "hand-outs [that] breed dependency on the state and a culture of patronage." People who receive state support, the DA argues, lose the ambition to look for work. Helen Zille warns that this recipe for dependency will only strengthen the ANC.

Political analysts point out that "in a country in which more than a quarter of its citizens are out of work and poverty is endemic, telling people to get on with their lives and enjoy the benefits of an 'opportunity society' is not an easy platform from which to win votes."[31] Thandiswa's life illustrates how difficult this desired possibility of self-reliance is for working-age adults like her. A mother of two, with no other stable income than her father's contributions to the household, child support grants, and the pension her own mother brings home, she is lacking educational credentials to propel her forward. Thandiswa nonetheless continues to try every conceivable avenue to extract herself from the endlessly depressing situation of unemployment and poverty.

She has looked for work, tried to start her own business, inquired about how to get back into school, and taken out loans from relatives and people she knew and trusted to take short vocational courses. Her efforts have been as endless as they have been fruitless. It is hard for her to imagine finding a way out of her dire situation, and the idea that a political party could set its sights on insuring that she loses her child allowance is, for Thandiswa, simply terrifying.

Government subsidies are, of course, nothing new. When they flowed to the privileged, the practice did not trouble them. For many years, the White farmers, already a politically powerful group, were beneficiaries of state largesse. Subsidized fertilizer, derived from costly oil and price supports, enabled farmers to compete effectively against world commodity prices. In the United States, policies like these have been dubbed "welfare for the rich" and "corporate welfare," and farm subsidies have been a mainstay of midwestern agriculture (and the politics that goes with it). To South African farmers, these policies were investments in the country's economic engine.

When the ANC came to power, it set about reducing those subsidies, requiring farmers to share ownership with their workers and opening the door for reform that aimed at a more equitable ownership of land in the country. The escalating cost of making good on ANC promises for homes, jobs, and education for the impoverished majority, created pressures to economize elsewhere. From the Black point of view, it was high time the state served the majority. From a White perspective, this was economic reprisal.

What to think then, of the argument about dependency? Those familiar with the welfare reform debates of the Clinton presidency have heard this story before: generosity toward the poor encourages laziness, reduces the motivation to work, and creates a powerful downdraft on the public treasury. It is worth noting that while the South African safety net is a lifeline, it is hardly generous. The child support grant is less than R300 per month per child up to the age of seventeen. The old-age pension tops out at R1,260 per month, and this money is generally shared among family members on a variety of household expenses. Few critics of the system could make do on this level of monthly income. The child support grant system is part of a patchwork quilt of resources that prop up poor households. We get a glimpse of how tenuous it is from Nwabisa's field notes from an interview with Thandiswa about where her money comes from:

> *Firstly Thandiswa gets the child grant of R240 per child. She receives the money through the bank. Her other two sisters also receive the child grant for their children. Before she found work, Thandiswa was dependent on her parents' income: the mother's pension of approximately R1000, and whatever her father earns as a farm worker outside of town: he contributes R250 to the household's funds every week. Part of the money received is also sent to the Eastern Cape, to help . . . with the children [there] and money for electricity.*
>
> *Basic services such as electricity are paid off Mam'Cethe's pension and the additional R250 per week. Some money is set aside to pay up on "lay away" clothing accounts held at large shops. Nomonde also helped out by providing groceries for the family every month end after she was paid. When it comes to buying things for herself like toiletries, Thandiswa relies on supplies purchased by Thumeka, Mam'Cethe, or Zikhona who sometimes also received some money from her boyfriend.*
>
> *Food has gotten expensive lately, especially food for the children. And diapers are expensive too. In fact, Thandiswa no longer buys them at Shoprite but at the Somali owned shops because they sell singles at R2.50 a diaper.*

Having to depend financially on others and on the grant system is exactly what bothers Thandiswa. She hates feeling infantilized. Millions of people in her position must agree. Aiming for the sky, the majority seems to continue to believe in upward mobility, wishing for independence, education, employment and inclusion in the broader South African experiment of democracy.[32] If they could, they would do without nibbling on the grants or pensions of their mothers or grandmothers.

Amanda's situation is a case in point. During her spells of unemployment, she could have accessed a child support grant to help her with Lindiwe's expenses, but when we asked her whether she had done so, she shook her head in surprise: "The grant? No. I wasn't going to stand in the queue among those who are so much worse off than me. No, they *need* the grant. I managed, together with my family. We managed."

We found little evidence of a "grant dependency syndrome" among the people of this book. What we did see was a nation of people desperate for work, willing to sell snacks, toys, or windshield covers in the middle of the road just to earn a few rand. Official national unemployment rates remain at 25 percent, but with as many as 57 percent of young Black South Africans and 63 percent of young Black women out of work, the country faces an employment crisis that the grant system can scarcely address. The ANC's efforts at job creation have not paid off at scale, and the educational system, which is supposed to provide young people with the skills and knowledge necessary to make it in an ever more competitive environment, is failing dismally. Almost twenty years after the end of apartheid, the harsh reality is that less than half of all grade-one-enrolled pupils eventually graduate with a grade-twelve certificate. Only 15 percent get good enough marks to allow them entrance into universities, and, of those who do, less than half eventually graduate.[33] Inequalities fall along racial lines: less than 40 percent of Black South Africans between the ages of twenty-one and twenty-five are passing their high school completion exams ("matric"), compared to 80 percent of White and Indian South Africans.[34] The majority of Black youths who do make it through secondary or even higher education do so with lower levels of skill than their White and Indian peers.[35]

One cannot help but wonder why the outcomes remain so dismal after all the effort made since the onset of democratic rule to equalize government investment in the nation's schools. The answer lies both in differential resources and mismanagement of what is available. Although schools receive the same amount per capita from the government, they are able to charge families additional fees that vary dramatically by the social class of the students. Paarl Boys' High can obviously afford to charge higher fees to the mainly wealthy parents whose children attend the school. Schools in far poorer areas like Manenberg and Khayelitsha can ask very little of parents who often struggle to provide enough food for the family. This difference in resources inevitably impacts the number[36] and skill levels of teachers,[37] the availability of books, and virtually every other aspect of the educational infrastructure.[38] In the poorest areas, widespread reports describe unmotivated teachers who do not manage to keep often-unruly pupils under control, do not teach, or simply remain absent.[39] Violence in schools is a serious problem: in August 2013, authorities closed sixteen schools in Manenberg because a wave of gang violence left teachers too afraid to go work.[40]

These problems combine to create impossible poverty traps for young people like Thandiswa and Ambrose, who understand that education would improve their lives but cannot find the means to return to school while simultaneously needing to look for work, let alone to try to return to a school that would offer a better quality education than the ones in their immediate environment. Without access to social welfare—they're too old to receive child support and too young for a pension—they are vulnerable and have few other options but to remain dependent on others around them.

The political system in South Africa is a work in progress, and its elected officials have only begun to grapple with these serious problems of social inequality. The post-apartheid generation has never known a time when there were no grants to help the most desperate and no child allowance to stop little ones from going hungry. Their parents remember all too well.

CHAPTER TEN

After Freedom

THE AFRICAN NATIONAL CONGRESS INHERITED a country with one of the highest levels of inequality in the world, created and sustained by a political system designed to keep the races apart in all spheres of life and to exclude the majority population from the nation's wealth, its best schools, and labor market opportunities. Extreme rural poverty pulled workers into a migrant labor system that was strictly regulated by the race laws of the apartheid system and hence tore African families apart, leaving millions of women in mostly barren, under-serviced homelands while men lived and worked in single-sex hostels on the outskirts of cities, sending their pay back to the homelands.

Legislation reshaped the racial landscape of the cities, ejected people of color, and cleared the way for Whites to take control of the most valuable real estate. A Coloured colleague at the University of Cape Town recalls that her grandmother was forcibly removed in the late 1960s from an area that is today known as the Waterkant, a lively tourist enclave that looks out on the magnificent Table Bay Harbor. The family filed a land restitution claim after apartheid fell and had to wait until 2004 to receive compensation of R40,000 (about $4,000). Similar houses in the Waterkant are now on the market for R6–7 million ($600,000–$700,000), but the family will see none of that appreciation.[1]

By the time the Group Areas Act was fully implemented, the country's urban Black and Coloured populations had been dumped in forbidding, distant settlements that had no stores, jobs, or green space. Parents spent long hours commuting back into the cities they had been ejected from, leaving their children on their own in increasingly violent, drug-plagued townships. "The Americans," the Bad Boys, and all the other gangs of Manenberg were the predictable result of the destruction of existing social structures, the absence of adults, lack of privacy, and the sense of total exclusion from the larger city. What started as a form of territorial protection morphed into a lethal drug market that continues to plague the apartment blocks in the township.

The result of apartheid policies was a population burdened by illiteracy, violence, high rates of infectious disease, and malnutrition, in slums that provided nothing in the way of a springboard when apartheid ended. On the eve of the first free election in 1994, 51 percent of the South African population was living below the United Nations Development Programme poverty line of R354 per month, close to 25 percent could not read, and more than two million South Africans had no formal housing.[2] Meanwhile, the country's vast holdings of diamonds, gold, platinum, chrome, manganese, and other valuable minerals belonged to mining companies who employed Black labor at exploitative wages. The rich agricultural land that had made South Africa self-sufficient as a food producer and an exporter of dairy products, beef, and wine was almost entirely in the hands of the wealthy White minority.

It is small wonder that the victory of the ANC over apartheid and the first free election, which swept Nelson Mandela into office, ignited an explosion of hope. Political exiles who had fled for their lives began returning by the hundreds. Apartheid legislation was repealed, and the National Party and ANC—once mortal enemies—together drafted an interim constitution that provided for a "Government of National Unity" and a five-year transition. The new South Africa was to strive for equality, non-racialism, and non-sexism; acknowledge the supremacy of the constitution and rule of law; and be governed via democracy.[3] The 1993 interim constitution enshrined free elections and guaranteed ethnic groups representation in Parliament. In June 1994, the ANC and NP jointly developed what would be finalized in 1996 as the Constitution of the Republic of South Africa. Mandela set about deploying the national treasury to improve the living conditions of the poorest Blacks, while simultaneously encouraging Whites who had both the human and the "real" capital to stay put. Stabilizing foreign investment was a high priority in a country so dependent on extractive industries, particularly mining. Where post-colonial countries like Zimbabwe had expelled Whites or expropriated land from them, Mandela counseled patience and inclusion.

The Truth and Reconciliation Commission, inaugurated in 1995, took up the task of exposing human rights abuses and fixing responsibility, but it avoided the bitter fruit of punishment. Discovering what had really happened in the dungeons of the apartheid system and exposing perpetrators to the court of public opinion was a daunting task. It required stripping back layers of secrecy, digging into government archives, and publicly interviewing survivors, soldiers, and police. Families like the Sophoteles and far-more-famous families like the Bikos, who lost their loved ones without explanation or with transparently bogus ones (usually that the disappeared had committed suicide), were eager, at a minimum, to heap public shame on the perpetrators. Though it undertook a wrenching process, the commission was responsible in many ways for the relatively peaceful transition to democracy in South Africa. The country was likened to Northern Ireland—another place filled with murderous strife and class/religious division—in the annals of successful political evolutions.

For ordinary people, the most visible changes were the disappearance of "Whites only" signs, separate queues in shops, and other humiliating forms of forced segregation and labor control that divided families. People who once had to carry passes and fear a police force that operated with impunity were now free to walk where they wanted, to love and marry without regard to skin color, and to criticize the government and its institutions when the spirit moved them. It was an intoxicating time. Amanda and the other women in her family bought new dresses to go to the polls, and Amanda, though just a child at the time, stood alongside her grandmother and thousands of eager voters, celebrating the freedom that had been almost unthinkable ten years before.

Since that time, South Africa has continued its evolution toward modern democracy. Elections are hotly contested, and voter participation, though lower now than in 1994, remains very high by international standards, eclipsing that of the United States.[4] Factions have erupted and new parties have arisen. In 2013, one emerged with Mamphela Ramphele, a former anti-apartheid activist and managing director at the World Bank, at the helm. Political leaders take to the airwaves and plaster posters all over the cities and townships. Party conventions are covered by a free press, and when corruption raises its ugly head, citizens are informed by their newspapers and can vote their conscience.

Of course, there is no perfect democracy, and this one has its flaws. To many, the dominance of the ANC leaves little room for truly meaningful opposition, especially at the national level, and there is concern that the overwhelming victories of the ANC in national and local elections will lead the party's leaders to be less responsive than they would be if faced with competitors.[5] Like Brandon and Anna, many in Cape Town and other urban areas do not feel politically engaged and look in vain for parties that express their interests or their political perspectives. Ambrose and Amanda are alternately angry and frustrated by the ANC's failings, either due to racial exclusion (favoring Blacks, in Ambrose's opinion) or because of blatant corruption (Amanda's chief complaint). Yet on the whole, democratic governance has worked and, although discontent with the government may be high in certain urban areas, and especially among Whites in the country, it remains for the voters and their representatives to set a course.[6] The people can throw their officials out if that is their will.

Economic justice and public safety have proven to be more challenging. Mandela's promises to the nation ignited pent-up desires for dramatic improvements in housing, education, and employment. Some of the promises to improve the life of ordinary people have come to pass, including an extended child grant system to help support the cost of raising the youngest generation, the opening up of public education, and state subsidies for housing. All of these policies have been instrumental in reducing the deepest forms of poverty. The positive consequences of their implementation can be measured in the increased height and weight of children, for whom malnutrition was once a serious barrier to adequate physical growth. Without these resources, families like Abbie's would be destitute and her children would be far worse off.

Households with a retired person can rely now on elder pensions that were extended to people of color at the time of the transition (finalized in 1993). These provide a stable (if not opulent) source of income, a measure of economic security previously unknown to poor South Africans.[7] That the taxes that support these measures are being paid almost entirely by White citizens is a demonstration of a commitment to redress the economic inequalities that accrued over the long history of apartheid. While complaints are loud and clear about the more aggressive forms of affirmative action, and there are murmurs around the unsustainability of the welfare system, there is rarely an open call for rolling back taxes that support these forms of social spending—unlike in countries like the United States, where a common refrain of opposition to "welfare spending" is heard virtually every election season.

Despite these improvements, economic and educational inequality—both between and within racial groups—has grown over the past twenty years. Race continues to play a huge role in where people find themselves on the socioeconomic scale. The majority of Black South Africans continue to live in poverty, in overcrowded townships or underdeveloped rural areas. They are the primary victims of the AIDS epidemic. South Africa is now the epicenter of that health crisis and its least fortunate citizens are often crushed by the social consequences (with increasing numbers of orphaned children needing to be absorbed by extended families or residential care programs).[8] A tiny elite has managed to capture the benefits of economic growth, while the vast ocean of the country's poor people has remained poor. Inequality has grown rapidly in most of the world's affluent countries, and in this regard South Africa is following a path unfolding in United States and western Europe as well.

What is striking for ordinary people, however, is that race is no longer the only dividing line between the good life and destitution. A new Black elite, the most visible members of which are politicians or self-made entrepreneurs who managed to capitalize on BEE deals, is now visible, their faces gracing the covers of popular magazines. Film stars, athletes, bankers, fashion models, and university leaders constitute a new legion of Black privilege. Like their White counterparts, they live in gated communities and houses surrounded by barbed wire, electric fences, and guards.

More ordinary but still upwardly mobile young Black people like Amanda and young Coloured people like Daniel enjoy affluence that earlier generations could never have accessed. Approximately five million Black South Africans are currently considered middle class—although the definition of who exactly constitutes this "new class" is debated.[9] They are homeowners with nice cars; they frequent the clubs where Amanda likes to spend her weekend nights. The lucky ones get to travel abroad and mix with international elites. Even so, many of them have an insecure hold on their good fortune and worry about whether they can maintain their comfortable place. A stroke of bad luck—a job loss, a sick relative who needs care—could see them slide back down into the lower classes.

As long as the middle class is doing well, the presence of the high-profile Blacks elicits no more resentment than one observes in other highly stratified societies. Indeed, most people hope to be able to emulate their good fortune. When Thandiswa's sister Abbie sees the famous singer Lira or model Rosette Nogomotsi strut their stuff on television, she isn't angry that these glorious women have so much more than she does. But when the whiff of scandal surrounds a wealthy Black politician, her fury is palpable. Solidarity within the race is an important social principle, and greed, bribery, and other forms of corruption are dismaying forms of betrayal in a country with so much need.

The deep tracks of inequality are perhaps most obviously displayed in the statistics on violent crime. South Africa has one of the highest murder rates in the developed world. Carjacking, break-ins, robbery, assault, and rape leave everyone feeling vulnerable on a daily basis. Higher-income neighborhoods look like fortresses. Houses are barricaded behind high walls with jagged broken glass sticking up along the tops. Windows, especially those that look out onto the streets or narrow side passages, are covered with bars, so that an unobstructed view of a hillside or a park is rare. Security companies do a brisk business in electrified fences, alarm systems, and cameras. In this, South Africa has a lot in common with other extremely unequal countries, such as Brazil, and it is not a happy comparison.

Families with few resources have also found it necessary to invest in burglar bars and fences at their front doors, although they are nothing compared to the high-tech security measures of suburbia. In the areas most troubled by

violent crime, poor people continue to live with abiding fear of physical assault and robbery and worry about their children's safety when they need to
use public latrines, play in a park, or walk home any time after the sun sets.
They are the most common victims of violent crime and have the least protection from it. There are predators in their midst who have few means of
legitimate earnings and turn to crime as an alternative. But necessity is not
the only reason for a spike in crime. The people of this book have sometimes
complained that a breakdown in civil society has led to crime that cannot be
explained by poverty or unemployment. Ambrose often looks out from his
furtive life in Manenberg to see a society plagued with a lack of trust and an
attraction to violence.

Some of the violence is organized. Street protest remains a ubiquitous
feature of South African politics, except that now it is mostly aimed at a Black
government that has failed to deliver. Protests during 2012 were especially
hard on the country, its economy, politicians, and poor people, with weeks of
industrial actions in the mining, transportation, and agricultural sectors that
threatened investors' trust and the country's economy. The social tensions and
strikes led financial analysts like Moody's to wonder out loud about the labor
laws and the persistent inequality and poverty, now almost twenty years after
the transition to a new democracy.

In December 2012, a strike at the Marikana platinum mine led to a bloody
confrontation between the state and its citizens, spreading rapidly to several
other mining sites. It started with workers in the North West Province who
went on strike against Lonmin, the company that holds a near monopoly on
platinum deposits. The miners demanded wage increases for the backbreaking work they do deep underground. Their jobs are dangerous and physically
exhausting, and few can work in the mines more than a couple of years before
their bodies give out. The South African police opened fire on striking miners
and killed more than thirty of them.[10]

Shockwaves went through the country and comparisons were readily
made with the apartheid-era Sharpeville massacre, when more than sixty civilians were murdered by South African security forces. It was a troubling display of force coming from a Black government, with Black police in the lead.

Still, the strikes continued. Truck drivers staged a strike in a wage protest that saw those who refused to participate attacked and bombed inside
their vehicles. Highways were blocked with burning tires, leaving drivers who
needed to get from one place to another terrified for their safety. In the summer months of 2012–13, farmworker strikes broke out in the Western Cape.
Agricultural laborers demanded an increase from R70 per day to R150 per day

and proper housing. As time went on, the conflicts became more strident and farms were set afire.

All the while, the ANC Youth League and its former leader Malema—by then expelled from the ANC after prolonged clashes with Zuma and his circle—spoke of expropriating the mines and other crucial industries, promising the poor that this was the solution, the only way out of misery.

The politics of ethnic division have not endeared the ruling party to many national and international observers, particularly since Zuma's first election victory. A Zulu firebrand who relies on his participation in the anti-apartheid struggle for political legitimacy, Zuma is better known for his personal flamboyance than for policy direction. In the run-up to the 2009 elections, Zuma seemed to encourage, or at least did not actively discourage, radical elements in the ANC who called openly for nationalization, land redistribution, and a firmer stance against elites who hold a disproportionate share of the country's resources. Flirting with these "dangerous elements" did not endear Zuma to White voters, including those on the left who believe in the project of a new South Africa.

Zuma's faction was also implicated in corruption. The president himself is constantly on the front page of newspapers for questionable use of the public treasury, including a vastly expensive, publicly financed upgrade to his private home in rural Kwazulu-Natal.[11] As a consequence, for many Black voters, the ANC is losing its ethical compass and no longer appears devoted to the causes that Mandela fought for. The masses continue to suffer from poverty while political elites enrich themselves. This is a disgrace in the eyes of ordinary people, for whom so much is at stake. Yet after each election round, the ANC stands as the winner, leaving the opposition parties with only a minority of voter support. Except in the Western Cape, where the battle between the ANC and DA party leaders can be vitriolic, the ANC remains in charge.

Whether people perceive South Africa hopefully, as a democracy with great potential, a country that has come a long way, or a corrupt nation that is squandering its moral heritage depends a lot on generation. Nosiphiwe and Zondwa, Amanda's grandmother and mother, point to the progress that has been made and that simply cannot be denied: everyone *does* have the right to vote, everyone *can* move freely, and families no longer have to be split up with men working in cities and women remaining in rural areas. Schools *have* opened up to all, houses *have* been built, and the expansive social grant system means that the deepest levels of poverty *have* been alleviated. Democracy is working, so they say, and though there may be regular contestation over the appointment of judges, the judicial system remains intact.

Civil society stands its ground, holding government accountable and demanding delivery on promises for health care and access to other services. If need be, the people can now bring the state to court: witness the Treatment Action Campaign, which forced the Mbeki government to provide antiretroviral medicine long denied to the millions of HIV-infected citizens. Equal Education, an advocacy group, opened a court case to demand quality education for all, especially in the townships. Farm strikes—that regrettably turned violent—forced negotiations over minimum wages and a critical look at the way in which food distribution in the country serves only the wealthy distributors and large-scale supermarkets. While talks about nationalization of mines and land confiscation remain, the ANC has not officially moved toward these measures and continues to search for ways to keep foreign investors at ease.

Amanda and Ambrose consider all this progress completely insufficient. Why should one have to take the state to court to demand access to life-saving medicine or the provision of quality education? Is it not the state's obligation to ensure all this? Where are the safe, green spaces in our townships, Amanda wants to know? Why does her life remain so insecure, her income lower than that of many of the Whites of her generation? Although she moves in multicultural circles and has White friends, why does she still feel "the look" that Whites direct toward her when she is visiting fancier parts of town with her Black friends? Do they believe she should not be there? Why does she not live in a mansion in the suburbs, while Whites remain comfortably hidden behind their high walls in those exclusive parts of town? Sure, there has been improvement. But equality is elusive and life remains an uphill battle largely unsupported by an ANC government that wallows in corruption, she insists.

Yet Amanda's life is vastly different from that of her parents. Born in a segregated but not desperately poor area of Port Elizabeth, her grandmother capitalized on the opportunity to send Amanda and her sister Alison to former "Model C" schools. Nosiphiwe activated whatever links she had with the educational system to push them into the opportunities she knew would change their lives. Both Amanda and her sister are living lives the older generation could have only dreamed of. They are educated, employed, and move in multicultural, upmarket circles.

Amanda's mother, therefore, asks for recognition of the things the ANC has achieved. She herself survives by setting up a range of informal businesses and is thankful that she no longer has to hide from police and carry a pass. Amanda maintains that life may be better, but it is not good enough, and that surely the promises of the ANC did not mean that she would have to share a three-bedroom flat with four couples, in continual insecurity about her employment and income.

Daniel's family capitalized on the same changes. As soon as the chance to send their children to former "Whites only" schools opened up, the Cornells seized it. Their starting position wasn't that desperate. They were able to count on advantages built into the apartheid system that legislated preferences for Coloured labor over Blacks in the Western Cape. The politics of apartheid translated into the ability of Coloured craftsmen like Daniel's father to build up a business. Sheer persistence, hard work, and a lighter skin color meant that they were more trusted by Whites, hence the family avoided the fate that befell Ambrose and his kin in Manenberg. Daniel's parents had a solid house, a proper family home, in a segregated section of Paarl that was far more pleasant and centrally located than the other Coloured "locations" in the Cape Town area. Sending his son to Paarl Boys' School, Daniel's father told him to work hard and keep his head high to ensure that no one would ever see him as anything less than completely worthy.

The payoff has been enormous. With a diploma from one of the best schools in the country, the path to higher education was a given for Daniel. The economic stability of his father's business, the connections into a more comfortable world, the warm nest of his family home—all meant he enjoyed a starting position far ahead of most of his Coloured peers. Ambrose could never imagine a life like Daniel's. It may as well be unfolding on another planet. He has no idea what kind of life people of his race group lead who have been blessed with a middle-class childhood.

Few people of color were equipped with the kind of networks and education Daniel managed to achieve so early on in the new democracy. Accordingly, when the employment equity legislation landed on the books, there were relatively few young men of color like him, technically qualified for a high-status occupation. He could practically write his own ticket in private industry since the advantages to firms complying with the law are enormous. He was in the right place at the right time with exactly the credentials they needed. So was Amanda. Relative to the vast majority of people in their racial and age group, both Daniel and Amanda came from middle-class households. Their parents had more education, larger and more property in better areas, and many more contacts than either Thandiswa or Ambrose. Class background helped to boost them into the professions they longed for because, when opportunity opened up, they were among the few of their color who were ready.

Growing up in the Manenberg Flats, with gang leaders the only models of professional advance, Ambrose was in trouble almost before he started. Isolated from the rest of Cape Town, and even within his own community, Ambrose doesn't lack the *will* to change—his dedication to our field study and to the community center where he volunteers are proof of his desire for a different life. But Ambrose runs a deficit of social and human capital, and without more of both he is not likely to work his way out of Manenberg. Of course, he could have made better choices along the way. Not everyone drops out of school; not everyone steals from his own family. Ambrose is far from a perfect man. But he is also far from incorrigible and has learned some lessons along the way that he is trying to put into play. He aligned himself with a community organization that was created to encourage pathways to better lives. He drew up a résumé with the help of people at the community center and hoped they would assist him in finding work. Yet the center is staffed by people who themselves know very little about the private sector and whose contacts are not particularly powerful. The advice they can provide and the interventions they might conceivably offer seem limited. How was it possible, we wondered, that no one had ever pointed out to Ambrose that it was crucial to give potential employers his correct address and phone number?

Ambrose's life is soaked in disappointment. He points out how dysfunctional Manenberg is, as if to say, "Someone who is worthy could not be living here." He is ashamed of the ways in which he has let his family down. Yet Ambrose lives in a country that he believes could not care less about his life. All the ANC talks about, he claims, is *Black* Economic Empowerment. Where do Coloured people figure? It feels to him as if the rest of South Africa has erased them from existence. There was more potential, he thinks, during apartheid, when Coloureds at least had a place in the hierarchy above Blacks. Today he is part of that vast group of "forgotten people," stranded out there in their tiny flats, in a distant corner of Cape Town. Disappointment coupled with racial distrust translates into support for the opposition Democratic Alliance, leaving Coloured citizens of Manenberg casting their lot with what many others still consider a mainly White party.

Thandiswa's life resembles Ambrose's in many respects, though her support for the ANC remains steadfast and the responsibility for her condition is, in her view, mainly her own. Having spent her childhood in the tumultuous African townships on the far outskirts of Cape Town, Thandiswa has found self-sufficiency an elusive goal. She is one of millions of Africans who continue to suffer the impact of the inequalities that were the very fabric of apartheid. Born into a family with little or no educational credentials, where the men worked the lowest kinds of jobs on a farm, while the women who followed were not legally allowed to be anywhere near the city, she lacked the resources that Amanda had to foster mobility. When Thandiswa felt lost in the educational system, there was no one to help her along, and when those valuable cattle in the Eastern Cape were threatened, her family left it to her to safeguard the only wealth they had been allowed to accumulate under apartheid.

Thandiswa's life has become an endless series of trials and errors designed to access further education and short-term, lower-end employment, though this has sometimes meant engagement with scams that promise a better life but actually result in financial debt. Nothing has worked, and this leads her to feel herself a failure and to sink into depression. We should admire her sense of agency, the ways in which she sees herself as responsible, since that is her source of motivation. Yet when nothing concrete materializes, Thandiswa is vulnerable to a fallacious post-apartheid sentiment: "Now there are opportunities for everyone." If that is true, then who else is to blame for her predicament but herself?

ANC social policies have helped her survive, but they cannot underwrite a new trajectory. Thandiswa can access the child support grants for Akhona and Andile, but she cannot cover the fees of the schools she would like to send them to. Thandiswa has been on a waiting list for a house for years, but even if she is lucky enough to get one, how would she earn money to buy food or pay for the utilities and taxes that come with it? Stuck in a morass of dependency, she continues to search for a way to create a better life, become a better mother, and shake off the sense of inertia that grabs her when she realizes nothing she does makes a difference. Thandiswa can do that when she has a job, and we saw her brighten visibly during the six months she worked for Renew and Reward. But when it was over, all that confidence dissolved.

Life is a challenge for Brandon as well. Born into a White Afrikaner neighborhood, Brandon had a childhood that was free and easy, without complications. Protected by apartheid regulations, the world of the Northerns was secure and stable. Jobs were not hard to find or keep. Higher education was available but not a necessity for a working-class man who just wanted a good wage and a steady contract. His father was able to secure a job in bank management without ever having gone near a university, something that would not have been possible without the color bar that protected Whites from competition in the labor market. Their homes were comfortable, their savings secure. Violence was not a serious problem and segregation kept those they feared far away. These conditions amounted to a head start that was significant in Brandon's life. But it all fell away in 1994. From then on, jobs were no longer automatically waiting, and therefore income too became less secure. Crime was on the rise and the fear for one's livelihood and even one's life became a reality. Brandon realizes that the old regime protected him, his family, and his friends, and he acknowledges the necessity of opening up opportunities for those who were forced to live with nothing in the past. But it is not a knowledge that sits easily.

"Taking the backseat" is a sour experience. It doesn't bring out the best in people. Yet Brandon might be more optimistic if all these remedial policies actually made a difference. If he could see vast improvements in the lives of the nation's majority population, he could take some pride in that, even if it had cost his own group. But what does Brandon see? He believes the ANC government does not care about the plight of Whites and really doesn't seem to care too much about the poorest Africans either. It mainly seems to be interested in shoring up special privileges for insiders.

Brandon and his friends cannot help but wonder about the country's direction. Will it repeat the neighboring fiasco that is Zimbabwe? Can they expect another decade of corrupt presidents who sing struggle songs and yet enrich themselves? Will they always have to live with the fear of violent attacks, murders on the farms? An uphill climb to get more education, only to crash into the barriers imposed by affirmative action? Brandon does not see— or perhaps does not want to recognize—the ways in which the privileges built into the apartheid system advantaged him. He has not had to contend with township life, rural poverty, or urban dispossession. His family was ahead of the game to begin with, but they can no longer hold on to those advantages, and hence, to him, the future is cloudy. Not desperate, just murky. He is not sure how Whites are supposed to shape their lives in this new South Africa. To his credit, he is committed to figuring it out and has not abandoned the country. He is here to stay, and for all his complaints and worries, he is invested in an effort to find answers to those questions about the future.

Class advantage, conveyed through the sieve of wealth and educational advantage, helps to explain why things are easier for Anna. Born into a German immigrant family that owns vast stretches of land in Namibia and several properties in South Africa, with a high school education from one of the best schools in Cape Town's quiet suburbs, there was never a question about Anna's professional ambitions. From childhood onward, it was a given that she would complete a university degree. True, she did not get her first vocational choice, unable to get into medical school, and settled for her second choice, architecture. But she could count on her family's financial support. When she decided to take a gap year, she knew how to find a paid part-time job that fit her qualifications, strengthened her résumé, and eventually allowed her to return to UCT to finish her degree. Anna went abroad as an exchange student for a year and later capitalized on her German identity and connections to find a job at a large architecture office in Switzerland.

As a child, Anna often wondered about the future of South Africa, especially what she could contribute, given her skills and background, but she happily lived unburdened by serious responsibility as she began to follow a path of personal growth. As she studied architecture, she thought that some day perhaps she might help redesign the cities that had been twisted by apartheid urban planning. Having finished her schooling, however, what she wanted first of all was to gain experience, earn Euros, and explore the world. Her reality could not be further removed from those of her less-fortunate peers, Black, White, and Coloured. Yet unlike Brandon, her friends are a rainbow of the South African middle class. She is close to Blacks, Coloured people, and immigrants from different countries—the entire spectrum of the educated. Perhaps this is why she has more confidence in the country's future than Brandon does. Her friends are living proof of what has worked.

Suzanne is an example of someone for whom politics, and the general question of the future of the country, translates into local worries rather than large issues of democratic representation or even corruption by elites. Like many other struggling migrants, she focuses on how the powerful—whoever they are—present obstacles to her economic security. Will they invoke a new licensing regime that will interfere with her craft market business? Is she going to have trouble getting a visa to go to India to buy the things she wants to sell in Greenmarket Square because her refugee permit has expired? If landlords try to pull a fast one on her—confiscating a deposit, jacking up her rent, refusing to fix a broken pipe—can she get help from someone, even though she feels like a person with few rights?

To say that Suzanne is focused only on the practical is, however, to sell her short. She bridles at the injustices and hardships that befall others who are not South African but are struggling to make a living here. She knows what they have been through to get here, what they have witnessed, who they have lost along the way, and how challenging it is to live in a place that will never really be home. Longing for the familiar, knowing that it is out of reach: this is the cross that refugees the world over must bear. For many, the experience induces an inward turn. They dwell on the mobility of their children and see the success of the next generation as the best bet for recapturing all that was lost in the transition from danger to safety, from a failed state to a functioning one. But Suzanne has become something of a rabble-rouser on behalf of refugees and migrants in the Cape Town settings where she is known. Her in-dignation at their treatment shows, and she has the skills to make a difference. She is not a lawyer, but she is something of a fixer who can operate in English and understand the rights that everyone, including refugees, is guaranteed.

She takes the less fortunate in hand and marches them to municipal of-fices, lawyers, judges, schools, and anyone in official settings who can make a difference. Stabbing at a piece of paper, she raises her voice and shows them where they are wrong or unfair or even corrupt. And she gets results, which is why Suzanne has come to be thought of as something of a hero in her migrant community. Although she has opinions about Jacob Zuma and Helen Zille, Suzanne is not likely to get on the political warpath and make the outcome of a national election her passion. She is quite likely to get down to business in the world of ordinary politics, the world most people live in and need help with.

It will be left to the next generation, Suzanne and Eduard's five children, to find their place in South African society and politics. They might leave behind their identities as Congolese or Burundian. In time, their command of Swahili and French may diminish. They will not know their grandparents. And they will remain on their guard because they are immigrants. If their current trajectories are any indication, though, these kids are going to be success stories in a country where education matters in setting the path to upward mobility. They are serious about school and their parents are fixated on their progress. This will propel them forward, and we will, no doubt, see them in a few years as university students, sitting in class next to people like Anna, who always knew they would have that privilege. In time, they may be joined by more people like Amanda, people whose grandmothers have ensured their own educational opportunities. The real challenge lies in the lives of young people in Khayelitsha and Manenberg who are in desperate need of the same opportunities.

THE PEOPLE OF this book have been party to two of the most dramatic politi-cal experiments in the history of the modern world. They were born into the first, a harrowing experiment in social engineering that sustained complete racial separation and White domination. Like its close cousin, the Jim Crow South in the United States, apartheid aimed to regulate every aspect of human contact in the name of racial superiority.

The second great experiment has engulfed their adult lives and is still a work in progress, twenty years after its inauguration. The new South Africa, forged in the heat of armed struggle but bathed in the light of democratic ideals, is attempting to reverse deep, destructive forms of racial inequality that have left some people ready to seize opportunities and others almost entirely unable to compete.

Their universe is not entirely unlike the one Hortense Powdermaker found in her journey long ago, to Indianola, Mississippi. She found parallel worlds there and people who bridled at injustice, some of whom would strike out for the urban North to escape the strictures they faced. African Americans of the 1930s were not unlike their counterparts in modern South Africa, who have found out how difficult it is to make up for a wholly inadequate education and to replace a racist system with one that can prepare all people equally for life in a modern, postindustrial economy. But Powdermaker's era was on the cusp of a huge expansion of industry, one that could absorb millions of migrants into factories gearing up to arm the nation's military for the Second World War.

The University of Cape Town is built into the hillsides below Table Mountain. Once a "Whites only" university, it is now home to a thriving multiracial student population. Scenes like this would have been very uncommon before apartheid came to an end.

Democratic South Africa emerged just as class and educationally driven inequality has made it difficult to provide for upward mobility in many post-industrial societies. In the United States, Germany, England, and elsewhere, the lion's share of income growth has benefitted high skilled workers, even though these countries already had well-functioning systems of education, from preschool to graduate school. Children from remote rural areas and crowded cities alike had access to universal literacy, well-provisioned school buildings, and trained teachers. South Africa, however, had none of these luxuries, with a population deeply divided by race and class, and with schools that ranged in quality from Paarl Boys' to overcrowded township schools in places like Khayelitsha and Manenberg with few books, dirt floors, and sixty children to a class. Rural regions of South Africa, where classes might be held outdoors under the shade of trees, were not magnets for teachers—and education was only part of the problem. Staggering wealth and wage inequality, millions without housing, countless thousands whose homes lacked running water and electricity, and catastrophic levels of infectious disease—all these conditions were on the very long list of challenges facing the African National Congress when it took the reins of the country. It would be sheer folly to expect these to be remedied entirely in the space of twenty years. Yet progress is

Taking shelter from the summer sun. Interracial contact no longer merits much notice.

clearly visible: 78 percent of households now live in formal houses, and 73 percent of families have access to piped water in their yards or houses. Education has been formally integrated and the country boasts near universal enrollment figures for its primary schools. The number of students of color enrolled at tertiary institutions is increasing.

The problem, as the people of this book see it, is that at this rate it will be centuries before their aspirations as the first anti-apartheid generation of South Africans will be realized. The pace seems agonizingly slow and the systems far from perfect. The educational system, though unified in theory, remains in shambles, and the unemployment rates are desperately high. Could change be faster? Here is where the problems of a troubled democracy become germane and pressing. When the people of this book look at their national leaders, they see a measure of idealism and appeals to legitimacy coming out of the great struggle against apartheid, but they also see greed, corruption, and inefficiency.

When they train their eyes on the alternatives to the ANC, which no longer commands automatic loyalty even though it routinely wins elections, they worry about the real intentions of their leaders. Zille, the leader of the Democratic Alliance, is spearheading a party that was in part, and not that long ago, a force for White nationalism. While acknowledging the role some of its founding members played in the anti-apartheid struggle, many cannot help but wonder whether the party is really interested in racial equality. Is Zille just cleverly trying to get enough votes to put those "Whites only" signs back on the drinking fountains? Many inhabitants of Khayelitsha remain convinced that her intentions are nefarious.

People died for the right to vote. But today confidence in what democracy has produced is declining and many South Africans look for other solutions. The rich take their wealth and barricade themselves behind barbed-wire fences, wondering whether one day the swelling population of have-nots might try to break through those defenses. Many pack their bags and leave for English-speaking countries where they have less to fear but may not feel at home.

Poor people are defenseless before a rising crime rate—and crime has claimed them as victims far more often than anyone else. For them, democratic authority may be the last great hope but it isn't one they feel in their bones, and the jury is out as to whether that hope is well placed. They know, however, since their older relations have instilled it in them, that this is what their people fought for and that this is what they must commit themselves to. There is no other real alternative.

The national flag in the colors of the African National Congress.

AS THIS BOOK DEALS EXTENSIVELY with racial groups, the question of how to refer to them in ways that make sense both in South Africa and elsewhere in the world arises quite naturally. We have opted to use the South African discourse of "Black people" or "Africans" to refer to indigenous South Africans, most of whom (in this book) are speakers of the Xhosa language, one of eleven official languages of the country. Similarly, we have used the apartheid government's official spelling for "Coloured" people, a category that does not exist in other countries (with the possible exception of Brazil, where the term "pardo" refers to "brown people"). The Coloured category was an artifact of the regime, but we have used it here because the term remains in common usage today. It refers to South Africans of diverse and mixed racial origins, including descendants of Khoisan peoples and Bantu-speaking people, most of whom speak Afrikaans or English or both. "White" refers to South Africans of European ancestry who received privileged treatment under apartheid.

Any book that tries to encapsulate the modern history of a country with as complex a population as South Africa runs the risk of overgeneralization. Every individual, when examined very closely, has unique attributes and perspectives. Pulling the lens way back to view massive groups leads to the opposite problem: lack of texture as individuals fade into the background. Particular regions of South Africa have different population groups and hence no one place can truly represent the entire country. We took a middle path in *After Freedom*, one familiar to sociologists and anthropologists who make use of ethnographic methods. We searched for seven young people through whose lives we could understand and could illustrate the main issues faced by the dominant social groups in the Western Cape: Coloured, Black, and White South Africans, as well as African immigrants and refugees who have made their way from neighboring countries to Cape Town in search of a better life.

Most young South Africans continue to be trapped in a cycle of isolation and destitution in the townships on the edges of Cape Town, faced with low levels of schooling, high levels of unemployment, poverty, crime, illness, and premature death. For some, however, life has changed significantly for the better. These upwardly mobile Black and Coloured people now reside in the affluent sections of inner-city or suburban Cape Town. Hence, for our South African participants, we aimed at finding paired young adults who, within the same racial group living in the Western Cape, belonged to more or less opposite ends of the socioeconomic spectrum.

We first selected areas that are home to the higher- or lower-income classes in the metropolitan area. We then introduced our study through individuals we already knew from previous fieldwork or previously existing social networks, through schools and local community organizations in each of the areas. We spread news about the study in the poorer Black township of Khayelitsha—where we eventually selected Thandiswa—and the poorer, Flats in Manenberg—where a local community group strongly suggested we work with Ambrose. To find the more socially mobile participants, we distributed information through institutes of higher education such as the University of Cape Town, University of the Western Cape, and other city colleges and inner-city NGOs. That is how we found Amanda, Anna, and Daniel.

We had a slightly different aim in the selection of our White participants, as we were explicitly looking for someone who could introduce us to the conservative Afrikaner community in the northern suburbs of the city and might accompany us on a field trip to interview White farmers in the Eastern Cape. These are fairly closed social groups that are difficult to access, and neither of us had many contacts that would have been helpful in gaining entrée. Snowballing through the existing network of contacts of our field workers, we eventually selected Brandon for the study.

All of our "key informants" were told of the extensive amount of time the study would ask of them. We had intentionally selected a small number of key informants to enable us to gather rich ethnographic data that would allow for the production of a narrative that exemplifies all of the issues described through their participants. Participants knew they could ask for a break from the study when they felt our presence in their lives was getting too much. Both the University of Cape Town and Princeton University reviewed our research and approved it via the "protection of human subjects" process.

Our field team worked together for eighteen months gathering the field material and an additional six months working through the analysis. Our participants kept diaries, which we collected periodically, photocopied, and returned to them. They were provided a very modest stipend to support their participation in the project, and, when the research ended, we offered to pay the fees required for an educational opportunity of their choice as a way of thanking them. Not everyone took us up on this offer, but it was made to all.

We promised our participants complete anonymity when the book was published, even though we were aware that some of them might have liked to have their real names used. Accordingly, we have used pseudonyms throughout the book, changed the names of their employers, and in some instances changed the kind of firm some work or have worked for. We realize that our key informants and those close to them will be able to recognize themselves, but we have done everything we can to make it impossible for anyone else to do so. This is for their protection but also to make it clear that their experiences are shared by thousands of people, even as none of them are fully representative of any category.

TO UNDERSTAND THE PERSPECTIVES OF the seven key figures in this book, we spent two years getting to know them and their families, friends, employers, neighbors, and even enemies. Katherine began this project as a professor at Princeton University, whose Institute for International and Regional Studies supported the research until she moved to Johns Hopkins University, which enabled its completion. Over the four-year period that covered the fieldwork and writing of this book, she was welcomed as a visiting scholar at the Children's Institute of the University of Cape Town, without whose hospitality and assistance this project would have been impossible.

Ariane led the fieldwork effort from the beginning, first as a doctoral candidate in the Center for Social Science Research at the University of Cape Town (UCT), then at the Children's Institute, where she is now a senior member of the research staff. While Katherine and Ariane came to know the people of this book well themselves, the daily fieldwork contributions of our remarkable multilingual and multiracial research team was essential to what we learned. They devoted two years to intensive research in the townships, refugee camps, middle-class enclaves, and downtown districts in and around Cape Town, Port Elizabeth, and commercial farms, abandoned sites, and rural hamlets in the Eastern Cape near the town of Fort Beaufort.

We owe an enormous debt of gratitude to this team and hope the book captures the depth of what we learned from them. Nwabisa Gunguluza was a graduate student in social anthropology who grew up in Gugulethu, one of the major Black townships in Cape Town. Without her ability to connect with people in both the poorest and relatively middle-class environments in these townships and the City Bowl, the work would have been impossible to complete. Seraj Chilwan, a sociology graduate of UCT, who came from Rondebosch East, a middle-class township built for Coloured people, devoted himself to fieldwork in Manenberg and Paarl, where his fluency in Afrikaans was essential. Zoe Duby, native of Swaziland, had just started working toward her PhD in public health and took on the enormous task of helping us to understand the lives of young White South Africans. Efua Prah was a graduate in social anthropology who conducted fieldwork in the refugee camps in the

Western Cape. Part Ghanaian and part South African, she was particularly attuned to the desperation of families and children in the desolate temporary residence area of Blikkiesdorp.

Several colleagues contributed important insights and encouraged us with the thought that a book like this was needed. Jeremy Seekings, professor of sociology and political science at UCT, is first among them. Director of the Center for Social Science Research when the project began, Jeremy is himself an authority on inequality in South Africa and along with his collaborator, economist Nicoli Nattrass, lent moral and logistical support to us. Shirley Pendlebury, the former director of the Children's Institute and a long-time advocate for the least fortunate in the country, as well as Shanaaz Mathews, current head of the institute, gave Ariane the latitude to work on the book when there were many competing demands for her time. We thank our editor at Beacon Press, Gayatri Patnaik, and our literary agent, Lisa Adams, who believed the book would matter to audiences far beyond South Africa.

Our deepest debt belongs to the people of this book. We promised that we would not use their names and hence they appear here under pseudonyms and could not be pictured in the many photographs contributed by our superb photojournalist, Jillian Edelstein. These seven individuals allowed our fieldwork team, as well as Katherine and Ariane, to spend hundreds of hours in their homes, talking with their family members, chatting with their neighbors. We traveled to their ancestral homes to meet their grandparents and siblings, visited their workplaces to interview their employers, celebrated with them when the good news arrived of a job, a marriage, or a vacation, and commiserated when nothing was going well. We trust they will find this account of their lives a fitting tribute to all they have been through and all they hope for.

PREFACE

1. Powdermaker, *After Freedom.*

2. Mattes defines the "born-free generation" in South Africa as those young people "who came of age politically after 1996." They were born in the mid-eighties, and "entered the political arena with little if any first-hand experience of the trauma that came before. . . . Their first political experience, possibly casting a vote in the 199 election, was with a relatively normal, though clearly reform-minded democratic political system" (7). Slightly different definitions circulate, too, with the press sometimes referring to the "born free generation" as "those born after apartheid ended in 1994" (Reuters, "ANC Risks Losing 'Born Free' Voters," News24 .com, January 28, 2013, http://www.news24.com/SouthAfrica/News/ANC-risks-losing-born -free-voters-20130128). All agree, however, that this young generation is a particularly large cohort in South Africa's population: the recent *Census 2011* data show that 29.6 percent of all South Africans are younger than fourteen, and 28.9 percent are between fifteen and thirty-four years old. Media, politicians, and academics have described the large group of youth alternatingly as a potential threat to social stability or a possible "dividend" for future development (Lefko-Everett, "Ticking Time-Bomb").

3. Organisation for Economic Co-Operation and Development, *Economic Surveys.* South Africa is considered as having the largest economy in Africa. The IMF lists South Africa as the richest country in Africa, when wealth is measured as GDP. It is then followed by Nigeria and Egypt. It would not rank first when measuring wealth as GDP per capita, in which case it would rank number 6, after countries such as Gabon and Botswana (International Monetary Fund, *World Economic Outlook Database*). The country's Gini coefficient is at 0.63, the highest of all countries listed in the UNDP's human development report of 2013 (www .hr.undp.org). StatsSA's income and expenditure survey for the period 2005–2006 even listed inequality in terms of income from work at the incredible high of 0.8. When taking social security grants and access to housing into account, however, the coefficient drops significantly but remains among the highest of the world.

4. *Census 2011* data, released by Statistics South Africa (www.statssa.gov.za), place the average annual household income of the Western Cape at R143,460. The province ranks only after Gauteng, which has the highest average household income of R156,243 per year, but far ahead of much poorer provinces such as Eastern Cape or Limpopo, with R64,539 per year and R56,844 per year, respectively. Inequality in the province remains high: almost 70 percent of the Black African households in the province have a monthly income of R3,200 or less, compared to 15 percent of White households; a meager 3.5 percent of Black African households report a monthly income of more than R25,600, compared to 38 percent of White households.

5. *Census 2011* data (www.statssa.gov.za) show that rural provinces such as the Eastern Cape and Limpopo have been experiencing huge out-migration over the past ten years. The Eastern Cape alone shows a net out-flow of more than 270,000 people. The wealthiest Gauteng and Western Cape provinces show the largest in-migration.

6. Smit et al., "Good Houses Make Good People?"

7. According to the latest *Census 2011* data (www.statssa.gov.za), the Black population group constitutes more than 75 percent of the entire South African population of 51.8 million. The Western Cape population, however, consists of 42 percent Coloured, 39 percent Black, 16 percent White, and 3 percent Indian/Asian and "other" people. It is the only province where the Black population group does not make up the largest proportion, but it is, together with Gauteng, also home to the largest percentage of White people.

8. *City of Cape Town—2011 Census* (Cape Town: Strategic Development Information and GIS Department, City of Cape Town, 2012). The majority of the new Black elite is, in fact, located in the wealthier Gauteng province; as census data indicate, the proportion of Black households with an income above R51,000 in the Western Cape, remains very small. Gauteng does, however, not have the same share of Coloured people.

CHAPTER ONE: THE PEOPLE OF THE BOOK

1. Xhosa surnames relate to clan, which in turn relates to ethnic origin. We have changed all Xhosa names and clan names to protect our participants' identities but in doing so may have lost the connection between surnames and clan names.

2. The 2011 census defines such informal dwellings as "makeshift structures not approved by a local authority and not intended as a permanent dwelling; typically built with found material (i.e., corrugated iron, cardboard, plastic). In Cape Town, 280,000 households are estimated to live in such informal houses. Statistics South Africa, *Census 2011*. Khayelitsha is the second-largest township in the country, after Soweto, and is thought to have the largest concentration of shacks (or informal dwellings, as they are officially called) in the Cape Town metropole. The *Affordable Land and Housing Dataset* estimates a continued growth in shacks of ten thousand per annum. Ward-level information for Khayelitsha from the 2011 census shows that just under half of all houses in the township are considered formal, just over half informal. Some of the areas (or sections) are older and with more formal houses than others. In places such as Harare and Llitha Park, 85 percent of all houses are formal, brick structures. In others, such as Nonqubela, squeezed in between the older part of Khayelitsha and the N2 highway, informal housing takes up more than 85 percent ("City of Cape Town–2011 Census–Ward Profiles," http://www.capetown.gov.za/en/stats/Pages/Census2011.aspx).

3. *Census 2011* data show that the Western Cape has the lowest level of unemployment in the country, using both the formal and expanded definitions. In the Western Cape, the official unemployment rate is at 21.6 percent compared to 37.4 percent in the Eastern Cape and, for example, 38.9 percent in Limpopo. Educational achievement is higher in the Western Cape, with 12.6 percent of people aged fifteen or older with no or only primary education, compared to 26.5 percent in the Eastern Cape (Statistics South Africa, *Census 2011*). Census data also show that 436,466 people migrated out of the Eastern Cape to other provinces in the period 2001-2011. Of those, 170,829 went to the Western Cape, 117,964 to Gauteng. The rest went to various other provinces. In total, the Western Cape received 432,790 people migrating in from

various other provinces, Gauteng saw an inflow of 1,440,142 of South Africans of other parts of the country.

4. Census data show the increase in service delivery in the entire country. In Cape Town, census 2001 data showed that just under 40 percent of all Black African households had no access to piped water inside their dwellings or yards. In 2011, this proportion had gone down to just under 30 percent. Access to sanitation had improved, with 81 percent of all Black households registered as being able to access flush toilets. Again, in some areas, however, access to such toilets remained very problematic, as we will describe in a later chapter. Close to 10 percent of all Black households in Cape Town were using pit latrines or buckets for their sanitation. In the poorest informal areas of Khayelitsha, only 20 percent have access to piped water inside their yard, just under 20 percent continue to use a bucket as a toilet, and more than 50 percent use paraffin or candles for their lighting. Close to 100 percent of White households have piped water in their houses and flush toilets (Statistics South Africa, *Census 2011*).

5. The 2011 census data put the average household size among the Black African population at 3–3.5 (Statistics South Africa, *Census 2011*).

6. All italicized passages in the book are taken either from written passages in the diaries of our key informants or written fieldnotes contributed by our research team. Indented passages that are not italicized represent direct quotes from interviews recorded, translated, and transcribed by our research team.

7. The official unemployment rate takes into account people aged fifteen to sixty-four who were without work in the week preceding the interview but who are looking for work and are available to work. That rate is 25 percent. The expanded definition, however, takes into account people who have altogether stopped looking for work. That rate is much higher, at 37 percent nationally (Statistics South Africa, *Census 2011*).

8. Southall, "Political Change and the Black Middle Class"; and J. Kew, "South Africa's Black Middle Class Doubles, Study Shows," Bloomberg.com, 2013. Exact numbers for this "new Black middle class" are still hard to come by, mainly because there are so many ways of defining its membership, but figures released in 2013 by the Unilever Institute of Strategic Marketing at the University of Cape Town claim the Black middle class grew to 4.2 million people in 2012, from 1.7 million in 2004.

CHAPTER TWO: APARTHEID LEGACIES

1. The original meaning of the Dutch word *apartheid* is "apartness," or "separateness."

2. A regulation that the Cape Province would not implement until the late 1930s.

3. Giliomee, *Last Afrikaner Leaders*.

4. Christopher, *Atlas of Changing South Africa*, 277.

5. For a detailed overview of the history of apartheid, see, among many others: Beck, *History of South Africa*; Christopher, *Atlas of Changing South Africa*; Wilson and Thompson, *Oxford History of South Africa*, 405; and Wilkinson, "City Profile."

6. Giliomee, *Last Afrikaner Leaders*.

7. She was from St. Helena, presumably descending from a family brought to South Africa as slaves.

8. Christopher, *Atlas of Changing South Africa*; Wilkinson, "City Profile."

9. Christopher, *Atlas of Changing South Africa*; Nuttall and Coetzee, *Negotiating the Past*.

10. Christopher, *Atlas of Changing South Africa*; Wilkinson, "City Profile."

11. Steinberg, *The Number*, 102–6.

12. At some points during our study, Mam'Cethe, Thandiswa's mother, would get the dates mixed up; it is not entirely clear whether the family left the Kat River Valley in the 1970s or early 1980s.

13. Vail, *Creation of Tribalism in Southern Africa*.

14. For more on the Kat River Valley, see: Nel, *Regional and Local Economic Development in South Africa*; Nel and Hill, *An Evaluation of Community Driven Economic Development*.

15. Christopher, *Atlas of Changing South Africa*.

16. Today, land density in Khayelitsha is still one of its main problems. The township is considered one of the largest—if not the largest—in the country. Reliable statistics are very hard to come by, with an ever-growing population and sprawling shack areas all throughout the township. In just six years' time, since its formation, the population is estimated to have risen from 50,000 in 1984 to 450,000 by 1990 and to an estimated 600,000 in 2000 (T. M. Tuswa, *Service Delivery in the City of Cape Town: A Case Study into Water Service in Khayelitsha*, MPA, University of the Western Cape, 2003). Some studies mention "some 10,000 new arrivals [setting up] home in Khayelitsha every year" (Bidandi, *Effects of Poor Implementation of Housing Policy*). The official census data, however, puts the population at 400,000 by 2014 (Statistics South Africa).

17. Wilkinson, "City Profile."

18. Christopher, *Atlas of Changing South Africa*, 5.

19. Steyn, *Whiteness*, xii–xiv.

20. Ibid., 130.

21. Nattrass and Seekings, "Citizenship and Welfare in South Africa."

22. Christopher, *Atlas of Changing South Africa*; ibid.

23. Ibid.

24. Seekings and Nattrass, "Class, Distribution and Redistribution."

25. Clark and Worger, *South Africa*.

26. Christopher, *Atlas of Changing South Africa*, 158.

27. Ibid.

28. As Seekings explains, "At the height of the township revolt, in early 1986, the state's authority in some townships was limited to periodic incursions by heavily armed military patrols, whilst anti-apartheid activists assumed many of the administrative, everyday policing and judicial roles usually monopolized by the state. A less dramatic form of resistance was the proliferation of shack accommodation in hitherto tightly regulated cities [. . .] the state was compelled to retreat steadily from its policies of influx control" (Seekings, "Introduction", 833).

29. Ibid.

30. 194,000 ballots were rejected on grounds of validity. There had been "serious irregularities" during the elections, noted by foreign observers, yet none of them were considered significant enough to affect the outcomes of the vote (Christopher, *Atlas of Changing South Africa*, 71).

31. Woolard, "Overview of Poverty and Inequality."

32. Lefko-Everett, "Ticking Time-Bomb."

33. Leibbrandt, "Trends in South African Income Distribution."

34. See Seekings, "Social Stratification and Inequality."

35. See Seekings, who hypothesizes about the existence of such sudden, sharp rises in social position at the time of the transition (ibid.). Also: Seekings and Nattrass, "Class, Distribution and Redistribution."

36. Three models were suggested by the then-minister of education: Model "A" schools would be those that chose to retain their exclusive, Whites-only status. "B" schools would be those that would open up partially while continuing to receive state funding. Model "C" schools were those that chose to open up completely and would continue to "receive subsidies for teachers' salaries but would assume responsibility for some expenses" (Soudien, "The Asymmetries of Contact").

CHAPTER THREE: THANDISWA'S STRUGGLES

1. Cape Town has a high burden of disease and high levels of health inequity. The estimated mortality rate for the city is 1,011 per 100,000 people. This is considerably higher than for most Western cities; for example, it is 60 percent higher than the latest mortality rate for New York City ("Summary of Vital Statistics 2011: The City of New York; Mortality," New York City Department of Health and Mental Hygiene, http://www.nyc.gov/html/doh/downloads /pdf/vs/vs-mortality-2011.pdf). Needless to say, health indicators are worse in the poorer parts of town, such as Khayelitsha; the mortality rate for communicable diseases there is about five times higher than it is in the adjacent Southern Peninsula Health District (550 deaths per 100,000 people per year, versus 112 deaths). Details in Groenewald et al., *Cause of Death and Premature Mortality*; and Smit et al., "Good Houses Make Good People?"

2. The national prevalence rate is at an estimated 30 percent among pregnant women tested at antenatal clinics. The Western Cape prevalence rate is lower, at an estimated 18.5 percent, but in some areas of Khayelitsha, prevalence is as high as the national rate ("The National Sentinel HIV and Syphilis Prevalence Survey in South Africa," 2010, National Department of Health).

3. Nattrass et al., "Poverty, Sexual Behavior, Gender, and HIV Infection"; and United Nations Development Programme, *South Africa Country Report*.

4. General Household survey data indicate that the vast majority of South Africa's children (close to 75 percent) live with one or both biological parents. Orphanhood is, however, on the increase. Data from 2010 showed that 17 percent of South African children did not have a living biological father, that 8 percent did not have a living biological mother, and that the numbers and proportions of double orphans are rising, mainly as a result of the AIDS pandemic. In the Western Cape Province, numbers of orphans are lower than those in many of the poorer parts of the country, with 10 percent in the Western Cape compared to, for example, 26 percent in the Eastern Cape. Approximately 25 percent of children in the poorest 20 percent of all households in the country are orphaned, and maternal orphans especially are at risk of lower educational and healthy outcomes (H. Meintjes and K. Hall, "Demography of South Africa's Children," in Hall et al., *South African Child Gauge*).

5. It is not at all unusual for households to be "fluid" and have extended families living in urban and rural homes. Family members frequently move between the two or between urban homes of different family members. Children especially often live with family members other

than their biological parents, most often because that enables mothers to look for employment. Though 30 percent of children in the country do not live with their biological mother, they do remain part of the extended network of kin. Descriptions of this kind of fluidity can be found in Spiegel et al., "Domestic Diversity and Fluidity"; Hall, "Children's Spatial Mobility."

6. According to Census 2011 data, the Boyas are an unusually large family. The average household size is just over three (Statistics South Africa, *Census 2011*).

7. Athol Fugard's play *My Children! My Africa!* chronicles the conflicts between generations and between the more educated and less educated in the townships over the wisdom of participating in the strikes and boycotts. The main character, a gifted, young Black man preparing for an academic quiz competition, is drawn to the streets, while his teacher is horrified at the thought that he will risk his life. The teacher ends up squealing to the police and dies at the hands of the mob.

8. Branson et al., "Education and Inequality."

9. Census 2011 data place the official unemployment rate in Khayelitsha at 37 percent; the extended definition would reflect an even higher percentage (Statistics South Africa, *Census 2011*).

10. "Ubuntu" is not a concept that can easily be defined, but Archbishop Desmond Tutu put it this way: "A person with Ubuntu is open and available to others, affirming of others, does not feel threatened that others are able and good, based from a proper self-assurance that comes from knowing that he or she belongs in a greater whole and is diminished when others are humiliated or diminished, when others are tortured or oppressed" (Tutu, *No Future Without Forgiveness*).

11. Not unlike how other young people in the African townships in Cape Town presented an understanding of their situation in other studies: Swartz et al., "Ikasi Style."

12. In this, Thandiswa is a lot like the individualistic middle-class managers in *Falling from Grace* (Newman). They cannot see the structure that fosters or denies opportunity. They can see personality or individual drive and think more in terms of the latter than the former.

13. The "real bottom" would, of course, consist of those who remain in the incredibly impoverished rural areas, but this is how Thandiswa described it.

CHAPTER FOUR: THE COCONUT DILEMMA

1. The use of different names, depending on the people Khanyiswa Sophotele introduced herself to, led to some confusing moments during the course of the study. Amanda had always only used her Christian name when introducing herself to us, but when Ariane visited her one evening with soup and fresh fruit, as she had heard "Amanda" was sick in bed, she was told there was no one by that name in the Sea Point apartment. Amanda and Ariane had a good laugh about it afterward, when it turned out everyone in the flat only knew her as Khanyo. At work, among colleagues, both names seemed to circulate, but when introduced to non-Black people Sophotele did not know, she would always choose to use "Amanda."

2. Later to be called Perseverance Schools.

3. Musson, *Johnny Gomas*.

4. Much has been written about the differences within Xhosa culture. Amanda's family belongs to an urban, Xhosa cultural world that was Christian (her grandmother is a staunch Christian and urges her granddaughters daily to make sure they attend church) and clearly

supportive of education and perhaps of a number of aspects of "Westernization." The elements of this cultural tradition differ from the forms of Xhosa culture that are prevalent in, for example, the deeper rural areas of the old Transkei. We only managed to visit Amanda's grandmother twice, and on both occasions, she would stall and become visibly tired when sharing memories. We, therefore, undoubtedly missed some important elements in our understanding of this urban Xhosa culture, but we have tried to capture as much detail as possible in this chapter (Banks, *Home Spaces*; Russell, "Understanding Black Households"; Southall, "Political Change and the Black Middle Class").

5. She mentioned attending school in Barkly Road, where, indeed, after the passing of the Group Areas Act, the Perseverance School erected a new building. The area was classified Coloured, though, so it is unclear how Nosiphiwe would have been able to attend the school there.

6. "Junior Certificate" seems to have officially referred to grade 10, but what Nosiphiwe refers to here is the fact that she wanted to continue until grade 12.

7. Nosiphiwe is referring to the long-standing tradition in various African cultures to have children reared by their grandparents or others within the extended kin network. In her work on kinship care in South Africa, Russell notes: "It is perfectly within the rules for a grandparent to claim a grandchild as one's own, especially if [the child's] mother is one's young, unmarried daughter." For a full overview, see Russell, "Understanding Black Households in Southern Africa."

8. Mamphela Ramphele's work *Steering by the Stars* describes in detail how young men from the townships around Cape Town faced similar danger when they decided they wanted to keep going to school, to focus on their individual path to what they believed would be a better future, while maintaining solidarity with their peers who had decided to join the boycott. The same dilemma is captured, most poignantly, in Athol Fugard's 1989 play *My Children! My Africa!*

9. Soudien, "Asymmetries of Contact."

10. The term "Model C" is officially no longer in use, but many "ordinary people" continue to use it to refer to historically White state schools. See Battersby, "Cape Town's Model C Schools."

11. Russell, "Understanding Black Households in Southern Africa."

12. Rough translation in English: "To pay for the stomach."

13. While the care of children by grandparents is not at all unusual in South Africa, it is not clear how common this emphasis on care within the matrilineal kinship group is.

14. Hall, "Children's Spatial Mobility."

15. Hall's analyses of 2011 General Household Survey data show that 30 percent of children do not have a co-resident mother; nuclear families are not the norm in the country, and 69 percent of children live in "complex" or "extended" household forms (ibid.).

16. Newman, *No Shame in My Game.*

17. A brief summary as this can of course not do justice to the many aspects related to the Xhosa initiation ritual nor can it fully capture the complexities this situation creates for Amanda and her sister: raised in a Christian family where the maternal line has been the important one for as long as Amanda can remember, she is now engaging with a ritual that she knows very little about and which is not usually the responsibility of women at all. It is

illustrative of the enormous resilience of the practice. Existing literature points out that "even [Christian] families who do not support it, do it as a requirement for becoming recognized men in the community. [. . .] Christian families tend to take their boys to doctors for circumcision [instead of going the more traditional, non-medical route of circumcision in 'the bush school']" (Mhlahlo, "What Is Manhood?," 82). For more detailed descriptions and theories, see Carstens, "The Socioeconomic Context of Initiation Ceremonies," and Cox, *Rites of Passage in Contemporary Africa*.

18. See Cherlin, *Marriage-Go-Round*.

19. See Jackson, *Real Black*.

20. This is precisely the question that Kevin Woodson asks in his remarkable doctoral dissertation based on extensive interviews with African Americans in Wall Street law firms and brokerage firms (Woodson, "Fairness and Opportunity").

21. Kopano, *Coconut*.

22. J. Kew, "South Africa's Black Middle Class Doubles, Study Shows," Bloomberg.com, 2013.

CHAPTER FIVE: FORGOTTEN

1. Kensington was by then already zoned as Coloured area, and so the move into Manenberg by Patrick's family is different from that of families who, for example, had been living in the inner-city area of District Six. The latter were forcibly removed; Patrick's family was offered a council house.

2. West, *Influx Control*.

3. Statistics South Africa, *Achieving a Better Life for All*. National census data of 1996 indicate that only 42.7 percent of Coloured women were employed at the time (Salo, "'Mans is ma soe'").

4. According to the Census 2011 data, approximately 45 percent of all Manenberg residents live in houses on separate stands, 13 percent live in semi-detached houses, 27 percent live in "flats," and 6 percent live in informal dwellings or backyard shacks. Income levels are generally higher in the areas where the houses are larger and freestanding, but all service delivery is much better here than, for example, in Khayelitsha: 99 percent of all houses have electricity and 90 percent have running water available in their houses or yards. Many people are, however, poor: 60 percent of the population earns less than R1,600 per month, and unemployment is at an estimated 34 percent (Statistics South Africa, *Census 2011*).

5. The apartment blocks that are locally referred to as "the courts" or "*die korre*" in Afrikaans.

6. See Salo, "Negotiating Gender and Personhood," on adolescent women and gangsters in Manenberg township on the Cape Flats. She describes the ways in which young men created and upheld the boundaries of these new, small communities through gang activities and how, in that process, they renegotiated the boundaries imposed by the apartheid state: "Through this process, they negated the legitimacy of state-imposed borders and, in so doing, reclaimed their gendered agency in the local context" (351).

7. Ibid., 345, describes in detail the life in the Flats of Manenberg. She points out that women too would be involved in the creation of this new social order. They would often deny the involvement of one of "their" young men in criminal activities outside their own block

of flats, while keeping a close eye on the behavior of young men and women who belonged to "their" court.

8. Statistics South Africa, *Census 2011*.

9. Steinberg, *The Number*.

10. Much has been written about the possible effects of living in a constant state of vigilance and a violent environment. For South African work, see Barbarin and Richter, *Mandela's Children*; Seedat et al., "Trauma Exposure"; and Van der Merwe and Dawes, "Prosocial and Antisocial Tendencies in Children."

11. Grade 10 is for many young people in the country a critical year for continued school attendance. The end of grade 9 is also the end of the compulsory years of education, and school attendance drops significantly after that. General Household Survey data of 2010 show a decrease in school attendance from 99 percent among thirteen-year-olds to 86 percent of seventeen-year-olds and 71 percent of eighteen-year-olds. Attendance among Coloured youth is slightly lower than the national rates, and drop-out rates start to increase from the age of fifteen (K. Hall, "Children's Access to Education," in Hall et al., *South African Child Gauge 2012*).

12. Much of the literature on gangs points to the sense of belonging and status that young people receive through their gang-related activities, while they feel ever more cut off from the rest of their environment: Bility, "School Violence and Adolescent Mental Health in South Africa"; and Kinnes, "Gang Warfare in the Western Cape: Background," in *From Urban Street Gangs*.

13. Steinberg, *The Number*.

14. Kinnes, *From Urban Street Gangs*; Sullivan and Bunker, "Drug Cartels, Street Gangs, and Warlords"; September, "Drugs Fuelling Cape Gang Wars," Eye Witness News, May 14, 2013, http://ewn.co.za/2013/05/14/Drugs-fuelling-WC-violence; and IRIN, *South Africa: Gang Culture in Cape Town*, February 27, 2007, http://www.irinnews.org/report/70038/south-africa-gang-culture-in-cape-town.

15. Isaacs, "Small-Scale Fisheries Reform."

16. It also corroborates other pieces of ethnographic work, such as Bray et al., *Growing Up in the New South Africa*, and De Lannoy, "Educational Decision Making." Ethnographic and survey data both indicate higher levels of "negativism" among Coloured adults and adolescents. They express a lower sense of control over their own lives, a weaker belief in a better future, worse self-reported health, and so on.

17. A view corroborated by a study by the International Security Studies: Leggett, "No One to Trust."

CHAPTER SIX: THE OTHER SIDE OF THE COLOURED DIVIDE

1. Soudien, "Assymetries of Contact," describes how, behind the symbolic victory, however, the decision-making power in schools such as Paarl Boys High and, for example, the renowned South African College School in Rondebosch, remained in the hands of the vast majority of White parents, teachers, and management staff. They were (and in many instances still are) the ones who decided what language the school would use and which school fees would be charged. The "opening up" of previously all-White schools remained limited to those who could, in fact, find a way to "fit in" and pay the required school fees.

2. Statistics South Africa, *Census 2011: Municipal Report.*

3. This is not to say that Mbekweni does not also struggle with problems of, for instance, crime and violence. The South African Police Service reported 136 sexual crimes, 50 common robberies, and 9 murders over the period 2009–10 (*Crime Research and Statistics,* South African Police Service).

4. It is difficult to tell, though, what that percentage means in terms of absolute numbers because the population of Manenberg is so hard to count. When the "back yard dwellers" are added in, perhaps as many as 95,000 people are in residence.

5. Salo, "'Mans is ma soe.'"

CHAPTER SEVEN: THE PAST WAS WRONG, BUT IT WAS THE PAST

1. Census 2011 data show that the vast majority of people living in the Northern suburbs remain White (71 percent) and that 99 percent of the residents live in a formal house with access to piped water, sanitation, and electricity in their houses; 60 percent of households in the area have a monthly income of R12,801 or more (Statistics South Africa, *Census 2011*).

2. The 2011 census data show that 41 percent of all inhabitants in the Northern suburbs, where Brandon grew up, above the age of twenty have a higher-education degree. More than 95 percent of all Whites in the area are employed.

3. Though analysis of several waves of General Household Survey data indicates that "even controlling for years of education, white, coloured, and Indian labour market participants continue to receive strong premia relative to Africans both in terms of employment and earnings." This is mainly a consequence of the *quality* of education received. See Branson et al., "Education and Inequality."

4. Giliomee, *Last Afrikaner Leaders*; Seekings, "Continuing Salience of Race."

5. Crapanzano, *Waiting.*

6. Lizette Lancaster, "Is South Africa an Inherently Violent Country?," *ISS Today*, Institute for Security Studies, March 25, 2013, http://www.issafrica.org/iss-today/is-south-africa-an -inherently-violent-country.

7. Institute for Security Studies, "National Victims of Crime Survey Highlights Progress but Challenges Remain," news release, December 15, 2011, www.issafrica.org; South Africa Police Service (SAPS), *Crime Report*. The ISS and SAPS indicate that crime figures actually seem on the decrease: the murder rate today is less than half of that registered in 1994, and incidences of violent housebreakings and carjackings have decreased, too. But public perception takes long to change, and distrust in the presented figures is high.

8. It should be noted that these estimates remain of questionable quality and would not take into account those who at some point left but later returned (Polzer, "Population Movements"). See also "How Many South Africans Have Left the Country?," *Politicsweb*, August 14, 2012, http://www.politicsweb.co.za/politicsweb/view/politicsweb/en/page71619?oid= 318618&sn=Detail; and Peet Van Aardt, "Millions Whites Leave SA—Study," *Fin24*, September 24, 2006, http://www.fin24.com/Economy/Million-whites-leave-SA-study-20060924.

9. South African Institute of Race Relations, *South Africa Survey Online 2008/2009* (Johannesburg: SAIRR, 2008), 54–56, http://www.sairr.org.za/services/publications/south-africa -survey/south-africa-survey-online-2008-2009/?searchterm=south%20africa%20survey %202008.

10. Ibid., 55.

11. Wilson et al., "Digging into Ourselves."

12. G. Karstens-Smith, "White South African Seeking Refugee Status Won't See Case Go Before the Supreme Court," *National Post*, April 26, 2012, http://news.nationalpost.com.

13. Numbers of returning immigrants are very hard to determine (Polzer, "Population Movements").

14. Bobotjie is a national dish, consisting of a layer of minced meat, with an egg-based topping, all oven-baked.

15. White minority rights had been guaranteed during the CODESA (Convention for a Democratic South Africa) negotiations in the run-up to the 1994 elections. Many Whites today feel their rights are not protected, a sentiment fed by "the issues of black economic empowerment, affirmative action, nationalisation and land reform"—and Malema's recent demands of reclaiming land without compensation to the White farmers—by the continued rhetoric used by many of the ANC youth league's members, and by "smaller acts" such as the renaming of streets and towns from formerly Afrikaans names to African names or the university reforms that ask, for example, a previously Afrikaner university to no longer teach only in Afrikaans (Hugo Kruger, "Swart Gevaar Is Still Very Much Alive," letter to the editor, *City Press*, April 30, 2011).

16. Ibid.

17. Durrheim, "White Opposition to Racial Transformation."

18. Interventions that are meant to assist women, disabled people, and retirees are much more easily accepted than those that put the emphasis on race (ibid.).

19. Ibid.

20. Moolman, "The Role of Threat on Afrikaner Attitude."

21. Durrheim, "White Opposition to Racial Transformation."

22. Electoral analysis in 2009 pointed at a continuously strong influence of party identification as a decisive factor in voting behavior, followed by "issue based voting" and "personal factors." Party affiliation is generally on the decline in South Africa, with 34 percent of voters now claiming they do not feel close to any political party. The African National Congress (ANC) continues to have the highest level of party identification. However, the Western Cape has the lowest level of party affiliation, among both White and non-White voters. The majority of Whites in the Western Cape voted Democratic Alliance (DA), indicating that problems such as crime (93 percent), unemployment (71 percent), and corruption and dishonesty on the part of government officials (49 percent) need to be sorted out.

23. Since 1994, only 7 percent of land has been reallocated. Most land claims have involved urban land, not rural, and in the rural areas, the vast majority of farms remain in the hands of White owners. More details on the country's land-reform policies can be found in Hall and Williams, *Land Question in South Africa*; Statistics South Africa, *Census of Commercial Agriculture*.

24. She is referring to the *Voortrekkers* (pioneers) who left the Cape Colony at the time that it was under British rule and moved into the interior of the country. The (older) Afrikaner community regards that history with pride, from which Cara implies that many younger Afrikaners are trying to keep their distance.

25. South African Institute of Race Relations, *South Africa Survey*.

CHAPTER EIGHT: MOVEMENTS AND MIGRATIONS

1. Polzer, "Population Movements."

2. Patterns and underlying causes of internal migration remain underresearched in South Africa, but information is available in Posel, "Review of Current Literature"; Kok et al., *Post-Apartheid Patterns*.

3. Lowenberg, "Why South Africa's Apartheid Economy Failed"; Crawford and Klotz, *How Sanctions Work*.

4. L. Donnelly and C. Benjamin, "China and SA Cement Relationship," *Mail and Guardian* (Johannesburg), www.m.mg.co.za, March 22, 2013; South African Government News Agency, "SA Attracts Chinese, Indian, Russian Investors," SAnews.gov.za, April 30, 2013; South African Government News Agency, "New Factory to Stimulate Job Creation for W Cape Youth," SAnews.gov.za, June 7, 2013; *Mail and Guardian*, "Africa Isn't a Big Bull in China's Shop," www.m.mg.co.za, June 20, 2013.

5. Stanwix, *Minimum Wages*; Simbi and Aliber, *Agricultural Employment Crisis*.

6. *Independent Online*, "Busa Worried by Farm Retrenchments, February 8, 2013, www.iol.co.za.

7. Official unemployment rates in the Western Cape were at an estimated 21.6 percent, according to the latest census data. This is far lower than the unemployment rates of, for example, Limpopo and the Eastern Cape, with 38.9 percent and 37.4 percent respectively, but they can easily go up to more than 50 percent in townships such as Khayelitsha (Statistics South Africa).

8. Segatti, "Mobilisation Against Foreign Traders."

9. S. Mama, "Church Saved Refugees from Attack by Locals; Echoes of the Massacres Back Home," *Weekend Argus*, April 13, 2013.

10. Misago et al., *May 2008 Violence*; Segatti, "Mobilisation Against Foreign Traders"; ibid.; E. Mabuza, "South Africa: Xenophobic Rage Leaves Trail of Havoc in Gauteng," *Business Day*, AllAfrica.com, May 19, 2008.

11. Segatti, "Mobilisation Against Foreign Traders"; S. Mama, "Church Saved Refugees from Attack by Locals. Echoes of the Massacres Back Home," *Weekend Argus*, April 13, 2013; S. Evans, "Orange Farm: Feeding the Xenophobia Beast," *Mail and Guardian*, May 2, 2013.

12. Youth unemployment in general is at an all-time high with approximately 48 percent of those aged twenty to twenty-five unemployed (compared to 25 percent in the general population). That figure does *not* include discouraged workers. Since the global economic downturn, discouragement has seen a dramatic increase among the unemployed, especially among young Black men (S. Verick, "Unravelling the Impact of the Global Financial Crisis on the South African Labour Market," Employment Working Paper no. 48, Economic and Labour Market Analysis Department, Employment Sector [Geneva: International Labour Organisation, 2010]).

13. Morrell et al., "Hegemonic Masculinity/Masculinities."

14. PASSOP, *Blue Waters Safety Site*.

15. Pieterse, *Urbanization Imperatives for Africa*.

16. *Bantu* means "people" and *stan* means "land of." The term *Bantustan* was first used in the 1940s and referred to a tribal reserve for Black inhabitants of South Africa. The Ciskei was one of the ten Bantustans created in South Africa during the Apartheid rule. The "homeland"

for Xhosa people received nominal independence in 1981, but was never recognized as an independent country by any other country worldwide.

17. Several studies have indicated that families who moved from one of the previous Bantustans have maintained connections between rural and urban homesteads. Cattle ownership has remained important, especially in the fragile context of deprivation. It allows households such as that headed by Tata Boya a sense of economic and social independence. See, among others, Ainslie, "Farming Cattle."

18. Smit et al., "Good Houses Make Good People?"

CHAPTER NINE: POLITICAL HEAT

1. B. Berger, "Thabo Mbeki's Resignation: Jacob Zuma Endorses Interim South African Leader," *Telegraph* (UK), September 22, 2008; M. Mofokeng et al., "Why Mbeki Was Fired," News24.com, September 22, 2008; Pienaar, "Separation of Powers"; M. Rossouw, "ANC Dumps Mbeki, Moves to "Heal Rift," *Mail and Guardian* (Johannesburg), www.mg.co.za, September 20, 2008.

2. Berger, "Thabo Mbeki's Resignation"; Mofokeng et al., "Why Mbeki Was Fired"; Pienaar, "Separation of Powers"; Rossouw, "ANC Dumps Mbeki"; Congress of the People, http://www.congressofthepeople.org.za/.

3. Democratic Alliance, http://www.da.org.za/.

4. Plaut and Holden, *Who Rules South Africa?*

5. "Malema: Helen Zille a 'Racist Little Girl," *Mail and Guardian*, May 1, 2009, http://mg.co.za.

6. Statistics South Africa, *Census 2011*.

7. Plaut and Holden, *Who Rules South Africa?*; Southall, "Political Change and the Black Middle Class."

8. Plaut and Holden, *Who Rules South Africa?*; E. Naidu, "Black Middle Class Growing and Spending, *Independent Online*, March 2008.

9. Just under half of South Africa's population lives below the minimum living income calculated at R600 or $75 per month. The vast majority of those who are poor are Black (93 percent) (Leibbrandt et al., "Trends in South African Income Distribution and Poverty").

10. D. Smith, "The New Black Elite: Eating Sushi While Sitting on a Ticking Time Bomb," *Guardian* (UK), November 12, 2010; J. February, "The ANC's Plague of Corruption," *Pretoria News*, November 5, 2012; Plaut and Holden, *Who Rules South Africa?*

11. Plaut and Holden, *Who Rules South Africa?*

12. Lefko-Everett, "Ticking Time-Bomb?"

13. J. Herskovitz, "'Born Free' Voters May Not Choose ANC," *Mail and Guardian* (Johannesburg), January 29, 2013.

14. P. Alexander, "A Massive Rebellion of the Poor," *Mail and Guardian*, April 2012; Lauren Heese and Kevin Allan, "Are Fiery Street Protests Replacing the Vote?," *Business Day*, February 18, 2011; Nashira Davids, "Service-Delivery Protests Getting Uglier—Report," *Times* (London), October 11, 2012.

15. Smith, "New Black Elite."

16. *Independent Online*, "Corruption Threatens the NDP—Manuel," 2013.

17. BBC News, "Tutu Warns of Poverty 'Powder Keg,'" 23 November, 2004, http://news .bbc.co.uk/2/hi/africa/4035809.stm.

18. Grade R is the final year of pre-school education or kindergarten. Ambrose refers to the fact that some ANC leaders never completed levels of higher education.

19. Herskovitz, "'Born Free' Voters."

20. Ibid.

21. Plaut and Holden, *Who Rules South Africa?*

22. Thandiswa and many of her neighbors were very worried. Perhaps their sentiments are shared by the majority of those around her: so far, the Democratic Alliance has not managed to secure strong support in the African townships such as Khayelitsha, Nyanga, and Langa: "Its poll share reached 1%, only of 7 of the 81 voting districts of Khayelitsha . . . and was below 2% everywhere" (Plaut and Holden, *Who Rules South Africa?*).

23. Anti-Eviction Campaign: Western Cape, "Traders Evicted in Mitchells Plain Town Centre," March 8, 2010, http://antieviction.org.za/tag/informal-traders/.

24. M. Fraser, "Eastern Cape Refugees in the Western Cape," News24.com, March 22, 2012, http://www.news24.com/MyNews24/Eastern-Cape-refugees-in-the-Western-Cape-20120322.

25. City Press, "ANC Outraged at Zille's Refugee Comment," March 21, 2012, http://www .citypress.co.za/politics/anc-outraged-at-zilles-refugee-comment-20120321-3/.

26. Seekings and Matisonn, "South Africa"; Plaut and Holden, *Who Rules South Africa?*

27. African National Congress, www.anc.org.za.

28. Leibbrandt et al., "Trends in South African Income Distribution and Poverty"; Seekings and Matisonn, "South Africa."

29. IRIN News, "South Africa: Welfare Payments—A Panacea for Poverty?" http://www .irinnews.org/, February 2, 2011; Plaut and Holden, *Who Rules South Africa?*; Leibbrandt et al., "Trends in South African Income Distribution and Poverty."

30. Plaut and Holden, *Who Rules South Africa?*, and Seekings and Matisonn, "South Africa," point out that the ANC's position is, in fact, not so very different. The leading party has shifted its paradigm from creating a "Developmental State" to one that would promote self-sufficiency and sustainable development.

31. Plaut and Holden, *Who Rules South Africa?*

32. See Jan Hofmeyr, "Political Parties Ignore SA's Young Voters at Their Peril," *Business Day*, February 22, 2013, on Institute for Justice and Reconciliation website, http://www.ijr.org .za/; Swartz et al., "Ikasi Style."

33. Branson et al., "Education and Inequality."

34. Van der Berg and Louw, "Lessons Learnt from SACMEQII"; Van der Berg et al., *Low Quality Education*; Taylor, Fleisch, and Shindler, *Changes in Education*.

35. South Africa scores consistently low on international numeracy and literacy tests, with children from the poorest, most dysfunctional township schools performing the worst. See Anderson et al., "Grade Repetition and Schooling Attainment"; Lam and Seekings, "Transitions to Adulthood"; and Bray et al., *Growing Up in the New South Africa*.

36. Phurutse, *Factors Affecting Teaching and Learning*, a report prepared by a research consortium comprising the Human Sciences Research Council and the Medical Research Council of South Africa, shows that classrooms in poorer areas remain overcrowded. Figures for the Western Cape Province alone—which generally scores higher than other provinces

on educational outcomes—indicated that more than 70 percent of educators were teaching classes of more than thirty-six learners.

37. In 2000 it was estimated that the number of un(der)qualified teachers in the South African educational system was at a level of 22 percent; the Western Cape rate was 11 percent (Bot, *Macro Indicators in Education*).Teacher performance in both reading and mathematics is appallingly low, especially in poorer areas (Van der Berg et al., *Low Quality Education*).

38. "Having almost three million youth between eighteen and twenty-four unemployed and not in education or training not only points to a grave wasteland of talent but to the possibility of serious social disruption. Almost one million students leave school after completing grade 10. Providing ten years of educational resources—an education to youth who do not complete their final two years of schooling—is an enormous waste of educational resources and leaves this group extremely vulnerable to unemployment" (N. Cloete, ed., *Responding to the Educational Needs of Post-School Youth: Determining the Scope of the Problem and Developing a Capacity-Building Model* [Centre for Higher Education Transformation, 2009]).

39. Crouch and Mabogoane, "No Magic Bullets, Just Tracer Bullets," show that these problems are not only due to a shortage of resources but also to school mismanagement. Also, Fleish and Christie, "Structural Change"; Simkins and Paterson, *Learner Performance in South Africa*.

40. Associated Press, "South Africa: 16 Schools Closed Over Fears of Violence by Gangs," *New York Times*, August 15, 2013, accessed August 17, 2013.

CHAPTER TEN: AFTER FREEDOM

1. The settlement of land restitution claims has been very slow in the country. To speed up the process of restitution, the Commission of the Restitution of Land Rights started to apply Standard Settlement Offers (SSO) of cash compensation for all urban land claims. They were usually set at R40,000 per household of former owners. Most claimants who were offered these SSOs accepted them, "even though these do not adequately compensate for the market value of what was lost. As a result, restitution has made little contribution to confronting and eroding spatial apartheid in the cities" (Hall, *Land and Agrarian Reform*).

2. Calculations on poverty levels differ, but there seems a general consensus that, indeed, between 1993 and 1995 "at least 50 to 60% of Black and 22–32% of Coloured South Africans were living in poverty" (Friedman and Bhengu, *Fifteen Year Review of Income Poverty Alleviation Programmes*).

3. Human Sciences Research Council, *Survey on South African Voter Participation*.

4. Voter turnout was 87 percent in 1994, and decreased to 77 percent in 2009 (International Institute for Democracy and Electoral Assistance, www.idea.int, 2013).

5. Human Sciences Research Council, *Survey on South African Voter Participation*.

6. In 2005, 40 percent of South Africans claimed being "satisfied" and 16 percent "very satisfied" with the way democracy works in the country, but levels of contentment were much lower in the formal urban areas of the Western and Eastern Cape (10 percent in both). Dissatisfaction with the way in which democracy was working was highest among Indians (31 percent) and Whites (23 percent). Data from the Human Sciences Research Council, *Survey on South African Voter Participation*.

7. Case and Menendez, "Does Money Empower the Elderly?"

8. AIDS is, undeniably, a serious problem in the country that causes enormous strain on networks of care and exacerbates poverty for individuals and households. That we do not report in more detail on the pandemic's impact on our participants' lives is perhaps because we did not explicitly probe into its consequences, but it is also a clear sign that AIDS is but one of the many issues faced by this generation of young South Africans. Poverty, unemployment, lack of access to quality education, and precariousness in the lives of those who have made it into the new middle class—all play an enormous part in the lives of our interviewees.

9. Southall, "Political Change and the Black Middle Class."

10. The police, along with the Ministry of Safety and Security, maintained that the shooting happened in self-defense, with some of the strikers heavily armed and allegedly having fired a gun at one of their police members.

11. A. Makinana, "Parliament Stunned as Full Cost of Nkandla Is Revealed," *Mail and Guardian*, March 14, 2013.

Affordable Land and Housing Dataset. Affordable Land and Housing Data Centre. http://www.alhdc.org.za/.

Ainslie, A. "Farming Cattle, Cultivating Relationships: Cattle Ownership and Cultural Politics in the Peddie District, Eastern Cape." *Social Dynamics: A Journal of African Studies* 31, no. 1 (2005).

Anderson, K. G., et al. "Grade Repetition and Schooling Attainment in South Africa." Unpublished paper. Population Studies Center, University of Michigan, 2002.

Bank, Leslie J. *Home Spaces, Street Styles: Contesting Power and Identity in a South African City.* London: Pluto Press, 2011.

Barbarin, Oscar A., and Linda M. Richter. *Mandela's Children: Growing Up in Post-Apartheid South Africa.* London: Routledge, 2001.

Battersby, J. "Cape Town's Model C Schools: Desegregated and Desegregating Spaces?" *Urban Forum* 15, no. 3 (2004).

Beck, Roger B. *The History of South Africa.* Westport, CT: Greenwood Publishing House, 2000.

Bidandi, Fred. *The Effects of Poor Implementation of Housing Policy in the Western Caoe: A Study Case of Khayelitsha, Site C.* University of the Western Cape, 2007.

Bility, K. M. "School Violence and Adolescent Mental Health in South Africa: Implications for School Health Programs." *Sociological Practice: A Journal of Clinical and Applied Research* 1, no. 4 (1999): 285–303.

Bot, M. *Macro Indicators in Education 1994–2000* in *HRD Biennial Dtory,* chapter 13. 2001. http://hsrc.ac.za.

Branson, N., et al. "Education and Inequality: The South African Case." Southern Africa Labour and Development Research Unit Working Paper No. 75. Cape Town: SALDRU, University of Cape Town, 2012.

Bray, Rachel, et al. *Growing Up in the New South Africa: Childhood and Adolescence in Post-Apartheid Cape Town.* Cape Town: Human Sciences Research Council Press, 2010.

Carstens, P. "The Socioeconomic Context of Initiation Ceremonies among Two Southern African Peoples." *Canadian Journal of African Studies* 16, no. 3 (1982): 505–22.

Case, A., and A. Menendez. "Does Money Empower the Elderly? Evidence from the Agincourt Demographic Surveillance Site, South Africa." Supplement 69, *Scandinavian Journal of Public Health* 35 (2007): 157–64.

Cherlin, Andrew J. *The Marriage-Go-Round: The State of Marriage and Family in America Today.* New York: Vintage, 2010.

Christopher, A. J. *The Atlas of Changing South Africa.* London: Routledge, 2000.

Clark, Nancy L, and William H. Worger. *South Africa: The Rise and Fall of Apartheid.* London: Longman, 2004.

Cooper, Brenda, and Robert Morrell, editors. *Africa-Centred Knowledges? The Creative Space between the Immovable Rock and the Bad Place* (In press. London: James Curry).

Cox, James L., editor. *Rites of Passage in Contemporary Africa: Interaction between Christian and African Traditional Religions.* Religion in Contemporary Africa. Cardiff, UK: Cardiff Academic Press, 1998.

Crapanzano, Vincent. *Waiting: The Whites of South Africa.* New York: Vintage Press, 1986.

Crawford, N. C., and A. Klotz. *How Sanctions Work: Lessons from South Africa.* New York: St. Martin's, 1999.

Crouch, L., and T. Mabogoane. "No Magic Bullets, Just Tracer Bullets: The Role of Learning Resources, Social Advantage, and Education Management in Improving the Performance of South African Schools." *Social Dynamics* 27, no. 1 (2001): 60–78.

De Lannoy, A. "Educational Decision Making in an Era of AIDS." PhD diss., University of Cape Town. 2008.

Durrheim, K. "White Opposition to Racial Transformation: Is It Racism?" *South African Journal of Psychology* 33 (2003).

Fleish, B., and P. Christie. "Structural Change, Leadership and School Effectiveness/Improvement: Perspectives from South Africa." *Discourse: Studies in the Cultural Politics of Education* 25, no. 1 (March 2004).

Friedman, I., and L. Bhengu. *Fifteen Year Review of Income Poverty Alleviation Programmes in the Social and Related Sectors.* Durban: Health Systems Trust, 2008.

Giliomee, Hermann. *The Last Afrikaner Leaders: A Supreme Test of Power.* Cape Town: Tafelberg, 2012.

Groenewald, P., et al. *Cause of Death and Premature Mortality in Cape Town, 2001–2006: Key Findings.* Cape Town: South African Medical Research Council, 2008.

Hall, K. "Children's Spatial Mobility and Household Transitions." Working paper, forthcoming. Children's Institute, University of Cape Town.

Hall, K., I. Woolard, L. Lake, and C. Smith, editors. *South African Child Gauge 2012.* Cape Town: Children's Institute, University of Cape Town, 2012.

Hall, R. *Land and Agrarian Reform in South Africa: A Status Report, 2004.* Research Report No. 20. Programme for Land and Agrarian Studies, University of the Western Cape, 2004.

Hall, R., and G. Williams. *The Land Question in South Africa: The Challenge of Transformation and Redistribution.* Cape Town: Human Sciences Research Council Press, 2007.

Human Sciences Research Council. *Survey on South African Voter Participation in Elections.* Report for the Independent Electoral Commission. 2005. www.elections.org.za/.

International Monetary Fund. *World Economic Outlook Database.* April 2011. www.imf.org.

Isaacs, M. "Small-Scale Fisheries Reform: Expectations, Hopes and Dreams of 'A Better Life for All.'" *Marine Policy* 30, no. 1 (2006).

Jackson, John L., Jr. *Real Black: Adventures in Racial Sincerity.* Chicago: University of Chicago Press, 2005.

Kinnes, Irvin. *From Urban Street Gangs to Criminal Empires: The Changing Face of Gangs in the Western Cape.* Monograph 48. Pretoria: Institute for Security Studies, 2011.

Kok, Pieter, Michael O'Donovan, Oumar Bouare, Johan Van Zyl. *Post-Apartheid Patterns of Internal Migration in South Africa.* Cape Town: Human Sciences Research Council Publishers, 2003.

Kopano, Matlwa. *Coconut.* Johannesburg: Jacana Media, 2007.

Lam, D., and J. Seekings. "Transitions to Adulthood in Urban South Africa: Evidence from a Panel Survey." Paper prepared for International Union for the Scientific Study of Population General Conference, Tours, France, 2005.

Lefko-Everett, K. "Ticking Time-Bomb or Demographic Dividend? Youth and Reconciliation in South Africa." In *South African Reconciliation Barometer Survey: 2012 Report*. Cape Town: Institute for Justice and Reconciliation, 2012. http://www.ijr.org.za/.

Leggett, T. "No One to Trust: Preliminary Results from a Manenberg Crime Survey." *Crime Quarterly* 9 (2004).

Leibbrandt, M., et al. "Trends in South African Income Distribution and Poverty Since the Fall of Apartheid." OECD Social, Employment and Migration Working Papers, No. 101. Paris: OECD Publishing, 2010.

Lowenberg, A. D. "Why South Africa's Apartheid Economy Failed." *Contemporary Economic Policy* 15, no. 3 (1997): 62–72.

Mattes, B. "The Born Frees: The Prospect for Generational Change in Post-Apartheid South Africa." Centre for Social Science Working Paper No. 292. University of Cape Town, 2011.

Mhlahlo, A. "What Is Manhood? The Significance of Traditional Circumcision in the Xhosa Initiation Ritual." Master's thesis. Department of Sociology and Social Anthropology, University of Stellenbosch, 2009.

Misago, Jean-Pierre, Tamlyn Monson, Tara Polzer, and Loren B. Landau. *May 2008 Violence against Foreign Nationals in South Africa: Understanding Causes and Evaluating Responses*. Johannesburg: Forced Migration Studies Programme, University of the Witwatersrand/Consortium for Refugees and Migrants in South Africa, April 2010. http://www.cormsa.org.za/.

Moolman, J. F. "The Role of Threat on Afrikaner Attitude towards Affirmative Action and Its Beneficiaries." MBA thesis. University of Pretoria. 2010.

Morrell, R., et al. "Hegemonic Masculinity/Masculinities in South Africa: Culture, Power, and Gender Politics." *Men and Masculinities* 15, no. 1 (2012): 11–30.

Musson, D. *Johnny Gomas: Voice of the Working Class; a Political Biography*. South African History Online. Cape Town, 1989. www.sahistory.org.za.

Nattrass, N., et al. "Poverty, Sexual Behavior, Gender, and HIV Infection among Young Black Men and Women in Cape Town, South Africa." *Journal of AIDS Research* 11, no. 4 (2012): 307–17.

Nattrass, N., and J. Seekings. "Citizenship and Welfare in South Africa: Deracialisation and Inequality in a Labour-Surplus Economy." *Canadian Journal of African Studies* 31, no. 3 (1997): 452–81.

Nel, Etienne Louis. *Regional and Local Economic Development in South Africa: The Experience of the Eastern Cape*. The Making of Modern Africa Series. Aldershot, UK: Ashgate Publishing, 1999.

Nel, Etienne Louis, and Trevor Raymond Hill. *An Evaluation of Community-Driven Economic Development, Land Tenure, and Sustainable Environmental Development in the Kat River Valley*. Human Needs, Resources, and the Environment Series. Pretoria: Human Sciences Research Council Publishers, 2000.

Newman, Katherine. *Falling From Grace: Downward Mobility in the Age of Affluence*. Berkeley: University of California Press, 1999.

———. *No Shame in My Game: The Working Poor in the Inner City*. New York: Knopf/Russell Sage Foundation, 1999.

Nuttall, Sarah, and Carli Coetzee, editors. *Negotiating the Past: The Making of Memory in South Africa*. New York: Oxford University Press, 1998.

Organisation for Economic Co-Operation and Development. *Economic Surveys: South Africa 2013*. Paris: OECD Publishing, 2013.

PASSOP (People Against Suffering, Oppression, and Poverty). *Blue Waters Safety Site: Eviction Process Monitoring Report*. Cape Town: PASSOP, March 31–April 15, 2010. http://www.passop.co.za/.

Phurutse, M. C. *Factors Affecting Teaching and Learning in South African Public Schools*. Cape Town: Human Sciences Research Council/Medical Research Council of South Africa, 2005.

Pienaar, G. "The Separation of Powers: Are the Checks and Balances Working?" *South African Reconciliation Barometer* 6, no. 3 (November 2008).

Pieterse, E. *Urbanization Imperatives for Africa: Transcending Impasses*. Cape Town: African Centre for Cities, University of Cape Town, 2010.

Plaut, Martin, and Paul Holden. *Who Rules South Africa? Pulling the Strings in the Battle for Power*. Johannesburg: Jonathan Ball Publishers, 2012.

Polzer, T. "Population Movements in and to South Africa." Migration Fact Sheet 1. Forced Migration Studies Programme. University of Witwatersrand, 2010.

Posel, D. "A Review of Current Literature and Recent Research on Migration in Southern Africa." Working paper. University of Natal, 2002.

Powdermaker, Hortense. *After Freedom: A Cultural Study in the Deep South*. Madison: University of Wisconsin Press, 1939.

Ramphele, Mamphela. *Steering by the Stars*. Cape Town: Tafelberg Publishers, 2002.

Robins, Steven L., editor. *Limits to Liberation after Apartheid: Citizenship, Governance & Culture*. Athens: Ohio University Press, 2005.

Russell, M. "Understanding Black Households in Southern Africa: The African Kinship and Western Nuclear Family Systems." CSSR Working Paper No. 67. Centre for Social Science Research, University of Cape Town, 2004.

Salo, Elaine. "'Mans is ma soe': Ganging Practices in Manenberg, South Africa, and the Ideologies of Masculinity, Gender, and Generational Relations." In E. G. Bay and D. L. Donham, eds., *States of Violence: Politics, Youth and Memory in Contemporary Africa*. Charlottesville: University of Virginia Press, 2006.

———. "Negotiating Gender and Personhood in the New South Africa: Adolescent Women and Gangsters in Manenberg Township on the Cape Flats." *European Journal of Cultural Studies* 6 (2003): 345.

Seedat, S., et al. "Trauma Exposure and Post-Traumatic Stress Symptoms in Urban African Schools: Survey in Cape Town and Nairobi." *British Journal of Psychiatry* 184 (2004): 169–75.

Seekings, J. "The Continuing Salience of Race: Discrimination and Diversity in South Africa." *Journal of Contemporary African Studies* 26, no. 1 (2008): 1–25.

———. "Introduction: Urban Studies in South Africa after Apartheid." *International Journal of Urban and Regional Research* 24, no. 4 (2000): 832–40.

————. "Social Stratification and Inequality in South Africa at the End of Apartheid." CSSR Working Paper No. 31. Centre for Social Science Research, University of Cape Town, 2003.

Seekings, J., and H. Matisonn. "South Africa: The Continuing Politics of Basic Income." In *Basic Income Worldwide: Horizons of Reform,* edited by Matthew C. Murray and Carole Pateman. International Political Economy Series. Basingstoke, UK: Palgrave Macmillan, July 2012.

Seekings, J., and N. Nattrass. "Class, Distribution and Redistribution in Post-Apartheid South Africa." *Transformation: Critical Perspectives on Southern Africa* 1–2 (2002).

Segatti, Aurelia. "Mobilisation Against Foreign Traders in South Africa." African Centre for Migration & Society. Migration Issue Brief 5. June 2011. http://www.migration.org.za/.

Simbi, Tracy, and Michael Aliber. *Agricultural Employment Crisis in South Africa.* TIPS Working Paper 13. Durban: Department of Trade and Industry Policy Support Programme, 2000.

Simkins, Charles, and Andrew Paterson. *Learner Performance in South Africa: Social and Economic Determinants of Success in Language and Mathematics.* Pretoria: Human Sciences Research Council Press, 2005.

Smit, W., et al. "Good Houses Make Good People? Explorations in the Nature of Knowledge about the Relationship between Human Health and the Urban Environment at the Neighbourhood Scale in Cape Town." In *Africa-Centred Knowledges? The Creative Space between the Immovable Rock and the Bad Place,* edited by Brenda Cooper and Robert Morrell (In press. London: James Curry).

Soudien, C. "The Asymmetries of Contact: An Assessment of 30 Years of School Integration in South Africa." *Race, Ethnicity and Education* 10, no. 4 (2007): 439–56.

South African Institute of Race Relations. *The South Africa Survey.* Johannesburg, 2012. http://www.sairr.org.za/.

South Africa Police Service. *Crime Report 2010/2011.* Pretoria, 2011. http://www.saps.gov.za.

Southall, R. "Political Change and the Black Middle Class in Democratic South Africa." *Canadian Journal of African Studies/Revue Canadienne des Études Africaines* 38, no. 3 (2004): 521–42.

Spiegel, A., et al. "Domestic Diversity and Fluidity among Some African Households in Greater Cape Town." *Social Dynamics* 21, no. 2 (1996): 7–30.

Stanwix, B. *Minimum Wages and Compliance in South African Agriculture.* Development Policy Research Unit, University of Cape Town, 2013. www.econ3x3.org.

Statistics South Africa. www.statssa.gov.za.

————. *Achieving a Better Life for All: Progress between Census '96 and Census 2001.* Pretoria: Statistics South Africa, 2005.

————. *Census 2011: Municipal Report, Western Cape.* Pretoria: Statistics South Africa, 2012.

————. *Census 2011: Statistical Release.* Pretoria: Statistics South Africa, 2012.

————. *Census of Commercial Agriculture 2002.* Pretoria: Statistics South Africa, 2002.

Steinberg, Jonny. *The Number: One Man's Search for Identity in the Cape Underworld and Prison Gangs.* Johannesburg: Jonathan Ball Publishers, 2005.

Steyn, Melissa E. *Whiteness Just Isn't What It Used to Be: White Identity in a Changing South Africa.* Albany: State University of New York Press, 2001.

Strategic Development Information and GIS Department, City of Cape Town. *City of Cape Town—2011 Census*. Cape Town, 2012.

Sullivan, John P., and Robert J. Bunker. "Drug Cartels, Street Gangs, and Warlords." Special issue, Non-State Threats and Future Wars, *Small Wars & Insurgencies* 13, no. 2 (2002): 40–53.

Swartz, S., et al. "Ikasi Style and the Quiet Violence of Dreams: A Critique of Youth Belonging in Post-Apartheid South Africa." Special issue, Youth Citizenship and the Politics of Belonging, *Comparative Education* 48, no. 1 (2012): 27–40.

Taylor, Nick, Brahm Fleisch, and Jennifer Shindler. *Changes in Education Since 1994*. Braamfontein: JET Education Services, February 2008. http://www.jet.org.za/.

Tutu, Desmond. *No Future Without Forgiveness*. New York: Doubleday, 1999.

United Nations Development Programme. *South Africa Country Report*. 2013. www.undp.org.

Vail, Leroy, editor. *The Creation of Tribalism in Southern Africa*. Berkeley: University of California Press, 1989.

Van der Berg, Servaas, et al. *Low Quality Education as a Poverty Trap*. University of Stellenbosch, 2011.

Van der Berg, Servaas, and Megan Louw. "Lessons Learnt from SACMEQII: South African Student Performance in Regional Context." Paper presented at Investment Choices for Education in Africa Conference, Development Bank of Southern Africa, Johannesburg, September 2006.

Van der Merwe, A., and A. Dawes. "Prosocial and Antisocial Tendencies in Children Exposed to Community Violence." *Southern African Journal of Child and Adolescent Mental Health* 12 (2000): 19–37.

West, M. *Influx Control: The 1983 Statistics*. Cape Town: South African Institute of Race Relations, Cape Western Region, 1984.

Wilkinson, P. "City Profile: Cape Town." *Cities* 17, no. 3 (2000): 195–205.

Wilson, Monica Hunter, and Leonard Monteath Thompson. *The Oxford History of South Africa, Vol. 2*. London: Oxford University Press, 1969.

Wilson, Tim, et al. "Digging into Ourselves: Experiences of Public Health Sector Managers in Rural Areas." Paper presented at Towards Carnegie 3 Conference: Overcoming Poverty and Inequality in South Africa, University of Cape Town, September 2012. http://www.carnegie3.org.za/.

Woodson, Kevin J. "Fairness and Opportunity in the Twenty-First-Century Corporate Workplace: The Perspectives of Young Black Professionals." PhD diss., Department of Sociology, Princeton University, 2010.

Woolard, I. "An Overview of Poverty and Inequality in South Africa." Working paper prepared for the Department for International Development (SA); briefing paper for the Human Sciences Research Council. 2002.